TOWARD THE BELOVED COMMUNITY

TOWARD THE

MARTIN LUTHER KING JR.

BELOVED

AND SOUTH AFRICA

COMMUNITY

LEWIS V. BALDWIN

THE PILGRIM PRESS
CLEVELAND, OHIO

The Pilgrim Press, Cleveland, Ohio 44115
© 1995 by Lewis V. Baldwin

Chapter 1: Letter from King to Luthuli reprinted by arrangement with The Heirs to the Estate of Martin Luther King, Jr., c/o Joan Daves Agency as agent for the proprietor. All material copyright by Martin Luther King, Jr., copyright renewed by Coretta Scott King. **Chapter 2**: Material from *Christian Century* © 1966 Christian Century Foundation, reprinted by permission from the July 20, 1966 issue of *Christian Century*. Letters from King reprinted by arrangement with The Heirs to the Estate of Martin Luther King, Jr., c/o Joan Daves Agency as agent for the proprietor; all material copyright by Martin Luther King, Jr., copyright renewed by Coretta Scott King. **Chapter 3**: Material from International Tribute to Martin Luther King, Jr., 1979, used by permission of the United Nations Center Against Apartheid, Department of Political and Security Council Affairs. **Chapter 4**: Quotations from Galloway article used by permission of Cox News Service. Letters from King reprinted by arrangement with The Heirs to the Estate of Martin Luther King, Jr., c/o Joan Daves Agency as agent for the proprietor. All material copyright by Martin Luther King, Jr., copyright renewed by Coretta Scott King. Material from UNCAA used by permission of United Nations Committee Against Apartheid. **Chapter 5**: Material from Jim Wallis and Joyce Hollyday, eds., *Crucible of Fire: The Church Confronts Apartheid*, © 1989 by Orbis Books; used by permission. Same material also reprinted with permission from *Sojourners*, 2401 15th St., NW, Washington, DC 20009; (202) 328-8842 / (800) 714-7474.

00 99 98 97 96 95   5 4 3 2 1

Library of Congress Cataloging-in-Publication Data

Baldwin, Lewis V., 1949–
Toward the beloved community : Martin Luther King, Jr., and South Africa / Lewis V. Baldwin.
p.   cm.
Includes bibliographical references (p.   ) and index.
ISBN 0-8298-1102-8 (cloth : alk. paper). —ISBN 0-8298-1108-7 (paper : alk. paper)
1. King, Martin Luther, Jr., 1929–1968—Influence.   2. King, Martin Luther, Jr., 1929–1968—Views on apartheid.   3. Apartheid—South Africa.   4. Anti-apartheid movements—South Africa.   5. South Africa—Race relations.   I. Title.
E185.97.K354   1995
323'.092—dc20   95-18073
                        CIP

In memory of
Chief Albert J. Luthuli, Bantu Stephen Biko,
Chris Hani, Oliver Tambo, and Joe Slovo,
and for the millions of black men, women, and children
who suffered, bled, and died for a new
South Africa

CONTENTS

FOREWORD

Never in the widest stretch of my imagination would I have expected to see a book of this magnitude on Martin Luther King Jr.'s thought concerning South Africa. Lewis V. Baldwin has given me credit for suggesting early in 1983 that he write a book analyzing the impact of the black church and the black experience on King. However, if he had asked me about the feasibility of *Toward the Beloved Community*, I would have advised against it because I would not have thought enough sources would be available. But here it is, and it not only explores a subject heretofore unknown, it also marks the end of one period in King research and initiates a new one.

The latter remarks require an explanation. After the publication of Lawrence D. Reddick's *Crusader Without Violence: A Biography of Martin Luther King Jr.* (1959), no volume of significance on King was published until David L. Lewis's *King: A Critical Biography* (1970). Very little else of substance on King was published in the 1970s, except Kenneth L. Smith and Ira G. Zepp's *Search for the Beloved Community: The Thinking of Martin Luther King Jr.* (1974). Then within a short space of time, largely due to the availability of the King Archives in Atlanta and the FBI files, there followed in quick succession extensive works such as John J. Ansbro's *Martin Luther King Jr.: The Making of a Mind* (1982), Stephen B. Oates's *Let the Trumpet Sound: The Life of Martin Luther King Jr.* (1982), David J. Garrow's *Bearing the Cross: Martin Luther King Jr. and the Southern Christian Leadership Conference* (1986), and Taylor Branch's *Parting the Waters: America in the King Years, 1954–63* (1988). I think the period of such massive tomes has come to an end. I do not think we will see another 600–plus-pages volume of a general nature on King for a long time. If so, it will simply be a rehash of what has already been written.

Baldwin's volume does not follow the pattern of previous studies on King. There is a uniqueness about this volume that is obvious at first glance. "It focuses," Baldwin says, "on Martin Luther King Jr.'s *beloved community* ideal and its implications for the struggle against South African apartheid." The volume is focused on a specific topic. It is an example of the methodology future King researchers should follow. It is just the opposite of the methodology suggested by Thomas Mikelson in a 1991 review of James H. Cone's *Martin and Malcolm and America: A Dream or a Nightmare* (1991). Mikelson suggested that the next step is to place the insights King got from his theological training in the North in dialogue with what he inherited from the black cultural and religious experience in the South, thereby showing the genuine religious synthesis in King's faith, thought, and praxis. I do not think this is possible. King was not a systematic theologian. There were unresolved tensions in his thought up to the time of his assassination. Any synthesis of the kind suggested by Mikelson would be somebody else's synthesis, and thus a fabrication.

Baldwin's methodology is the best that King researchers can hope to do: select a specific topic, treat it intensely, and thus add another piece to the jigsaw puzzle King left us. In short, Baldwin's book points the way, and any further research that does not consult it will be deficient. This volume will be around for a long time, and I do not believe that it will be surpassed. All of us who labor in the vineyard of King research are indebted to Baldwin beyond measure.

Kenneth L. Smith
Professor Emeritus
Colgate-Rochester Divinity School
Rochester, New York

ACKNOWLEDGMENTS

My interest in the relevance and implications of Martin Luther King Jr.'s life and thought for the struggle against South African apartheid developed a decade ago while I was examining documents at the Martin Luther King Jr. Center for Nonviolent Social Change, Inc., in Atlanta, Georgia. I came across a couple of King's speeches on South Africa and a number of letters he received from South Africans, and this led to a more intense search for the civil rights leader's papers on South Africa at the King Center and at Mugar Memorial Library at Boston University. The search proved exciting and rewarding, and the ideas that resulted in this volume were conceived.

I have incurred a great many debts during the pursuit of this project. Louise Cook, Diane Ware, Sonya Jackson, and Bruce Keys, all of whom worked in the King Center Library and Archives during my research there, helped tremendously with the location and photocopying of documents pertinent to this study. While they no longer work at the King Center, they should be commended for the great contributions they made to the research of King scholars.

My thanks go to Dr. Howard Gotlieb and his staff in Special Collections at Boston University's Mugar Memorial Library for their kindness and assistance. They made available boxes of King's papers, and were enormously helpful in photocopying materials. The archivists, librarians, and other staff persons at the Mugar Memorial Library have devoted themselves to ensuring that the complete historical record of King's life, thought, and activities is preserved and made accessible to interested students and scholars.

Staff persons at the Amistad Research Center at Tulane University in New Orleans deserve special mention for making available the papers of the American Committee on Africa (ACOA). With the help of Rebecca Hankins, much material related to King and South Africa was discovered. I am highly grateful for the assistance so kindly rendered.

I am deeply indebted to several black South African leaders and students who afforded information and insights that strengthened my perspective on the historical and cultural context of their country, thus making it easier for me to avoid hasty and erroneous generalizations and conclusions. Adriaan "Aubrey" Jacobus Beukes, a minister in the Dutch Reformed Mission Church, whom I met at the University of Mississippi in April 1990, told me a lot about the psychology of growing up under the apartheid system. I in turn shared with him my own struggle under Jim Crow in the American South, and that exchange of ideas and experiences impacted this volume in decisive ways.

The anti-apartheid activist Dennis Brutus, who was for many years in exile from South Africa, and who recently taught at the Universities of Pittsburgh and Colorado, supported this work in so many ways. Brutus was gracious in referring me to other black South African activists, such as Oliver and Adelaide Tambo of the African National Congress (ANC). The recently deceased Oliver Tambo, who was president of the ANC for several years, and who reflected Martin Luther King Jr.'s spirit in profound ways, sent me a brief letter of encouragement.

Ramosotho Morgadi, Keith Appolis, Webster Mahlangu, and Roxanne Jordaan were among the South African students who provided moral and intellectual support. Morgadi, whom I met at Colgate-Rochester Divinity School in March 1991, corrected some of my misconceptions regarding black South African leaders. Appolis, a doctoral student on whose committee I served here at Vanderbilt, read parts of my manuscript and made me aware of its greatest strengths and weaknesses. Countless conversations with Keith over the last five years made this a better book than it would have been without his rich reflections and thoughtful criticisms. Mahlangu and Jordaan, both of whom had courses on King with me, were quite supportive. The insights I got from Roxanne and her husband Danny stimulated my thinking immensely.

George M. Houser, who worked with Martin Luther King Jr. while serving as executive director of the ACOA in the 1950s and 1960s, has been a tremendous source of support and inspiration. We communicated numerous times by mail and telephone, and I spent an hour interviewing him at his home in Pomona, New York. Houser assured me of the enormous value of this volume. I benefited greatly from his reflections on King and Africa.

The support from E. S. Reddy was of the kind few other sources could match. Having communicated with King during his work as Principal

Secretary of the UN Special Committee on the Policies of Apartheid, Reddy shared information and insights that advanced my work considerably. The assistance he provided proved particularly important because he has carefully studied Gandhi and South Africa. I shall always be grateful for Reddy's generosity and kindness.

I must express my deepest appreciation to Arun Gandhi, the grandson of the great Indian leader Mohandas K. Gandhi, for the intellectual stimulation and encouragement he provided. The long conversation Arun and I had at the University of Mississippi in April 1990 proved very beneficial as I sought to understand both Mohandas K. Gandhi and Martin Luther King Jr. in relation to the South African context.

My thanks go to Dr. Kenneth L. Smith, a former professor and dear friend, who read parts of the manuscript and graciously consented to write the foreword. Dr. Smith, who co-authored a fine book on King with Ira G. Zepp Jr., and who taught courses on King for many years at Colgate-Rochester Divinity School, set a noble example of devotion to King scholarship that I do not mind following. Unfortunately, Dr. Smith passed away on April 25, 1992. During the last three months of his life, he wrote me several times, always insisting that I complete this book.

I wish to thank Joseph Roberts, pastor of the Ebenezer Baptist Church in Atlanta, Georgia, for his kindness and assistance. As pastor and a close friend to the King family, he helped keep the lines of communication between me and the King Estate open during the early stages of this work.

I owe a very professional and personal debt to several colleagues who once worked with me here at Vanderbilt University. Walter Fluker, who currently holds the Deanship in Black Church Studies at Colgate-Rochester Divinity School, read parts of this work and offered editorial advice. Wallace Charles Smith, who now pastors a large congregation in Washington, D.C., gave timely words of support and encouragement. Julius Scott, who taught at Vanderbilt in 1987, and who is now retired, used his influence as a former high-ranking staff person at the King Center to help get this volume published.

I would like to acknowledge Vanderbilt University's Students Against Apartheid (VAA), an organization that no longer exists. As an adviser of this organization for three years, I was challenged by its moral claims and by its efforts to sensitize an often hostile Vanderbilt community to the South African apartheid problem. Some of the members of VAA exemplified the spirit of Martin Luther King Jr. in the 1980s in calling upon

Vanderbilt and other institutions of higher learning in Tennessee to sell their stock in South Africa.

My heartfelt gratitude goes out to many former members and leaders of the ACOA, and of defunct organizations such as the American Negro Leadership Conference on Africa (ANLCA) and the National Union of South African Students (NUSAS). While their names are too numerous to list, the information they gave through letters helped make this book a worthwhile endeavor.

I gratefully acknowledge Shelly Rayome, Wanda Graves, and Pamela L. Yates, who are responsible for the photographs included in this work. They always responded to my request on the shortest notice.

One of my greatest debts is to my wife, Jacqueline, who provided a sounding board for my ideas, and who simply would not let me give up on this project. Her love and support helped ease the tremendous anguish, frustration, and loneliness I often felt while writing this book.

Finally, I am grateful beyond measure to God the liberator, whose unwavering goodness sustained me in this effort. The divine spirit renewed my strength and faith at those times when the outcome of this volume was much in doubt in my mind. This book testifies to the fact that even the most difficult obstacles are no match for God's power.

INTRODUCTION

Very little has been written about Martin Luther King Jr.'s significance in relation to international issues and concerns. Most literature on King has either explicitly or implicitly limited him to the American context, presenting him as a southern black leader, a civil rights activist, an "American Gandhi," or a national symbol. While this approach has some merit, especially considering King's tremendous role in transforming American life and culture, it undermines King's importance as a world leader and a world symbol, and fails to capture the extent to which he addressed the global realities of racism, poverty, and war.[1]

King's contributions *to the uplift of the poor and oppressed in South Africa in the 1950s and 1960s provide an important angle from which his global significance can be assessed. Given the time, energy, and resources King devoted to the struggle of people of color against South African apartheid, it is strange that scholars have left this angle largely unexplored. King's many references to South Africa in sermons and writings, his attacks on South African apartheid in public speeches and interviews in the United States and abroad, his friendship with black South African leaders like Chief Albert J. Luthuli of the African National Congress (ANC), his admiration and respect for anti-apartheid activists such as Nelson Mandela and Robert Sobukwe, and his activities on behalf of oppressed South Africans through organizations like the American Committee on Africa (ACOA) and the American Negro Leadership Conference on Africa (ANLCA), have received only superficial treatment in books and articles written about him.[2] This pattern of neglect must be corrected if the full range of King's thought and activities as a prophet of peace and social justice is to be known and appreciated.

This book focuses on Martin Luther King Jr.'s *beloved community* ideal and its implications and relevance for the long and continuing struggle against racism, tribalism, classism, and sexism in South Africa. Its purpose

1

is threefold. First, it examines King's reflections on and contributions to the anti-apartheid struggle in the 1950s and 1960s. Second, it assesses his impact on anti-apartheid activists and movements in and outside South Africa in the 1970s and 1980s. Finally, it explores the applicability of King's ideas and methods to the South African context in the 1990s and beyond. The central question to be addressed here is: Is King's communitarian ideal, and the nonviolent means by which he pursued that ideal, relevant for South Africans in their continuing quest for a more peaceful, just, and inclusive society? The contention here is that ethical and theological dialogue with King concerning the meaning, character, and actualization of human community can be very fruitful for South Africans as they seek to create a society in which all persons live together in harmony and with equal opportunity.[3]

The contents of this work—which draw heavily on the many references King made to South Africa in letters, interviews, sermons, public speeches, articles, and books—rest on the conviction that apartheid in any form, rooted in the assumption that people of color are inferior to and cannot live on terms of equality with white people, is the very antithesis of the beloved community ideal.[4] Apartheid constitutes both social evil and theological heresy because it denies at least four basic principles that formed the core of King's conception of community: (1) the impartiality of God in creating and dealing with human beings; (2) a sacramentalistic idea of the cosmos as echoed by the psalmist, "the earth is the Lord's, and the fullness thereof—the world, and they that dwell therein"; (3) a belief in the dignity and worth of all human personality; and (4) a solidaristic view of society and the world, which holds that each person is a distinct ontological entity who finds growth, fulfillment, and purpose through personal and social relationships based on the agape love ethic.[5] This final principle is best characterized in King's use of the metaphor of the "great world house" or the "world-wide neighborhood," which suggests a totally integrated human family, unconcerned with human differences and devoted to the ethical norms of love, justice, and community:

> We have inherited a large house, a great "world house" in which we have to live together—black and white, Easterner and Westerner, Gentile and Jew, Catholic and Protestant, Moslem and Hindu—a family unduly separated in ideas, culture and interest, who, because we can never again live apart, must learn somehow to live with each other in peace.[6]

The beloved community was essentially "the capstone of King's thought"—"the organizing principle of all his thought and activity."[7] It has been variously called "the Christian eschatalogical ideal," "the ideal corporate expression of the Christian faith," and "the mutually cooperative and voluntary venture" of all moral and rational persons.[8] The beloved community vision was consistent with King's understanding of the Christian doctrine of the kingdom of God on earth, and with his view of democratic socialism as an economic and political ideology. For King, this conception of community represented a peculiar blend of insights from black culture, the Bible, liberal Christian theology and ethics, the American democratic heritage, Niebuhrian Christian Realism, and Eastern and Western philosophical traditions.[9] While the African American church, the extended family network, and the southern black experience, in which King was nurtured, constituted the most important formative influences in the shaping of his ideas about community, Boston Personalism and the Social Gospelism of Walter Rauschenbusch provided him with the intellectual framework to articulate those ideas.[10] This must be clearly understood before King's communitarian ideal can be extended beyond the American context and perceptively related to the unique South African situation.

The critical importance of the beloved community in King's intellectual concerns is evident from a reading of his sermons, public speeches, interviews, and writings from Montgomery to Memphis.[11] Convinced that community is the ultimate goal of human existence, King insisted that it was imperative for all persons of goodwill to struggle nonviolently against sin and the evil forces that work against harmony and wholeness in God's creation.[12] This view had powerful implications for the struggle against America's racism three decades ago, and it is relevant to the continuing efforts to destroy the last vestiges of the South African apartheid system.

King refused to isolate South African apartheid from the larger, global problem of racism as promoted by white people. "In country after country," he wrote in 1967, "we see white men building empires on the sweat and suffering of colored people." He continued:

> Portugal continues its practices of slave labor and subjugation in Angola; the Ian Smith government in Rhodesia continues to enjoy the support of British-based industry and private capital, despite the stated opposition of British Government policy. Even in the case of the little country of South West Africa we find the powerful nations of the world incapable of taking a

moral position against South Africa, though the smaller country is under the trusteeship of the United Nations. Its policies are controlled by South Africa and its manpower is lured into the mines under slave-labor conditions.[13]

Thus, the apartheid regime in South Africa was symptomatic of a world problem; namely, the irrational preoccupation with skin color, the need for whites to dominate and control peoples of color, and the failure of persons to grasp the extent to which they are interrelated and interdependent. This perception was fundamental to King's theological, philosophical, and ethical arguments against apartheid.[14]

Three points will become abundantly clear throughout this book. First, King's interest in and contributions to the struggle against South African apartheid grew largely out of his experiences as a black man in a racist society, and also out of considerable travel, observation, study, and reflection. Knowing the pain that came with being black in a society founded on white supremacy, King was able to relate to people of color in South Africa, and to identify those intellectual, moral, and spiritual values so essential for their liberation and advancement. Had he not been a person of color, with a keen intellect and a sense of life beyond the boundaries of the United States, his insights into the South African situation would have been less searching and sophisticated, to say nothing of his actions on behalf of a free South Africa.[15]

Second, King's concern for and contributions to the movement against apartheid were in phase with his deepening and expanding involvements, coupled with his mounting interest in the oppressed worldwide. As he increasingly studied the vast sweep of humanity, and advanced his obligations as a social activist over time, King became more and more convinced that the success of Blacks in America would remain questionable as long as black South Africans, and peoples of color generally, suffered on grounds of race and economics. Indeed, he came to the conclusion that African Americans and people of color in South Africa were engaged in essentially the same struggle, a conclusion that reinforced in his thinking the unity of the struggles of the oppressed on a global scale. Such a perspective came naturally for one who possessed a remarkable ability to empathize with others.[16]

Finally, King's interest in and contributions to the struggle against South African apartheid linked him to a tradition of African American thought and leadership dating back to Richard Allen, Robert A. Young, and David Walker in the eighteenth and nineteenth centuries, and as recent as the Republic of New Africa, the Nation of Islam, and Ron Karenga.[17] King's spiritual and cultural bond with this tradition of thought and leadership, a tradition shaped primarily by black nationalists, was his concern for the freedom and uplift of all people of African descent. This is not to say that King was a full-blown black nationalist or a Pan-Africanist, for the range of his concern and vision, at least in his own mind and in the thinking of those who have explored his life and thought, ultimately transcended such ideological categories.[18]

Chapter 1 discusses King's efforts to understand the South African freedom struggle within the broader context of the human struggle in the 1950s. His earliest views on South Africa, and the forces that shaped and informed them, are treated, and so are his activities for South African liberation through the ACOA. The chapter ends with a discussion of how King's perspective on South Africa, coupled with his anti-apartheid activities, connected him in mind and spirit with W. E. B. Du Bois, Paul Robeson, Adam Clayton Powell Jr., and other African American leaders in the fifties.

Chapter 2 explores the various ways in which King addressed the apartheid problem in South Africa in the 1960s. Special attention is devoted to the manner in which he repeatedly compared and linked the oppression of people of color in South Africa to that of African Americans. Attention is also given to King's mounting activities on behalf of South African freedom through the ACOA and the ANLCA, and to his correspondence with Americans, South Africans, and others about the apartheid problem. The chapter concludes with a focus on the responses of South Africans to King's assassination, and on King's general influence on various sectors of South African society in the sixties.

King's fading legacy in South Africa in the 1970s is the subject of Chapter 3. The struggle on the part of people worldwide to keep alive King's dream of a new, nonracial and democratic South Africa, achieved through nonviolent action, is discussed in contrast to the indifference and complacency of world leaders and institutions, and against the background of a retreat from Kingian-Gandhian principles and methods among certain radical elements in South Africa. The impact of Black Consciousness, liberation theology, and other forces on King's fading legacy in South Africa is underscored. King's influence on the ideas and methods of Desmond Tutu and Allan Boesak is also highlighted. The chapter closes with an extensive discussion of the international tribute to King by the United Nations Special Committee Against Apartheid (UNSCAA) in 1979.

Chapter 4 targets the continuing retreat from Kingian-Gandhian ideas and methods, and the search for new alternatives in South Africa in the 1980s. The extent to which King continued to influence anti-apartheid leaders, perspectives, and movements around the world is also treated. Furthermore, the discussion provided here will show how world leaders honored King for his impact on the movement against apartheid in 1982, and the degree to which some countries applied in a practical way his earlier call for the imposition of nonviolent economic and diplomatic sanctions against South Africa.

Chapter 5 examines the relevance and implications of King's thought for the creation of a new South Africa in the 1990s. Emphasis is placed on how King's dream for South Africa found partial fulfillment with the freeing of Nelson Mandela and other political prisoners, the dismantling of apartheid laws and institutions, the first all-race elections, and the selection of Mandela as South Africa's first black president. King's ideas on the major barriers to human community are applied to the South African context, and important similarities and differences between the civil rights leader and Nelson Mandela are considered.

Chapter 6 offers reflections on how the beloved community might be truly realized in South Africa, today and in the future, through a serious application of King's views on education, religion, legislation, court action, and nonviolent direct action to the social order. These reflections simply serve to emphasize King's continuing relevance for South Africa, despite its rapidly changing character.

Toward the Beloved Community is an attempt to generate more discussion concerning King's importance as a world figure and as one who significantly influenced liberation movements throughout the world. It is not excessive to expect greater attention of this nature to one whose birthday is celebrated in at least one hundred countries.[19] We need to know more about how King moved beyond conceptions of "a new South" and "the American dream" to articulate a vision of "the world house."[20] Also, we need to better understand the means by which he sought to translate this vision of "the world house" into practical reality. We have much to gain from studies of the relevance and applicability of King's global vision for contemporary and future human situations.

CHAPTER 1

THE POLITICS OF RACE
Viewing South Africa in Context in the 1950s

*No people can sympathize more with these black African,
brown Indian and mixed colored populations of South
Africa than we Americans of African descent.*

Paul Robeson, 1951[1]

*The purpose of the Apartheid policy is that, by separating
the races in every field in so far as it is practically possible,
one can prevent clashes and friction between Whites and
non-Whites.*

J. G. Strijdom, 1955[2]

*The struggle for equality among men continues in
Montgomery, Alabama and in Johannesburg, South Africa.
In America the battle is aided by public opinion and to
some extent federal action. In South Africa the government
itself has fostered the short-sighted doctrine of apartheid.*

James A. Pike
Martin Luther King Jr., 1958[3]

Several interesting and important developments occurred in the life of
Martin Luther King Jr. in the 1950s. First, King completed his seminary and graduate school education, receiving a bachelor of divinity
degree from Crozer Theological Seminary and a doctor of philosophy
degree from the Boston University School of Theology. Second, he assumed the pastorate of Dexter Avenue Baptist Church in Montgomery,
Alabama. Third, King figured prominently in the Montgomery bus boy-

cott and in the founding of the Southern Christian Leadership Conference (SCLC), involvements that established his role as a civil rights leader and catapulted him to national and international fame. Fourth, he embraced nonviolence as a personal and social ethic, as a method undergirded by a strong intellectual platform. Finally, King emerged as a spokesman for oppressed South Africans, raising their struggle to international consciousness and relating it to movements of the oppressed worldwide.[4]

This chapter examines King's public witness and activities on behalf of oppressed South Africans in the 1950s. Special attention is devoted to his early awareness of the South African context, to his anti-apartheid activities through the American Committee on Africa (ACOA), and to the ways in which those activities linked him at the levels of ideology and praxis with other African American leaders in this period.

Early Awareness of the South African Context

It is impossible to identify precisely the point at which Martin Luther King Jr. developed an interest in the racial situation in South Africa. His earliest knowledge of and perspective on South African apartheid probably owed much to letters exchanged in the early fifties between his father, Martin Luther King Sr., and black South African leaders such as Walter Sisulu of the African National Congress (ANC).[5] The elder King's ties to black anti-apartheid activists from South Africa may have begun as early as the summer of 1948, when the Zulu chief and ANC spokesman Albert J. Luthuli (also spelled Lutuli) visited Atlanta, Georgia, and preached and lectured to African American educators, students, and church persons.[6] The younger Martin had recently graduated from Atlanta's Morehouse College, and would have certainly heard of Luthuli's activities in his hometown.[7] The extent to which he and his father discussed South Africa cannot be determined, though it is known that they occasionally shared views on the struggles of peoples of color against oppression across the globe. In any case, it is difficult to avoid the conclusion that Martin Luther King Jr.'s initial interest in the problems of oppressed South Africans grew partly out of a family background that encouraged a concern for world affairs.[8]

The importance education may have had in the shaping of King's early understanding of and views on South Africa deserves some consideration. African affairs were often discussed in the classrooms and in chapel during his years at Morehouse College (1944–48).[9] Benjamin E. Mays, the college president, occasionally talked about Africa during the Tuesday morning chapel services in the mid- and late 1940s, events that required the attendance of all students and faculty. As early as 1936, Mays visited Africa and subsequently had extensive conversations with South African delegates at world conferences.[10] Exposed to a collegiate environment where interest in Africa ran high, and where Africans sometimes appeared, it would have been only natural for King to develop a sense of the conditions under which the masses of South Africans lived.[11]

King's exposure to the life and work of Mohandas K. Gandhi in 1951 undoubtedly afforded deeper insights into the impact of the South African system on peoples of color. A student at Crozer Theological Seminary at that time, King learned of Gandhi's activities through a sermon by Mordecai Johnson, the dynamic black preacher, theologian, and president of Howard University. King left the meeting and purchased six books on Gandhi's life and works.[12] Even if Johnson failed to mention Gandhi's anti-apartheid activities in his sermon, it would have been impossible for King, in reading about Gandhi, to overlook the Indian leader's participation in South Africa's history from 1893 to 1914, for "it was during these years that Gandhi developed his ideas of nonviolence, practicing them as a means of opposing European racial discrimination against Indians living in South Africa."[13]

King's study of Gandhi at Crozer, though not very intense, heightened his sense of the world, despite the fact that he then found some of Gandhi's views on love and nonviolence difficult to consume. He related Gandhi's ideas to the broader context of his studies at Crozer, particularly around questions of the unity of humankind and the need to merge the intellectual and the practical in effecting social change, a quest that continued with his exposure to personal idealism and theological liberalism at Boston University from late 1951 to 1954. In short, the education King received at Crozer and Boston reinforced his view of the world as a single community, a perspective that had significant implications for positions he later took regarding South Africa.[14]

Interestingly, King had a keen sense of the problems shared by people of African ancestry worldwide when he became pastor of Dexter Avenue Baptist Church in Montgomery in 1954. From the beginning of his pastoral experience, he saw the African American struggle within the larger framework of the African struggle. "Martin always saw a close relationship between the black struggle in America and the struggle for African independence," writes Coretta Scott King. "In his early speeches and sermons he had often compared European colonialism with Negro oppression in America."[15] With this understanding, King was not apt to make important distinctions between Jim Crow in the American South and apartheid in South Africa. His early references to African liberation movements at Dexter, made even before his first trip to the continent, seem to support the view that his education helped shape his consciousness of Africa.

King's trip to Ghana in 1957 provided opportunities to discuss South Africa with leaders quite familiar with the workings of the apartheid system. In March of that year, while attending Ghana's independence celebrations, King discussed apartheid at great length with Michael Scott, an Anglican priest who had worked with unwanted lepers in South Africa, and who shared his nonviolent approach. On that occasion, King "expressed admiration for the bus boycott outside Johannesburg, with thousands of Africans actually walking ten to fifteen miles a day." King and Scott agreed that violence would not work for the oppressed in South Africa. "Nonviolence in India and in Alabama 'did something to the oppressor,'" King declared, "and so it will even in South Africa." The willingness to suffer "will eventually make the oppressor ashamed of his method," he continued, "and the forces of both history and Providence are on the side of freedom."[16] King's conversation with Michael Scott was similar in content and moral tone to the ones he had around the same time with Bishop Ambrose Reeves of Johannesburg and Archbishop Trevor Huddleston of Tanganyika. Both Reeves and Huddleston were also associated with the struggle against apartheid, and they were as idealistic as King in assessing the need and potential for peaceful, democratic change in South Africa.[17]

South African apartheid loomed very much in the sphere of King's moral vision when he left Ghana to visit Nigeria in 1957. His knowledge of the problem had increased significantly, but his reflections on the possibility of a nonviolent solution to apartheid appeared, at this point, very uninformed. Fresh from the successful Montgomery bus boycott, with "a rather simplistic and exaggerated conception of the power of nonviolence," King assumed that that method would be as productive in South Africa as it had been in Montgomery.[18] He noted that "the independence of the Gold Coast was gained largely by nonviolent methods and with a minimum of force," and that violent revolution in South Africa or anywhere else in Africa would be as immoral and impractical as the use of violence by blacks in the southern United States. "For one thing," said King in 1957, "the Negroes both in America and in Africa do not have the weapons." His analysis at this juncture failed to adequately consider how even peaceful demonstrators in South Africa had been brutally beaten, maimed, murdered, and jailed over long periods without legal redress by the South African government, despite expressions of outrage from the rest of the world. Moreover, King apparently failed to seriously consider the lack of a natural rights tradition in South Africa, and the problems that posed for a nonviolent approach to apartheid. Only later would he come to a keen sense of South Africa as a unique historical, political, and cultural context, a development that made his insights on the question of means to eliminate apartheid more penetrating and refined.[19]

When King returned to Montgomery from Africa in April 1957, he had decided to be a voice for South Africa's oppressed majority. He began to read more about South Africa's history, devoting special attention to anti-apartheid movements. His knowledge undoubtedly expanded to new levels as he studied the Defiance Campaign led by Chief Albert J. Luthuli and the ANC in 1952–53, a campaign that drew strong support from Indian activists such as Manilal Gandhi, the son of Mohandas K. Gandhi.[20] During this campaign, Luthuli, president of the ANC, took the lead in organizing sit-in demonstrations against segregation in libraries, on railway seats, and in other facilities, activities quite similar to the sit-ins staged later by black students in the United States. Because Luthuli was a Christian minister and a strong proponent of nonviolent direct action, struggling to free people of color from white racism and domination, King identified with him and saw him as one of the brightest hopes for the creation of the beloved community in South Africa.[21] While King never visited South Africa, his study of and experiences with racism in the United States and colonialism in Africa prepared him to understand quite clearly the physical and psychological impact of apartheid on its victims, and to relate on a personal level with Luthuli and others engaged in struggle against that evil.[22]

Black South Africans also identified with King and the civil rights movement in America. In fact, it was during the Montgomery bus boycott in 1956 that King became known among the oppressed in South Africa. Many South Africans developed a special interest in King because they felt that in his struggle against racism and segregation in America, he was working for the liberation of peoples of color everywhere. This perception found reinforcement as King publicly expressed support for the 156 activists arrested on suspicion of treason by the South African government in December 1956.[23] King's *Stride Toward Freedom: The Montgomery Story* (1958) became a favorite text for many South African activists, especially ANC leaders, who found inspiration in the manner in which the civil rights leader translated nonviolent principles into practical action.[24] The views that King and black South African activists held concerning each other, and their gestures of friendship and sense of obligation toward each other, offer important clues into the nature of the relationship between the civil rights movement in America and the anti-apartheid movement in South Africa in the 1950s.

King and anti-apartheid activists in South Africa were quite conscious of the traditions of nonviolent protest that united them. Gandhi's use of nonviolence to liberate Indians in South Africa, and the ANC's adoption of that method in 1912, became quite significant for King as he struggled with the means by which his people might best win freedom in the United States. King's consciousness of the importance of these traditions for the African American struggle probably grew when he visited India in 1959, a trip during which he discussed nonviolence with Gandhi's relatives and groups of African students studying in India. Recalling the impact of those experiences upon his personal growth, King wrote: "I left India more convinced than ever before that nonviolent resistance is the most potent weapon available to oppressed people in their struggle for freedom."[25]

While considering the spirit and methods that connected him to Gandhi and the ANC, King said nothing in the fifties about how the ANC tradition of nonviolence differed somewhat from that associated with him and Gandhi. He must have discovered, through his study of the Defiance Campaign, that the ANC's use of nonviolence did not develop out of a large degree of special training and discipline. Moreover, he must have considered the high levels of government-sponsored violence that followed the ANC's nonviolent campaigns, problems not so typical of movements led by him and Gandhi. Mokgethi Motlhabi maintains that the "reasons for the difference" between movements like the Defiance Campaign in South Africa and the activities of Gandhi and King "might not be as simple as they appear at first sight." Motlhabi goes on to explain that the fact that

> civil disobedience in South Africa always seemed to end in violence whereas *on certain occasions* in India and the USA it did not, is not an indication that South African nonviolence advocates were less ethical or less disciplined than Gandhi or King, though this might well have been the case. It

must be granted, though, that for them nonviolence was mostly only a strategy, while for Gandhi and King it was also a way of life as well as a theological and moral principle.[26]

Considerable travel, observation, study, and reflection made it possible for King to connect in mind and spirit with oppressed South Africans. He learned a lot about South Africa by being among, conversing with, and observing the conditions of Africans from various countries. His experiences at these levels, coupled with his exposure to and struggle against Jim Crow in the American South, prepared him to speak consciously and directly to the apartheid problem in South Africa.[27] Having decided to become a voice for oppressed South Africans, King then moved to establish the kind of organizational links that would make his public witness against apartheid most effective and known to the world.

Work Through the American Committee on Africa

Martin Luther King Jr.'s interest in joining an organization that made meaningful contributions to South African liberation became known in many circles soon after his return from Africa in 1957. His interest in this regard had been inspired by his trip to Ghana, where he had discussed South Africa with religious and political leaders, and by his increasing awareness that the civil rights movement in America could not be separated from movements of the oppressed in other parts of the world.[28] King's interest in the proper organizational channel to challenge apartheid naturally took him beyond his SCLC, an essentially regional organization designed to serve as an arena through which local protest organizations in the American South could coordinate their protest activities.[29]

A couple of strong and well-known possibilities existed. One was the Council on African Affairs, an organization founded in London by the black artist and activist Paul Robeson and others in the 1930s, and which "was the most important one in America working for African liberation during the 1940s and '50s."[30] King knew of this organization, and of Robeson's and W. E. B. Du Bois's activities through it, but his reluctance to associate with the most radical elements of the left in America would have militated against his joining the council, despite its long-standing interest in the problems of South Africa.[31] King's reluctance would have been to some degree understandable. Any close association with the likes of Robeson and Du Bois, widely known for their strong communist ties, would have strengthened the claims made by southern segregationists and other more well-meaning Americans that the civil rights movement was inspired, supported, and infiltrated by communists. At this early stage in his career, King seemed determined to undermine such claims. Furthermore, King knew of the harassment and isolation to which Robeson and Du Bois were subjected by the federal government, a concern that would have been uppermost in his mind in this period of lingering McCarthyism and the cold war.[32] He desired to maintain a friendly alliance with the federal government, one most conducive to the progress of civil rights.[33]

The American Committee on Africa (ACOA) stood as another possibility for King. This organization had initially been formed in 1951 as Americans for South African Resistance (AFSAR), by Donald Harrington, Charles Y. Trigg, George M. Houser, Bayard Rustin, A. Philip Randolph, Norman Thomas, Roger N. Baldwin, and Conrad Lynn. Based in New York, AFSAR sought to lend what assistance it could to those defying the South African government.[34] In May 1953, a month or so after the end of the Defiance Campaign, AFSAR became incorporated as the American Committee on Africa. From that point, it continued to address South African issues while relating "to the whole anti-colonial struggle in Africa."[35] Having a growing reputation around the world, and an increasing thirst for freedom that transcended the American context, King accepted an invitation to join the ACOA in 1957.[36]

This decision on King's part most likely resulted from several considerations, aside from the ACOA's strong support for organized resistance to South African apartheid. First, the ACOA existed as a national organization with strong international connections. Second, it developed as an interracial organization, concerned with the building of a truly multiracial and democratic South Africa. Thus, it reflected both King's goal of the beloved community and the composition of the civil rights movement.[37] Third, the inner circle of ACOA organizers and leaders consisted of activist clergymen and established civil rights leaders who shared King's belief in the morality and practicality of nonviolence as a social ethic. Harrington, Trigg, and Houser were Christian ministers with a history of pacifism dating back to World War II; Rustin and Randolph were long-time nonviolent activists; Thomas stood as a strong critic of capitalism; Baldwin had served for several years as director of the American Civil Liberties Union (ACLU); and Lynn had a solid reputation as a civil rights lawyer.[38] Fourth, the ACOA committed its resources to creating a broader, deeper, and more positive relationship between the United States and all of Africa. Finally, the ACOA did not isolate its concern for South Africa from the civil rights movement and anticolonial struggles throughout Africa.[39] King ultimately viewed the ACOA as one of the most vital links between American and African interests.

In June 1957, King was nominated to serve on the National Committee of the ACOA by that organization's Special Nominating Committee. By September of that year, his name appeared on all ACOA stationery imprinted with a letterhead.[40] A member of the organization's National Committee throughout the late fifties, King found in it an important vehicle for keeping abreast of events and important developments in South Africa. He received reports on a regular basis from George Houser, who served as the ACOA's executive director during King's years of involvement with the organization.[41] King also discovered in the ACOA another medium, aside from the SCLC, for publicizing activities related to the civil rights movement in America. During the late 1950s, Houser sent out hundreds of letters to ACOA members, supporters, and potential supporters, urging them "not only to relate yourself to the very important work being carried on in regard to our racial situation in the United States, but also to the very tragic problem as it exists in South Africa."[42]

King occasionally read and signed ACOA appeals, letters, petitions, and declarations concerning the apartheid problem. In July 1957 he joined Eleanor Roosevelt and Bishop James A. Pike as initial sponsors, under the auspices of the ACOA, of the *Declaration of Conscience,* a document proclaiming "December 10, 1957, Human Rights Day, as a Day of Protest against the organized inhumanity of the South African Government and its *apartheid* policies."[43] Eleanor Roosevelt served as international chairman of this campaign, Pike as U.S. chairman, and King as U.S. vice chairman.[44] Noting that the South African government "continues to extend relentlessly its racist policy of *apartheid* into the economic, educational, religious, and other areas of life," the *Declaration of Conscience* insisted that

The time has come for a worldwide protest against the racist policies of the Government of the Union of South Africa. Freedom-loving people throughout the world have watched with great concern as the doctrine of white supremacy has gained increasing acceptance among South African whites. This racist doctrine—apartheid—has denied the African, Asian and Coloured people in South Africa even the elementary rights granted by any democratic state. Totalitarianism increasingly grips almost every area of human activity in South Africa. It is the only system by which apartheid can be imposed upon the South African people. As such, apartheid is a threat to the liberty of every South African, white or non-white.[45]

Proclaiming that "We support the overwhelming majority of the South African people, non-white and white, in their determination to achieve the basic human rights that are the rightful heritage of all men," the sponsors of the *Declaration* went on to explain, "in the spirit of the Universal Declaration of Human Rights adopted on December 10, 1948, by the General Assembly of the United Nations," how people of goodwill worldwide could best contribute to the struggle against apartheid:

> We ask them to join us in calling on the Government of the Union of South Africa to honor its moral and legal obligations as a signatory to the United Nations Charter by honoring the Declaration of Human Rights. We call upon members of all free associations—churches, universities, trade unions, business and professional organizations, veterans and other groups—to petition their organizations and their governments to use their influence to bring about a peaceful, just, and democratic solution in South Africa. We call upon all men and women to mobilize the spiritual and moral forces of mankind on this day of Protest to demonstrate to the Government of the Union of South Africa that free men abhor its policies and will not tolerate the continued suppression of human freedom. We seek to persuade the South African government, before it reaches the point of no return, that only in democratic equality is there lasting peace and security. [46]

In more specific terms, the sponsors of the *Declaration* urged all supporters to take the following steps:

> *Write your Mayor or Governor* suggesting that he issue a proclamation declaring Human Rights Day, December 10, 1957, in your city, state or province as the Day of Protest against South African racism.
>
> *Urge your own local clergyman* to devote an appropriate day on or before December 10th as a day of prayer for the suppressed South African people.
>
> *Ask your own local or regional voluntary organizations or groups* to issue statements of policy in support of the *Declaration of Conscience* and to call upon their members to participate in the Day of Protest.
>
> *Organize a public Day of Protest* demonstration in your own community. Seek the widest cross-section of sponsorship from among religious, labor, business, veteran, professional, political, educational and civic groups.

Add your name to the signers of the *Declaration of Conscience*... and support this campaign with your most generous contribution. Your financial help is necessary to make this a truly effective world-wide effort.[47]

King's role in sponsoring and promoting this *Declaration of Conscience* provides additional evidence that he, very early in his career as a civil rights leader, had a clear sense of how the African American struggle connected to the struggle of people of color in South Africa. "It was the realization of this link," King maintained, "which drew me to join in a worldwide *Declaration of Conscience* concerning apartheid, a campaign organized by the American Committee on Africa in 1957."[48]

The *Declaration* generated enormous publicity, due mainly to its international appeal. It bore the signatures of some 123 world leaders, among whom were Martin Buber, Pablo Casals, Chief Anthony Enahoro, Erich Fromm, Rabbi Israel Goldstein, Trygve Lie, Albert Luthuli, Reinhold Niebuhr, Martin Niemoeller, Julius Nyerere, Alan Paton, Ambrose Reeves, Arnold Toynbee, and Bruno Walter.[49] News of the *Declaration* reached millions in the United States and abroad through newspapers and radio. In the United States, articles on it appeared in *The New York Times, The Christian Science Monitor, The Washington Post and Times Herald, The Oregon Daily Journal,* and *The Anderson Herald* of Anderson, Indiana.[50] The personal benefit King derived from the campaign proved considerable. His popularity increased across the world, especially among peoples struggling against apartheid.

Generally speaking, the international community gave mixed responses to the *Declaration.* In the United States, endorsements came from several sources, including Mayor Robert F. Wagner of New York City, Senator Wayne Morse of Oregon, The Council of Churches of Greater Kansas City, and *The Oregon Journal* of Portland, Oregon.[51] Many government officials and ordinary citizens in America refused to endorse the *Declaration,* a position not surprising in a nation where responses to King and the civil rights movement often ranged from silence to outright opposition.[52] The World Assembly of Youth in Paris expressed its approval of and support for the *Declaration,* and so did Vice President W. R. Tolbert Jr. of Liberia, Chief Minister Norman W. Manley of Jamaica, The National Union of Students of India, The Danish Youth Council, and hundreds of other persons and organizations based in Africa, Asia, and Europe.[53] Michael Scott, the director of the Africa Bureau in London, sent King a long letter expressing support for the *Declaration* and calling for "the exertion of a well-considered pro-gramme of moral pressures" to force change in South Africa.[54]

King and others in the ACOA anticipated with great interest the re-sponses of South Africans to the *Declaration*. As expected, the South African government expressed anger over the international protest against its racial policies. On December 12, 1957, two days after the protest, it deputized External Affairs Minister Eric Louw to make a thirty-minute national broadcast in reply to the charges made in the *Declaration*. Louw launched a strong attack against King, James Pike, Eleanor Roosevelt, and George Houser, denouncing them as "known leftists" and insisting that the ACOA had "a decidedly pinkish tinge."[55] Already hated by white su-premacists throughout the world because of his activities in the American South, King would never be allowed to visit South Africa.[56]

Many liberal whites and persons of color in South Africa greeted the *Declaration* with enthusiasm and hope. Words of praise for the sponsors of the campaign came from the Liberal Party of South Africa, the interracial National Union of South African Students (NUSAS), Bishop Ambrose Reeves of Johannesburg, *Rand Daily Mail* of Johannesburg, and *The Cape Times* of Cape Town. *The Cape Times* echoed the sentiments of many free-dom-loving South Africans when it declared that "The trouble about our troubled country is that unless the Government changes its ways there is no real answer to criticism of race policies here."[57] The expression of such senti-ments by liberal elements in South Africa helps explain why King remained hopeful for a peaceful solution to apartheid in that country, even as he con-sistently attacked its government for its intransigence and repressive acts.

King's association with the *Declaration of Conscience* signaled the begin-ning of a period of fruitful correspondence between him and some black South African leaders. In a letter to King, Oliver Tambo, the secretary-general of the ANC, expressed appreciation for the civil rights leader's pro-motion of the *Declaration,* and noted that "we now appeal to you to give your full support to the crusade for South African freedom."[58] Similar sen-timents came from Albert Luthuli, the president-general of the ANC, who exchanged letters with King. In defense of King, James Pike, and Eleanor Roosevelt, Luthuli explained that "By branding the sponsors of the *Declaration of Conscience* as ultra-Liberalistic and smearing them as Communist, the Minister of External Affairs, Mr. E. H. Louw, did not ab-solve South Africa from the charges made by leading individuals and statesmen throughout the world."[59] The *Declaration* helped create a bond between Luthuli and King that embraced their common concern for the liberation of all people of African ancestry through nonviolent means.[60]

King's involvement in the ACOA's anti-apartheid activities went beyond the *Declaration of Conscience* to include the raising of funds for political prisoners in South Africa. His interest in the problems of South African political prisoners and their families initially surfaced after 156 anti-apartheid activists were arrested on suspicion of treason in December 1956.[61] In 1957 and 1958, King wrote and signed letters requesting donations of ten dollars or more to help cover the legal fees of political prisoners and to assist their families.[62] Convinced that Albert Luthuli, Oliver Tambo, and others of different races were arrested because "they desire a democratic, multi-racial society," King was asked to join nineteen other American leaders in signing "A Letter to the Religious Press," a document issued on March 5, 1958, to increase fund-raising efforts and to inspire worldwide condemnation of the treason trials in South Africa. The letter read in part:

> As Christians and Americans we feel a grave responsibility to help meet the need in South Africa. The treason trials are a challenge to the people of goodwill around the world who realize that much is at stake. Not unmindful of our own failures in race relations in the United States, we nevertheless call for your support to help a people whose government sponsors a most rigid program of segregation.[63]

Much of King's fund-raising activity on behalf of South African political prisoners occurred in connection with the ACOA's South Africa Defense Fund. The Fund came into existence in 1956, soon after the arrest of the 156 opponents of apartheid. King reported in 1959 that the ACOA had "sent $50,000 for aid in the extensive legal costs and family hardships of the accused."[64] At that time, the South Africa Defense Fund developed into the broader Africa Defense and Aid Fund, and King served as one of its sponsors.[65] Although the budgetary restrictions of his SCLC prevented him from consistently contributing large sums of money to the Fund, the use of his name in connection with it brought contributions from various parts of the world.[66]

King also allowed the ACOA to use his name and influence in promoting special days of protest and conferences and workshops on South Africa. This action stood in line with his view that Americans had much to learn about South Africa and its role in the revolutionary change taking place worldwide in the fifties. King attached his name to ACOA letters calling for freedom rallies in support of oppressed South Africans.[67] Though not always present at the ACOA's Human Rights Day celebrations, held each year on December 10, and its Africa Freedom Day Activities, observed annually in April, King occasionally got involved as a sponsor and honorary chairman.[68] These involvements occurred in the late 1950s, when King was pushing for change in Montgomery, calling for a "White House Conference" to resolve the school crisis in Little Rock, Arkansas, and advocating the cessation of nuclear tests, actions that further substantiated his view that a truly democratic South Africa could be achieved only within the confines of a democratic and peaceful world.[69]

As the fifties came to an end, King viewed with deep interest developments in South Africa. He still believed that nonviolent direct action offered the best hope for a new and inclusive South Africa, a hope that stood a chance of being realized as long as Albert Luthuli headed the ANC. But Luthuli's nonviolent philosophy met a serious challenge from young militants in the ANC in 1958, creating fears of a shift toward armed struggle. Using the slogan "Africa for the Africans," the militants organized as the Pan-Africanists and repudiated "the broad South Africanism of the ANC."[70] Martin Luther King Jr. must have found this movement disturbing, mainly because its black separatism stood in stark contrast to Luthuli's and the ANC's policy of uniting all resisters to white supremacy, regardless of race. While it is unclear how King viewed the debate between Luthuli and the Pan-Africanists, in a practical sense he came down on the side of Luthuli, flatly rejecting the Pan-Africanist ideal of "Africa for the Aboriginals" and embracing Luthuli's ideal of "a raceless South Africa" based on "a universal franchise."[71]

King and Luthuli communicated with each other even as the latter faced the rising challenge of Pan-Africanism and the scrutiny and harassment of the South African government. When G. McLeod Bryan, a friend of King, visited Luthuli in September 1959, the South African activist, still mindful of the content, spirit, and impact of the *Declaration of Conscience,* informed Bryan of his tremendous admiration and respect for King. Bryan wrote King a month later, telling him what Luthuli had said about him:

> [H]e told me that the greatest inspiration to him was your *Stride Toward Freedom* [that Bishop Reeves had put into his hands]. Luthuli had been reading it in his cane fields the very day I visited him. He wished for copies to be put into the hands of his African National Congress. I told him I

would put the request to you, believing that you would contribute this much and more to South African freedom. His eyes were the brightest when I referred to him as the "King" of South Africa. His odds are so much greater, but he is a profound Christian sharing your views.[72]

Deeply touched by Luthuli's remarks, King responded with a letter to the ANC leader in December 1959. The letter stated in part:

May I say that I too have admired you tremendously from a distance. I only regret that circumstances and spacial divisions have made it impossible for us to meet. But I admire your great witness and your dedication to the cause of freedom and human dignity. You have stood amid persecution, abuse, and oppression with a dignity and calmness of spirit seldom paralleled in human history. One day all of Africa will be proud of your achievement.[73]

The words of praise and encouragement King and Luthuli expressed for each other must have been immensely reassuring at a time when both endured persecution and charges of being communists.[74] The tremendous moral, spiritual, and intellectual power they shared with each other developed out of their common commitment to the shaping of a new humanity. They presented the world with a special challenge in the 1950s, not only because they articulated clear visions of community for the United States, South Africa, and the world, but also because they committed themselves unselfishly to translating those visions into practical reality.[75]

One Among Many Black Voices

Martin Luther King Jr. was not the only African American leader to raise his voice in support of national and international protest against South African apartheid in the 1950s. Anti-apartheid rhetoric and activism came from radical and moderate elements in the civil rights movement. Representatives of both not only spoke out against white rule in South Africa, but also signed anti-apartheid declarations and appeals, contributed financially to the legal defense of South African political prisoners, and staged demonstrations against apartheid. Black leaders of various ideological persuasions engaged in deliberate efforts to lift the South African struggle to international consciousness, and to develop a voice for the oppressed masses outside South Africa.[76]

W. E. B. Du Bois and Paul Robeson had already established a long record of support for South African freedom when King first addressed the issue in

1957. Du Bois, the Harvard-trained scholar and father of Pan-Africanism, and Robeson, the well-known singer-actor-intellectual, considered African Americans and Africans elsewhere as essentially one family. Both preceded King in characterizing South Africa as the worst place in the world in terms of race relations, and in urging African Americans, as beleaguered as they were, to assist their South African brothers and sisters because they faced a common enemy.[77] While sharing King's view of bonds and obligations between African Americans and oppressed South Africans, Du Bois and Robeson, owing largely to their association with the radical left, lacked the resources and organizational support that were available to King to address the apartheid problem. The Council on African Affairs, through which Du Bois and Robeson sought to support oppressed South Africans financially and to educate the world concerning South Africa, succumbed to "the witch-hunt climate in the United States" and ceased to exist by the late fifties. This was a tragic development, because the council had served as the vehicle through which Robeson had supported the 1952 Defiance Campaign and other South African resistance movements with his writing, speaking, and benefit concerts.[78]

The "McCarthyite hysteria rampart in America" made it impossible for King to join Du Bois and Robeson in promoting the cause of the victims of apartheid. Despite their wide reputations as strong intellectuals with a social outlook, Du Bois's and Robeson's support was not seriously sought by the ACOA. Even so, they consistently made known their positions on South Africa. Du Bois and Robeson placed great emphasis on the struggle of the proletariat in South Africa for land and economic justice, a position not unusual for those who subscribed to the essential elements of marxism. They viewed the unity of oppressed South Africans—the coming together of blacks, Indians, and Coloreds in the struggle against white supremacy—as essential to the achievement of a South Africa along nonracial and socialist lines, a perspective with which King found some agreement.[79]

King shared Du Bois's and Robeson's perspectives on the similarities between South Africa and the American South. Recognizing the intensity of the racial oppression in both contexts, the three men felt that self-destruction for South Africa and the southern United States would be inevitable if they failed to yield to the forward march of civilization. They also held that the experiences of southern Negroes under Jim Crow made them more apt than other Americans to relate to and understand the oppressed of South Africa.[80] Be that as it may, Du Bois, Robeson, and King were equally clear in explaining that all Americans had a moral obligation to work for the elimination of apartheid. However, recognizing the extent of U.S. investments in South Africa, Robeson appears to have been more consistent and adamant than Du Bois and King in calling for a withdrawal of U.S. economic support for South Africa in the fifties.[81] Only in the 1960s would such a call be consistently and strongly emphasized by King.

African American leaders to the right of King also got involved in the South African cause in the 1950s. Max Yergan, who had worked many years with the Bantu of South Africa to improve educational facilities, became the best-known black conservative on this issue. He had worked at one point with Robeson in the Council on African Affairs. Yergan subscribed to King's dream of interracial cooperation and participatory democracy in South Africa, but his politics were not as radical as King's, a point substantiated in part by the fact that the South African government did not interfere with his activities on behalf of Bantu education.[82] In 1953, after being on assignment in Africa for *U.S. News and World Report,* Yergan wrote an article insisting that anti-apartheid activists cultivate "a sympathetic and constructive" attitude toward the South African government.[83] King and others in the ACOA preferred to rely on the politics of confrontation in dealing with the apartheid government, a fact that explains why conservatives like Yergan and George Schuyler never associated with them. Paul Robeson found Yergan's politics of cooperation most disturbing, and declared, after the latter's 1953 article, that "If one did not know that Yergan was a Negro . . . , one would have to assume that the article was written by a white state department mouthpiece assigned to working out a formula for maintaining white rule throughout Africa."[84] Such differences in politics reveal the nature of the debate between black leaders in the fifties concerning South Africa, even as they shared a commitment to ridding that country of apartheid and establishing it on a genuinely democratic foundation.

The ACOA became the point of connection between King and other popular and established civil rights leaders who included South Africa in their moral vision in the fifties. Adam Clayton Powell Jr., A. Philip Randolph, Jackie Robinson, and Howard Thurman served with King on the National Committee of the ACOA in the late fifties.[85] Powell and Thurman also joined King as supporters of the ACOA's Africa Defense and Aid Fund, along with other religious and political activists, such as

Mordecai Johnson, Charles Diggs, Benjamin E. Mays, and Sandy Ray.[86] Thurgood Marshall, so important to the civil rights movement from the standpoint of legislation and court action, became a signatory of the ACOA's worldwide *Declaration of Conscience* in 1957.[87] The support of such figures for the anti-apartheid cause shows that they had a clear vision of African liberation and its link to black Americans.

King and other African American leaders who promoted the ideal of a free South Africa in the fifties were intellectuals with a keen sense of the human struggle and their place in it. Indeed, they represented "the intellectual-activist types" that had constituted "the principal model" for W. E. B. Du Bois's leadership theory years earlier, and that was exemplified to the fullest in Du Bois, Robeson, and King.[88] In this sense, these leaders broke with that tradition of many educated blacks that separated the *intellectual* from the *social,* and which prevented intellectuals from devoting themselves completely to the liberation of people of African descent. For King, this dichotomy never really existed, despite the view that he was not socially and politically involved prior to the mid-1950s. Having grown up in an extended family network, a black church tradition, and a black college environment, where men were expected to succeed despite segregation and to become leaders in the quest for social change, King was not likely to be a detached intellectual who confined himself to the articulation of abstract, complicated ideas.[89] His view that the collective intellect should be put to the service of human liberation, and that ideas find meaning only when translated into practical action, became the impelling force in his fight for oppressed peoples.

CHAPTER 2

A COMMON DESTINY
Challenging Jim Crow and Apartheid in the 1960s

*I have said before and I still say so now that I see no reason
why, in a free democratic Africa, a predominantly black
electorate should not return a white man to Parliament, for
colour will count for nothing in a free Africa.*
Robert M. Sobukwe, 1960[1]

*My Negro friends were very eager to hear about South
Africa, and their readiness to help resolved itself many times
into the question, "Can we come over there to assist you?"*
Albert J. Luthuli, 1962[2]

*Our struggle for freedom in the United States is not funda-
mentally different from that going on in South Africa. . . .
We share a common destiny.*
Martin Luther King Jr., 1963[3]

I n the 1960s, no human being exceeded the prominence of Martin
Luther King Jr. His towering importance and vast influence can be
explained from two angles. First, he introduced something new into
American life and culture through his adherence to and practice of
creative nonviolent dissent.[4] Through the practical application of nonviolent principles in civil rights campaigns in Albany, Birmingham,
Washington, D.C., Selma, Chicago, Memphis, and other cities, King and
his followers forced Americans to reexamine the true meaning of democracy and the Christian faith. Second, King's prominence resulted from the
myriad ways in which he continued to challenge South Africa and other

parts of the world concerning the moral obligation to completely eliminate the great evils of racism, economic injustice and poverty, and war.[5]

King's meaning and significance for South Africa in the 1960s is the focus of this chapter. The discussion takes into account the ways in which he
compared and contrasted Jim Crowism in the American South and
apartheid in South Africa, his anti-apartheid activities through the American Committee on Africa (ACOA) and the American Negro Leadership
Conference on Africa (ANLCA), his correspondence with South African
students, and the impact of his death on South Africans and the anti-
apartheid movement.

Comparing and Contrasting Jim Crow and Apartheid

The links between the struggle of peoples of color in South Africa and the
civil rights movement in America remained a part of the consciousness of
leaders in both contexts in the sixties. The African National Congress
(ANC) leader Walter Sisulu, who corresponded with both Martin Luther
King Sr. and Martin Luther King Jr. in that period, said in an interview that
the freedom struggle in America "quite inspired us because of the manner
in which it was organized and the success it achieved."[6] In similar fashion,
Martin Luther King Jr. expressed his indebtedness to the Defiance Campaign and other nonviolent movements led in South Africa by Albert J.
Luthuli.[7] King's perspective at this point was rooted not only in a sense of a
special kinship with others of African descent, but also in the experiential
sources of the African American church and culture, which articulated the
community's suffering as linked to the well-being of humanity in general.[8]

It was out of this sense of a shared experience with oppressed South
Africans that King compared Jim Crowism and apartheid. In January
1960, he observed: "I have done a considerable amount of reading on the
whole of Africa and I have taken particular interest in the problems in
South Africa because of the similarities between the situation there and
our situation in the United States."[9] This tendency to compare the struggles was equally typical of African leaders. While meeting with King in
Atlanta, Georgia, in May 1960, Kenneth Kaunda, a leader from southern
Africa who later became president of Zambia, "compared the African fight
for freedom to the Negro's movement in the South and said that Africans
are very pleased with the 'desire and determination of the Negro citizen to
take his place in this country.'"[10]

King often spoke of apartheid in South Africa and Jim Crow in the

United States in the same vein, calling to mind W. E. B. Du Bois and Paul Robeson before him.[11] He devoted far more time to comparing and contrasting the two contexts in this period than he had in the previous decade. When the noted novelist and folklorist Harold Courlander wrote King in August 1961, claiming that there existed "more than a subtle difference" between the struggle in South Africa and that in the southern United States, King responded emphatically: "In some parts of the South there are persons who might even question your assumption that South African apartheid is categorically different from the situation of the unlettered Negro in the rural counties of the South in these United States." While King agreed that the media in the United States, unlike in South Africa, was free to make sure that "whatever happens today in the struggle for a better America is news around the world," he, on the other hand, reminded Courlander that "there are thousands of known cases of reprisal" against black people in the American South "which never come to the attention of the world."[12]

King pointed to the similarities between South African apartheid and southern Jim Crow with great specificity. For him, one similarity had to do with the fact that both systems were rooted in the doctrine of white supremacy. The struggle in both cases, then, was directed at the same enemy. While recognizing the problem of institutionalized racism in America, King held in 1967 that "the classic example of organized and institutionalized racism is the Union of South Africa." He continued: "Its national policy and practice are the incarnation of the doctrine of white supremacy in the midst of a population which is overwhelmingly black."[13] At the same time, King refused to reduce white supremacy to a mere "American phenomenon" or a "South African problem," and viewed it instead as a "global phenomenon," or a sickness that "knows no geographical boundaries."[14] Thus, many of the problems of peoples of color in America, Africa, Asia, and other parts of the so-called Third World could be traced to white supremacist doctrines:

> I think we have to honestly admit that the problems in the world today, as they relate to the question of race, must be blamed on the whole doctrine of white supremacy, the whole doctrine of racism, and these doctrines came into being through the white race and the exploitation of the colored peoples of the world.[15]

In King's view, another similarity between South African apartheid and southern Jim Crow involved the ways in which they exploited people of color economically, politically, psychologically, and otherwise, thereby degrading human personality and undermining human community. King clearly saw how both systems subjected people of color to segregation by law and custom, reduced them to the status of a laboring class with the lowest wages, denied them participation in the political processes, forced them to live and work under the worst conditions with the poorest of education, and exposed them to systematic public and private insult.[16] For King, the psychological violence stemming from such conditions could not be measured, especially since whites gained a false sense of superiority and people of color a false sense of inferiority. The inevitable result was the loss of a sense that humans are interrelated and interdependent.[17]

King also noted how apartheid in South Africa and Jim Crow in the American South divided and scarred the body of Christ. Such a comparison seemed only natural for one who claimed a serious devotion to the church and its ministry. He was disturbed that the theologies and practices of the Dutch Reformed Protestant Church in South Africa and the Southern Baptist Convention in America sanctioned white supremacy, thereby encouraging racial hatred and exclusiveness. King found this unacceptable, particularly in light of the church's mission to proclaim community as "a triadic relationship between persons, God, and the world."[18] "The vicious, inhumane" practices in South Africa, such as the Pass Laws and the delimiting of areas in which only members of a particular racial group or subgroup could reside, "are sanctioned and, to a large extent, set up by the Dutch Reformed Protestant Church," King complained. "Over and over again," he added, "Chief Luthuli, that great black leading Christian, has knocked on the door of the Church in South Africa, but always the response has been, 'Get away from this door. We're too busy reciting our creedal system.'" Referring to a similar situation in the United States, King expressed dissatisfaction that "my church could never join the Southern Baptist Convention because it is an all-white convention." "And if Negroes went into many of those churches today," said he of the typical Southern Baptist congregation, "they would be kicked out."[19] The Dutch Reformed Protestant Church and the Southern Baptist Convention were for King perfect examples of the church's failure to be, in accordance with the gospel mandate, "a symbol of the beloved community" and "a moral agent in the creation of community."[20]

Considering the natures of and similarities between the conditions in South Africa and the southern United States, King noted that it was easy to

understand why "the struggle against Jim Crow and apartheid has sometimes even taken similar tactical positions." He explained that

> When Negroes in Montgomery, Alabama became fed up with being pushed
> into the back of buses, they walked rather than continue in humiliation.
> When Africans riding on totally segregated buses to and from the shanty-
> town of Alexandra Township on the Witwatersrand became fed up, they
> also decided to walk for freedom.[21]

The fact that both people of color in South Africa and black southern-
ers in America embraced nonviolence in their struggles afforded, according to King, further evidence of that which bonded them spiritually and
intellectually:

> In our struggle for freedom and justice in the U.S., which has also been
> long and arduous, we feel a powerful sense of identification with those in
> the far more deadly struggle for freedom in South Africa. We know how
> Africans there, and their friends of other races, strove for half a century to
> win their freedom by nonviolent methods. We have honored Chief Luthuli
> for his leadership, and we know how this nonviolence and restraint were
> only met by increasing repression, culminating in the shootings at
> Sharpeville and all that has happened since.[22]

King saw yet another similarity suggested in the manner in which segregationists in both South Africa and the United States responded to
movements of the oppressed against the status quo. He found it very interesting, though not surprising, that the apartheid government in South
Africa, much like southern white politicians and other opponents of the
civil rights movement in America, often used the communist label to dis-
credit all activities against racist policies and practices:

> In South Africa today all opposition to white supremacy is condemned as
> communism, and in its name, due process is destroyed, a Medieval segrega-
> tion is organized with twentieth century efficiency and drive, a sophisti-
> cated form of slavery is imposed by a minority upon a majority who are
> kept in grinding poverty, and the dignity of human personality is defiled
> and world opinion is arrogantly defied.[23]

King's contact with Africans in various parts of the world in the sixties
reinforced his sense of the bonds and obligations that existed between
black South Africans and African Americans. He returned to Nigeria to

witness the independence celebrations in 1960, and the struggles of South Africa and Africa in general dominated his discussions with Africans. During that same year, King met with Adelaide Tambo and other ANC representatives at Africa Unity House in London, an experience that must have been transformative as far as his perspective on South Africa was concerned. The changing character of the ANC and the role of black South African women in the anti-apartheid crusade came into sharper focus for him.[24] The conference with black South Africans and other Africans in London in 1964 proved equally important as King sought to understand the pain and frustration of South African exiles.[25]

Given the parallels between the civil rights movement in America and the anti-apartheid crusade in South Africa, King found it exceedingly difficult to understand African Americans who denied all ties to oppressed South Africans. Bearing in mind the politico-economic forces that operated in both contexts, King declared that

> This is why I say it is impossible for a Negro, if he is at all conscious of the world around him, not to identify with the South African non-white, though we may speak different tongues and may never look into each other's eyes. We share a common destiny: to live on in poverty and rejection or to walk proudly as free men in our own nations.[26]

This statement, along with others scattered throughout King's speeches and writings, suggests that his interest in the problems of the poor and oppressed in South Africa must be viewed within the context of his broader concern for Africa and people of African ancestry everywhere. King focused on persons of African descent around the world, the unique links between them, the similarities in their condition, and the imperative need for them to work together to overcome oppression in all forms. An advocate of the view that black people everywhere are related in a special way by blood and condition, King asserted that "in many ways the futures of the emergent African nations (particularly those below the Sahara) and the American Negro are intertwined."[27] His perspective at this point found affinity with views expressed by generations of African American leaders and thinkers before him.

King was no less mindful of how the South African context differed from the situation in the American South. In fact, the extent to which historical and cultural factors contributed to the distinctiveness of apartheid as a system of oppression became increasingly clear to him in the 1960s.

For example, he came to a clearer understanding of how the problems in South Africa resulted from a lack of the kind of natural rights tradition that existed in the United States. Recognizing that there was no bill of rights or universal natural rights tradition even for white South Africans, King appealed to the South African government to "bring its policies in line with the Universal Declaration of Human Rights" as defined by the United Nations.[28]

The uniqueness of the South African context, historically and culturally, appeared in other ways to King, and especially with regard to tribalism, racial composition, and "the means available to the oppressor."[29] He discovered how tribal loyalties, the principal obstacle to unity across ethnic lines in South Africa, made unified struggle among the oppressed there more difficult to achieve than in the southern United States. Indeed, that sense of being a part of a suffering *community,* of having a common enemy, and of reaching toward a common destiny registered with less force among oppressed South Africans than among African Americans. This situation led King to conclude that a free and inclusive South Africa would be utterly impossible as long as the oppressed placed tribal loyalties above broadly based communal values.[30]

For King, racial composition loomed as perhaps the most obvious feature distinguishing South Africa from the southern United States. Peoples of color far outnumbered whites in South Africa, a situation unlike America, where blacks constituted a small minority amid a strong white majority. King felt that the numerical dominance of blacks and other peoples of color bred an unusually intense fear and insecurity in South Africa's whites regarding the future, causing them to adopt the most inhumane measures and tactics imaginable to sustain their power and privilege, and to prevent fundamental political change. Concerning the strikingly different political means used by oppressors in South Africa and the American South, King commented:

> Half a congress is, after all, better than none just as being a second-class citizen is a small improvement over not being one at all. . . . Even in Mississippi we can organize to register Negro voters, we can speak to the press, we can in short organize the people in nonviolent action. But in South Africa even the mildest form of nonviolent resistance meets with years of imprisonment, and leaders over many years have been restricted and silenced and imprisoned. We can understand how in that situation people felt so desperate that they turned to other methods, such as sabotage.[31]

In King's estimation, peoples of color in South Africa were involved in a far more difficult struggle, a struggle with which no other oppressed people could fully identify. "There can be no doubt of the fact that South Africa is the most stubborn and rugged place in the world in the area of race relations," he argued. He continued: "We read of tortures in jails with electric devices, suicides among prisoners, forced confessions, while in the outside community ruthless persecution of editors, religious leaders, and political opponents suppresses free speech and a free press."[32] Indeed, King pressed his analysis further, comparing South Africa to Nazi Germany. "The South African government, to make the white supreme," he observed, "has had to reach into the past and revive the nightmarish ideology and practices of Nazism. We are witnessing a recrudescence of that barbarism which murdered more humans than any war in history."[33]

The similarities and dissimilarities between South African apartheid and southern Jim Crow became one issue on which King found common ground with other African American leaders in the 1960s. The belief that apartheid and Jim Crow were basically indistinguishable in terms of their impact on vital areas of black life—economic, political, religious, social, and intellectual—were held by leaders as militant and controversial as Malcolm X and Adam Clayton Powell Jr., and as moderate as Congressman Charles C. Diggs Jr., Mordecai W. Johnson, Benjamin E. Mays, and Howard Thurman. The interest displayed by all of these leaders at this level proved contextual in the sense that the sixties constituted a period during which African Americans, under the influence of the black power and black awareness thrust, rediscovered and reaffirmed their ancestral roots in Africa.

Activities Through the ACOA and ANLCA

In the 1960s, organizations remained principal vehicles through which Martin Luther King Jr. challenged racism at home and abroad. His Southern Christian Leadership Conference (SCLC), headquartered in Atlanta, Georgia, afforded a network for attacking racism in the United States, and the New York–based ACOA provided a structure for protesting against South African apartheid. Although King's primary commitment was to the civil rights agenda of the SCLC, he made significant moral and financial contributions to the anti-apartheid activities of the ACOA.[34] This becomes all the more evident in view of the fact that King lived outside South Africa, and was thus seldom able to distinguish between the theoretical and practical possibilities of the South African situation.

King's work with the ACOA reached a new phase in March 1960, when South African police killed sixty-nine black peaceful protesters against Pass Laws at Sharpeville. The Sharpeville massacre angered King, especially since he had consistently criticized laws that restricted the freedom of movement of people of color in South Africa. The state of emergency that followed the massacre proved equally disturbing for him because numerous anti-apartheid organizations were banned and thousands of activists were detained without trial. In April 1960, the names of King, Hope R. Stevens, Eleanor Roosevelt, George Meany, A. Philip Randolph, and others involved in the ACOA's Africa Freedom Day celebration appeared on a statement declaring that "the massacre in South Africa has shocked the world." The statement called upon people of goodwill worldwide to "protest the cruel, inhuman massacre in Sharpeville," and to help "meet the needs of the families of those killed and wounded in South Africa."[35] During that same time, King and others in the ACOA united with more than fifty leaders in the Americans for Democratic Action (ADA) in urging the United States government to impose diplomatic and economic sanctions against South Africa. After commending Secretary of State Christian Herter "for the declaration of the State Department deploring the use of violence by the South African government against its people," the protesters asserted that

> In view of the determination of the South African government to continue on its present appalling and disastrous course of action, we believe that further steps are urgently needed to impress upon it the deep concern with which the American people view its actions. We therefore urge that our ambassador be recalled to Washington for consultation on the situation and that, while these consultations are in progress, American purchases of gold from South Africa be suspended. As you know these are measures long sanctified by diplomatic usage, and are a form of language among nations—strong language, but amply justified by the gravity of events. We are confident that the U.S. people will support you in these actions.[36]

King and others on the National Committee of the ACOA also supported the formation of the South Africa Emergency Committee in April 1960. Made up of twenty-five "key organization leaders" from the ACOA, Americans for Democratic Action, the National Council of Churches (NCC), the National Association for the Advancement of Colored People (NAACP), the American Jewish Congress (AJC), and other groups, the committee launched "a nation-wide campaign against the racist policies of the South African government." As a first step, the committee echoed King's call for the mobilization of American public opinion, for a consumer boycott of South African goods, for pressure on private American investors in South Africa, for the raising of legal defense and welfare funds for the recent victims of repressive police action, and for pressure on U.S. policy makers and UN delegations to influence South Africa "to abandon its ruthless *apartheid* program."[37]

King, George Houser, and others in the ACOA opposed the idea of an American or UN military response to the events surrounding the Sharpeville massacre. After the massacre and the declaration of a state of emergency by the South African apartheid regime, King became unalterably convinced that economic and diplomatic pressure from the civilized world was absolutely essential for peaceful change in South Africa.[38] Given his hope for South Africa, he must have been quite concerned when many in that country viewed Sharpeville as symbolic "of the failure of nonviolent attempts by blacks to achieve justice." At this stage, the ANC and the Pan-Africanist Congress (PAC) went underground and resolved that the era of armed resistance had begun:

> After Sharpeville some began to reassess the fifty-year-old tradition of nonviolence in the ANC. Since its inception the ANC had been resolutely committed to nonviolence, but in 1961 Nelson Mandela and others abandoned this policy. There were, they argued, two alternatives—to submit or fight. Four forms of violence were examined: sabotage, guerrilla warfare, terrorism, and open revolution. Fears of open interracial civil war led to the deliberate limitation of violence to sabotage, and then with the proviso that, firstly, it should not injure or kill people, and, secondly, it should be directed at targets which would bring economic pressure on the white electorate to change. Thus was born *uMkhonto weSizwe* (Spear of the Nation); and the first acts of sabotage were committed in 1961. The ANC's policy of nonviolence was thus finally abandoned by men who felt that all channels of peaceful protest had been closed.[39]

The nations of the world did not respond favorably to this shift in tactics. Some world leaders predicted a race war, echoing fears that Martin Luther King Jr. had frequently expressed. In the midst of this changing scene, world leaders looked to Albert J. Luthuli as the best hope for peaceful coexistence between the races in South Africa. In December 1960, Luthuli, who had led nonviolent campaigns in the fifties, was named the recipient of the prestigious Nobel Peace Prize, an honor he was not allowed to receive until 1961.[40] This gesture on the part of the global community, however well-meaning, would not revive the era of nonviolent protest as previously known in South Africa.

Apparently, King did not respond publicly to the ANC's and the PAC's announcement of an era of armed struggle in South Africa. This was not unusual for him, especially considering his policy of refusing to tell the oppressed in other countries how to conduct their struggles. While he publicly supported the release of the ANC activist Nelson Mandela and the PAC leader Robert Sobukwe from prison, he never questioned their tactics in a public forum.[41] However, King's continuing admiration for and contact with Luthuli seem to suggest something about his feelings on the matter. King continued to see Luthuli as the voice of reason, operating between the extreme forces of complacency and violence in his country. In other words, Luthuli at this point represented what Mohandas K. Gandhi had previously symbolized for India; namely, a spirit of love and nonviolence in a society torn by complacency, indifference, hatred, and violence. King's sense of Luthuli's importance for South Africa found reinforcement in the very nature of what the two men said about each other. When James W. King, a Baptist minister from Ohio, visited Luthuli in 1964, he asked the South African activist "what he would want Americans to know." Luthuli replied: "Give my highest regards to Martin Luther. It is not often that we see clergymen taking a stand on social issues. It means a lot to us here. Martin Luther King is my hero."[42] King responded to Luthuli's comments with the same measure of generosity. "I cannot begin to say to you how delighted I am to hear from Chief Luthuli," he said in a letter to James King. "I consider him one of the truly great men of our age. So you can see how flattered I am to receive his generous words concerning my work."[43] It was probably through Luthuli that King had his greatest impact on oppressed South Africans in the 1960s.

But it was virtually impossible for Luthuli to continue to live up to the image that King and others had of him. As the more radical voices of the ANC and Pan-Africanism emerged, Luthuli's leadership confronted a serious challenge, calling to mind King's own struggle against Malcolm X and black power militants.[44] As was the case with King, the challenge helped radicalize Luthuli, causing him to consider new methods in the crusade for freedom and justice. Even as he praised King for nonviolent victories in America, Luthuli failed to embrace a thoroughgoing pacifism, noting on one occasion that "when a man attacks my Kraal, I must take my spear and defend my family."[45] He remained with the ANC even after its shift to armed struggle, an issue that should not be overlooked by those who would compare him to King.[46] Be that as it may, Luthuli and King were drawn together by their essential belief in a peaceful, nonracial society. Furthermore, they received strength from each other at a time when both were denounced by the forces of black power and separatism, and when the epithet "communist" was still volleyed at them from white supremacists.[47]

The ACOA symbolized the meeting of the minds of Luthuli and King, especially since both used their names and influence to attract moral and financial support for the organization. Luthuli often repeated Alan Paton's claim that the ACOA "represents the conscience of America," concluding that "I do not know what we would do without it."[48] While Luthuli's work on behalf of the ACOA was necessarily confined to the drafting and signing of appeal letters, King continued to promote the organization's agenda in various ways. He frequently signed appeal letters on behalf of the ACOA's Africa Defense and Aid Fund, allowed his name to appear on its letterhead and on brochures about its work, accepted financial contributions on its behalf, served as honorary chairman of its Africa Freedom Day and Human Rights Day observances, remained on its National Committee, and occasionally served as its guest speaker.[49] There was for King no necessary and practical distinction between these involvements, geared primarily toward South African freedom, and his efforts to secure basic constitutional rights for his people in Albany, Birmingham, Selma, and other cities in the American South.

Convinced that matters had deteriorated in South Africa, King became part of a new ACOA campaign to evoke positive worldwide action against apartheid in 1962. The ACOA director George Houser described the campaign as being "in the nature of a follow-up on our 1957 *Declaration of Conscience*," which had been sponsored by King, James Pike, and Eleanor Roosevelt.[50] The idea involved the drafting of a similar declaration, and King, Albert Luthuli, and Eleanor Roosevelt were asked to initiate the campaign and to invite "world leaders to sign this declaration." Roosevelt declined to participate due to poor health.[51] Thus, King and Luthuli became the initial sponsors of the ACOA's *Appeal for Action Against Apartheid*. Luthuli explained the *Appeal* in these terms:

> The *Appeal for Action Against Apartheid* is projected to bring pressure on South Africa on an international scale—pressure for change before it is too

late—before we are caught in a bloody revolt which would necessarily po-larize along racial lines and blot out all hope for justice in South Africa. Such a cataclysm would destroy our movement here; it would endanger hard-won progress everywhere, including America. That is why Martin Luther King joins me as an initiating sponsor for this *Appeal for Action*. The *Appeal* must not remain merely a document; it must become the base of an international campaign.[52]

The *Appeal for Action Against Apartheid* was powerfully symbolic in that it united the voices of two of the century's greatest champions of non-violent direct action. Built around the ACOA's Africa Freedom Day and Human Rights Day celebrations, the *Appeal* advocated the following:

(1) Hold meetings and demonstrations on December 10, Human Rights Day.
(2) Urge your church, union, lodge, or club to observe this day as one of protest.
(3) Urge your government to support economic sanctions.
(4) Write to your Mission to the United Nations urging adoption of a resolution calling for international isolation of South Africa.
(5) Don't buy South Africa's products.
(6) Don't trade or invest in South Africa.
(7) Translate public opinion into public action by explaining facts to all peoples, to groups to which you belong, and to countries of which you are citizens until *an effective international quarantine of apartheid is established.*[53]

The response to the *Appeal* worldwide was quite positive and in some respects overwhelming, a development not surprising since Luthuli was a recent Nobel Prize recipient and King an internationally known civil rights leader. It was signed by approximately 150 world leaders, aside from Luthuli and King. Signatories from the United States included James Baldwin, Senator Clifford P. Case of New Jersey, Ossie Davis, U.S. Con-gressman Charles C. Diggs Jr., Harry Emerson Fosdick, Harry Golden, George Houser, Donald Harrington, U.S. Congressman Adam C. Powell Jr., Reinhold Niebuhr, A. Philip Randolph, Walter Reuther, Lillian Smith, and Paul Tillich, all of whom were connected in some way to the ACOA.[54] The list of sponsors of the *Appeal* from abroad was as long and equally im-pressive, including such figures as Prime Minister Ahmed Ben Bella of

Algeria, Samuel Hugo Bergman, Max Born, Martin Buber, Madame Simone De Beauvoir, Danilo Dolci, Tom Mboya, Martin Niemoller, Bishop Ambrose Reeves, Michael Scott, Oliver R. Tambo, and a host of others.[55] This effort to achieve a worldwide condemnation of apartheid reflected something quite profound about the visions of Luthuli and King in the early 1960s. The *Appeal* provided more than ample proof of their refusal to separate the freedom struggles in the United States and South Africa, and of their conviction that the moral obligation for eliminating racism rested ultimately with the global community.

King's and Luthuli's effectiveness in initiating and promoting the *Appeal for Action Against Apartheid* led some in the ACOA to raise new questions about the relationship of black Americans to South Africa in particular and Africa in general. "Believing that pressure from the black community could have great influence on U.S. policy toward Africa," writes George M. Houser, "the A.C.O.A. proposed to leaders of civil rights groups that an organization be set up in which they could join forces to press the government on African issues."[56] The result was the formation of the American Negro Leadership Conference on Africa (ANLCA) in New York in June 1962, and the naming of Theodore E. Brown as its director. The "Call Committee" of the organization consisted of the "Big Six" of the civil rights movement; namely, Martin Luther King Jr. of the SCLC, Roy Wilkins of the NAACP, Whitney Young of the National Urban League, A. Philip Randolph of the Brotherhood of Sleeping Car Porters, James Farmer of the Congress of Racial Equality (CORE), and Dorothy Height of the National Council of Negro Women (NCNW).[57] King's role in the ANLCA squared perfectly with his conviction that the civil rights movement in America, the anti-apartheid crusade in South Africa, and the battles against colonialism throughout other parts of Africa were a common struggle, a point that could be made concerning the other leaders as well.

The ANLCA provided yet another organizational umbrella under which King contributed to organized movements against South African apartheid. Twenty-eight national organizations and several U.S. congressmen became sponsors of the ANLCA, ties that appeared initially to give it the resources necessary to make a strong case against South Africa.[58] Given its base of support, the new organization held a number of successful and influential conferences in the sixties. The ANLCA's interest in the problems of South Africa found powerful expression from the outset, especially since that country was on the verge of a classic revolutionary situation:

> In South Africa, the possibility of wholesale violence seems all the more imminent. Organizations of Africans have been banned, leaders have been imprisoned, freedom of movement has been almost completely curtailed, the white supremacist government has built up its military power to smash any possible revolt, and an atmosphere of bitterness, fear and frustration is over the whole country. Not until freedom and equality have been won can the new spirit prevail.[59]

The "Call to the American Negro Leadership Conference on Africa" went on to note that both the General Assembly and the Security Council of the United Nations had condemned the South African regime, "but these resolutions have not been implemented by substantive action."[60]

The first major conference of the ANLCA occurred on the Arden House Campus of Columbia University in New York, November 23–25, 1962. Martin Luther King Jr. and the other leaders present put forth strong resolutions on the Congo, Kenya, the Central African Federation, Angola, Mozambique, South West Africa, and South Africa. The resolutions on South Africa were stated in terms compelling enough to merit extensive quotation:

> The American Negro Leadership Conference condemns apartheid as a system to exploit the African, Asian, and Colored majority in South Africa by white supremacists and endorses the campaign of *Appeal for Action Against Apartheid.*
>
> We deplore our government's opposition to the United Nations resolution calling for sanctions against South Africa. We urge the United States to support such action by the United Nations against South Africa and to seek its implementation through effective policing of the modes of entry.
>
> We recognize that the United States prohibits the shipment of arms to South Africa designed for use in the implementation of apartheid, but we call upon the Government to undertake a total embargo of war material to the South African Republic, because no practical distinction can be made between weapons for maintaining apartheid and weapons for any other purpose.
>
> We call upon the United States business firms to cease lending money to South Africa and to withdraw investments from that country since such financial transactions can only strengthen the present racist government.

We urge the United States Government to actively discourage any public or private economic aid to South Africa.

We urge the State Department to include opponents of the apartheid policy among the South African recipients of leadership grants.

We call upon individual Americans to join the growing international boycott of South African goods.

We demand that the United States Armed Forces cease military maneuvers in cooperation with South African forces and the use of South African waters or bases.

We urge that the United States abandon the practice of excluding American Negroes from its missions to the Republic of South Africa and Africans from affairs sponsored by the American Embassy and all other United States Missions in that country.

We urge the American Olympic Committee to fight for the exclusion of South Africa from the coming Olympic games unless that nation permits all South African athletes to compete for places on its team without regard to race or color.

We oppose the efforts of the Republic of South Africa to incorporate the three High Commission Territories, namely, Basutoland, Swaziland, Bechuanaland into the Republic of South Africa.[61]

Martin Luther King Jr. delivered one of his most important statements on Africa at this 1962 ANLCA conference. In that statement, which later appeared in a more extensive version in *New York Amsterdam News,* he underscored the hypocrisy that typified America's relationship to Africa in general and South Africa in particular:

It is tragic that our foreign policy on Africa is so ambivalent; for example, on the one hand, we decry in some mild manner the apartheid policy of the Union of South Africa but economically we continue "business-as-usual" in spite of the stringent racist policies being enforced and intensified. We do not support economic sanctions in the United Nations though we impose them ourselves.[62]

Convinced that U.S. policy toward Africa had to be shaped in conformity "with our own democratic posture," King held that the American government's stand against "racism at home" meant nothing if it failed to evolve into "a strong functional attitude" against racism abroad.[63]

Plans for a White House conference with President John F. Kennedy on South Africa followed the ANLCA meeting. Representatives of both the

ANLCA and the ACOA were involved. The conference was initially scheduled for December 10, 1962, Human Rights Day, but did not take place until a week later. While the problems of Africa as a whole figured high on the agenda, King, Theodore Brown, James Farmer, Dorothy Height, A. Philip Randolph, Roy Wilkins, and Whitney Young urged President Kennedy to impose economic sanctions against South Africa.[64] They reminded Kennedy that his commitment to civil rights in America would remain questionable as long as the administration refused to comply with the United Nations' *Resolution A/RES/1761* regarding the need for international pressure against the apartheid regime. Moreover, they solicited Kennedy's support for the *Appeal for Action Against Apartheid.*[65]

The year 1962, then, proved enormously important in terms of King's mounting activities against South African apartheid. His involvement with the *Appeal for Action Against Apartheid,* his speech on the Arden House Campus of Columbia University, and his participation in the White House conference were important enough, but perhaps more significant was his decision to work through both the ANLCA and the ACOA. By participating as best he could in the anti-apartheid activities of both organizations, he hoped to convey a twofold message. The first message was that his campaign against racism was not regional but universal. Second, he hoped to show black Americans in particular that it was both useful and necessary for them to understand the problems of South Africa and to contribute what they could to the elevation of the oppressed in that land. King warned against the perils of isolationism, declaring in December 1962 that the American Negro must have "a growing awareness of his world citizenship."[66]

When 1962 came to a close, it was not difficult for King to see positive evidence of his efforts on behalf of a free South Africa. That evidence most certainly existed at the social level, for he had been involved, through the *Appeal for Action Against Apartheid* and the emergence of the ANLCA, in making people of all races and ethnic backgrounds around the world more sensitive to the apartheid problem. But there were also notable examples of how King's stand against apartheid caused changes in the personal lives of even avowed racists. The conversion of Beyers Naudé, a Dutch Reformed and South African clergyman, made the point in a most remarkable way. Naudé, a ranking member of a secret white racist organization in South Africa called the *Broederbond,* was transformed "from a narrow racist to an inclusive Christian" after sitting with King and hearing him speak in a black church in Winston-Salem, North Carolina, in 1962. Naudé publicly resigned from the *Broederbond* early in 1963, and "at once became the main white opponent to the Nationalist Government, and formed both a journal, *Pro Veritate,* and an ecumenical organization, The Christian Institute, to lead the way to a free and open and non-racial South Africa."[67] Examples of this nature undoubtedly convinced King that racism, however deeply it penetrated the psyche of white people, would not be a permanent condition.

The close alliance between the ANLCA and the ACOA after 1962 excluded any possibility of King's valuing one organization more than the other. His contributions to the fund-raising activities and programmatic thrusts of both, when considered alongside his many other involvements, proved quite impressive. From 1963 until his death five years later, King drew on the resources of both the ANLCA and the ACOA as he sought to heighten his influence on the movement against South African apartheid.[68]

A pivotal role in the civil rights campaigns in Birmingham, Washington, D.C., and other American cities made 1963 less productive than 1962 as far as King's anti-apartheid activities were concerned. Although his signature continued to appear on the ANLCA's and ACOA's fund-raising letters and petitions calling for U.S. government action against South Africa, King played essentially no part in other events they sponsored. The ACOA's Africa Freedom Day and Human Rights Day celebrations went on without him, and he even missed the meetings of the Call Committee of the ANLCA.[69] While pointing out the need "for some type of continued organizational setup to relate the American Negro with Africa and its many problems," King noted in a letter to the ANLCA director Theodore Brown in April 1963 that the SCLC did "not have the financial resources to support such a permanent thrust." However, King offered to participate in urging foundations to support continuing organizations like the ANLCA and the ACOA.[70]

One of King's greatest opportunities to further impact world opinion on South Africa came when the UN General Assembly set up a special committee on the apartheid policy of South Africa early in 1963. In April 1963, shortly before that committee began hearings on South Africa, the ACOA director George Houser wrote King urging him to testify before it. "I am reinforced in my opinion that it would have tremendous effect if you would be able to appear before the committee at a time agreeable to you and to their schedule," said Houser. Houser went on to say that

> They are very enthusiastic about this. It would be quite appropriate for you to do this, not only because of your position here in this country, but also because you, along with Chief Luthuli, helped to initiate our *Appeal for Action Against Apartheid* campaign around Human Rights Day last December 10th. Your appearance before the committee to make a brief statement would have great impact around the world and certainly in South Africa. It also would help to bring this whole problem of the U.S. relationship to South Africa forcibly to the attention of officials in Washington. . . . Your participation in that struggle (in Birmingham) will make all the more effective what you can say about the struggle in Africa as well.[71]

Houser's request of King was supported by Enuga S. Reddy, an Indian activist and Gandhi admirer who served as the Principal Secretary of the UN Special Committee on the Policies of Apartheid of the Government of the Republic of South Africa. Reddy wrote King in June 1963, and actually tried to arrange the civil rights leader's testimony at the United Nations.[72] Collin Gonze, an ACOA staff person, prepared the rough draft of a statement for King to read on that occasion.[73] King appeared genuinely interested, but a convenient time could not be found.[74] George Houser put the idea before King again in September 1963, soon after his famous "I Have a Dream" speech in Washington, D.C., but again commitments to the struggle in America made an appearance before the UN impossible.[75] It would be a mistake to conclude that King's unavailability added up to a declining interest in the battle against South African apartheid. This would not have been possible for one who so consistently linked the freedom struggles in the United States and South Africa.

There was initially no strong indication that 1964 would be any different from the previous year in terms of King's efforts against the racist system in South Africa. He remained on the National Committee of the ACOA, and on the Call and Policy Committees of the ANLCA, but the growing demands of the civil rights movement seemed to make his presence more symbolic than substantive. Once again, King's contributions to the anti-apartheid efforts of these organizations were reduced largely to an occasional financial gift and to the signing of appeal letters, declarations, and petitions. His desire to draw major attention to the tragic situation in

South Africa during appearances before the platform committees of the Democratic and Republican conventions never materialized.[76] Although King supported the ACOA's and the ANLCA's attempts to press a stronger South Africa policy upon President Lyndon B. Johnson in the summer of 1964, he had reasons to doubt the success of such attempts, especially in light of the government's preoccupation with civil rights at home and war in Southeast Asia.[77]

Evidence of King's continuing influence on the South Africa–related agendas of the ANLCA and the ACOA surfaced in profound ways toward the end of 1964. He was quite instrumental in the planning process that led to the ANLCA's second major conference on U.S.-Africa policy, a conference held at the Shoreham Hotel in Washington, D.C., September 24–27, 1964. ANLCA and ACOA representatives came together at this conference, and a number of resolutions were adopted concerning the Congo, Southern Rhodesia, South West Africa, the Republic of South Africa, and the U.S. aid program for Africa in general.[78] The resolution passed on South Africa reflected, in remarkable measure, the ideas and spirit of King:

> We condemn South African *apartheid* as a denial of basic human rights to the majority of the people of that unhappy land.
>
> We identify with the struggle for justice and freedom in South Africa.
>
> We recognize the evolution in United States' policy toward South Africa in past years, but call for bold initiatives and a more dynamic approach in the immediate future.
>
> Although U.S. foreign policy has formally opposed *apartheid* and racial oppression in South Africa, it must now move beyond this. The unwillingness of the government of the United States to support any concrete proposals for economic, financial and related sanctions against the South African government is a major obstacle to the efforts of the United Nations and independent African states to solve the South African problem. Accordingly, we urge:
>
> (1) A United States Government policy designed to prohibit future investment in South Africa and to discourage continuance of American-owned plants or subsidiaries in South Africa.
>
> (2) United States Government support for economic sanctions by the United Nations against South Africa.
>
> (3) Specific and immediate attention to the imposition of an oil embargo against South Africa.
>
> (4) Rigid implementation by the United States Government of the arms embargo to which it has already subscribed.

(5) Abandonment of the present United States practice of excluding American Negroes from its Missions to the Republic of South Africa.

(6) A United States initiative to implement the United Nations resolution (General Assembly *Resolution No. 1978,* December 16, 1963) calling for aid to families of political prisoners in South Africa and refugees from that country.[79]

Milfred C. Fierce speculates that, "At the 1964 conference, the seed for the creation of TransAfrica (the black American lobby for Africa and the Caribbean) more than a decade later may have been planted with the resolution calling for the birth of a permanent organization to carry out the objectives of the conference."[80] It is well known that through the ANLCA and ACOA conferences, Martin Luther King Jr. and other civil rights activists heavily influenced the next generation of African American leaders who related the flowering of freedom in America to the rights of the oppressed in South Africa.[81]

King became even more conscious of the need to struggle against apartheid when he was named the recipient of the Nobel Peace Prize in December 1964. This recognition enhanced his sense of having a global mission and of the need to shift to a broader base of issues. On December 7, 1964, while en route to Oslo, Norway, to receive the prize, King gave his "Address on South African Independence" in London.[82] In that address, delivered before persons from America, India, Pakistan, the West Indies, South Africa, and other parts of Africa, King alluded to an underground escalation of frustration and resentment among the oppressed in South Africa, noting that the situation there was frightening and ripe for violent rebellion:

> Today great leaders—Nelson Mandela and Robert Sobukwe—are among the many hundreds wasting away in Robben Island prison. Against the massively armed and ruthless State, which uses torture and sadistic forms of interrogation to crush human beings—even driving some to suicide—the militant opposition inside South Africa seems for the moment to be silenced. The mass of the people seems to be contained; seems for the moment unable to break from oppression. I emphasize the word *seems* because we can imagine what emotions and plans must be seething below the calm surface of that prosperous police state. We know what emotions are seething in the rest of Africa and indeed the dangers of a race war—of the dangers we have had repeated and profound warning.[83]

King went on to accuse the United States and Great Britain of "bolstering up the South African tyranny" through "our investments" and "through our governments' failure to act decisively." "We must join in a nonviolent action," he added, "to bring freedom and justice to South Africa by a massive movement for economic sanctions." Considering the sheer gravity of the South African situation, King found the actions of the United States and Britain most perplexing:

> In a world living under the appalling shadow of nuclear weapons, do we recognize the need to perfect the use of economic pressures? Why is trade regarded by all nations and all ideologies as sacred? Why does our government, and your government in Britain, refuse to intervene effectively *now*, as if only when there is a bloodbath in South Africa—or a Korea, or a Vietnam—will they recognize the crisis? If the U.K. and the U.S. decided tomorrow morning not to buy South African gold, to put an embargo on oil; if our investors and capitalists would withdraw their support for that racial tyranny, *then* apartheid would be brought to an end. Then the majority of South Africans of all races could at last build the shared society they desire.[84]

Though King was already very well known in South Africa, the "Address on South African Independence" enhanced his image as one concerned about the oppressed everywhere. This proved particularly significant for the South African students who heard the address. It was impossible for these students not to feel a special sense of intimacy with the civil rights leader, especially when, in concluding the address, he suggested that the destinies of black Americans and oppressed South Africans were interlocked. "Clearly there is much in Mississippi and Alabama to remind South Africans of their own country," King declared. "Though we in the civil rights movement still have a long and difficult struggle in our own country," he continued, "increasingly we intend to influence American policy in the UN towards South Africa."[85] The address revealed, in no uncertain terms, King's view of the South African struggle as one profoundly affecting the course of freedom in America and in other parts of the world.

The experience in London, and the larger issue of South African liberation, registered heavily on King's mind and heart even as he received the Nobel Peace Prize on December 10, 1964, three days after the "Address on South African Independence." In his "Nobel Prize Acceptance Speech," King mentioned Chief Albert Luthuli of South Africa as one of "the dedicated pilots of our struggle," and as a leader "whose struggles with and for his people, are still met with the most brutal expression of man's inhumanity to man."[86] The spiritual bond King felt with Luthuli in that moment of ecstasy and heightened expectation must have been overwhelming, especially since Luthuli had also received the Nobel Peace Prize three years earlier.

King entered 1965 with a revitalized interest in the problems of South Africa and of the oppressed worldwide. This renewed spirit came mostly as a result of his Nobel Peace Prize, but it also owed much to ACOA and ANLCA members who kept before King the sense that his leadership was critical in making Americans more conscious of their moral responsibility toward South Africa. George Houser of the ACOA and Theodore Brown of the ANLCA were particularly important in this regard. They continued to inform King of various events in connection with the South African situation, and to remind him of SCLC's financial and moral obligations to the ACOA and the ANLCA. Despite growing budgetary problems, the SCLC contributed hundreds of dollars to these organizations in 1965, to say nothing of the amount secured through appeal letters signed by King.[87]

In January 1965, King reiterated his call for sanctions against South Africa, and for a kind of "Marshall Plan" to benefit all of Africa economically.[88] In July of that year, the ACOA director George Houser targeted King as the one who could most effectively address the South African tragedy as the main speaker at the organization's upcoming Human Rights Day program. Concerning the event, Houser remarked to King:

> We feel that the American Committee on Africa should observe this day with a large meeting in New York, presenting speakers which will link the freedom struggle in our South with that in South Africa; where the fight is becoming so almost humanly impossible that they need every bit of hope and brotherly encouragement that we on the outside can possibly give them.[89]

Houser left no doubt about the importance of a King appearance at the Human Rights Day activities, scheduled for December 10, 1965. In a letter to the civil rights leader, Houser explained:

> I know how very busy your own work keeps you. But I have noted your increasing concern for the deteriorating and humanly horrible situation in South Africa, and for this reason I feel sure that if it is in your power you will do this for us—not for ACOA—but for the millions of our co-workers who suffer in the land of apartheid.[90]

King kindly accepted Houser's invitation. Much of the planning for the event was set in motion by Mary Louise Hooper, "who herself lived in South Africa for two years and worked closely with Chief Luthuli."[91] Flyers were distributed, fund raising proceeded with some success, and the activities occurred on schedule. The program itself, held in the Hunter College auditorium in New York, drew 3,500 people, and it proved to be one of the very best sponsored by a major interracial organization in America for the benefit of South Africa. The freedom songs of Miriam Makeba, the South African singing star, and of Pete Seeger, the American folk and civil rights singer, rose and fell in perfect melody, indicating something of the profound spirit that easily joined the aspirations of the oppressed in the United States and South Africa. Robert Resha of the ANC of South Africa was among the speakers, thus providing yet another opportunity for King to receive firsthand information on the workings of the apartheid system. In his "South Africa Benefit Speech," which rivaled the songs of Makeba and Seeger in language quality and raw power, and which echoed some of the concerns of Resha's talk, King denounced the white South African oppressors for violating even the most elementary standards of civilized behavior:

> Africa has been depicted for more than a century as the home of black can-
> nibals and ignorant primitives. Despite volumes of facts controverting this
> picture the stereotype persists in books, motion pictures, and other media of
> communication. Africa does have spectacular savages and brutes today, but
> they are not black. They are the sophisticated white rulers of South Africa
> who profess to be cultured, religious and civilized, but whose conduct and
> philosophy stamp them unmistakably as modern day barbarians.[92]

The "South Africa Benefit Speech," combined with the powerful black American and South African freedom songs, was not only a testimony to how the civil rights and anti-apartheid movements intersected, but also a perfect demonstration of how the yearning for freedom finds expression through art.

The speech underscored America's failure to deal seriously and firmly with the apartheid regime, a concern raised a year earlier in King's "Address on South African Independence" in London, and one which, on close examination, suggests that there was no necessary relationship at this time between King's perspective on South Africa and his need to rely on the backing of the U.S. government in the civil rights movement:

With respect to South Africa, . . . our protest is so muted and peripheral it merely mildly disturbs the sensibilities of the segregationists, while our trade and investments substantially stimulate their economy to greater heights. We pat them on the wrist in permitting racially mixed receptions in our Embassy, and by exhibiting films depicting Negro artists. But we give them massive support through American investments in motor and rubber industries, by extending some forty million dollars in loans through our most distinguished banking and financial institutions, by purchasing gold and other minerals mined by black slave labor, by giving them a sugar quota, by maintaining three tracking stations there, and by providing them with the prestige of a nuclear reactor built with our technical cooperation and fueled with refined uranium supplied by us.[93]

King ended his speech at Hunter College with major attention to the means by which South Africans could best eliminate apartheid and establish community. "The time has come," he affirmed with intense feeling, "for an international alliance of peoples of all nations against racism." While recognizing the need for the oppressed to lead their own nonviolent struggle inside South Africa, King concluded, at the same time, that such an internal struggle would be futile devoid of external nonviolent pressure from the international community:

Have we the power to be more than peevish with South Africa, but yet refrain from acts of war? To list the extensive economic relations of the great powers with South Africa is to suggest a potent nonviolent path. The international potential of nonviolence has never been employed. Nonviolence has been practiced within national borders in India, the U.S., and in regions of Africa with spectacular success. The time has come fully to utilize nonviolence through a massive international boycott which would involve the USSR, Great Britain, France, the U.S., Germany, and Japan. Millions of people can personally give expression to their abhorrence of the world's worst racism through such a far flung boycott. No nation professing a concern for man's dignity could avoid assuming its obligations if people of all states and races adopted a firm stand.[94]

The most optimistic part of King's conclusion covered the tremendous possibilities that interracial alliances presented for the creation of a new South Africa. "Even more inspiring is the fact that in South Africa itself incredibly brave white people are risking their careers, their homes and their lives in the cause of human justice," he reported. Thus, King did not discount assistance even from whites. To be sure, the possibility of whites and people of color struggling together against apartheid, and eventually living in harmony, is an important theme coursing through the "South Africa Benefit Speech"—a powerful corroboration of the beloved community ideal that King embraced and projected:

> Negro and white have been separated for centuries by evil men and evil myths. But they have found each other. The powerful unity of Negro with Negro and white with Negro is stronger than the most potent and entrenched racism. The whole human race will benefit when it ends the abomination that has diminished the stature of man for too long. This is the task to which we are called by the suffering in South Africa, and our response should be swift and unstinting. Out of this struggle will come the glorious reality of the family of man.[95]

During the period from 1966 until his death in 1968, King found it more and more difficult to exert a powerful and positive influence on developments in South Africa. Few African American intellectuals of his stature shared his commitment to the oppressed in that country, and the masses of his people in America seemed too consumed by their own struggle for liberation and survival to aid the anti-apartheid cause in significant ways. Even as King lashed out at the treatment of people of color in South Africa, and even as he called for a new human spirit and community in that land, he found increasingly less time and resources to act on these concerns. When George Houser wrote him in January 1966, asking him to participate in hearings on American policy toward South Africa before the Sub-Committee on Africa of the House Foreign Affairs Committee, King appeared interested but was compelled by other commitments to decline the request.[96] The flow of financial contributions into King's SCLC was beginning to decrease at this time, mainly due to his growing militant positions on Vietnam and economic justice, thus making it difficult for him to continue to support simultaneously his own civil rights agenda and the anti-apartheid thrust of the ACOA and the ANLCA.[97]

There were still other challenges at home that interfered with King's potential impact on the South African freedom struggle. His public opposition to U.S. policy in Vietnam, coupled with his push for basic structural changes in the capitalistic system, led the federal government, the media, segregationists, and even white and black supporters to attack and abandon him.[98] Moreover, King found his leadership and philosophy increasingly undermined by the challenges of black power, urban riots, and the white backlash. These forces combined plunged him into an isolation and frustration far more painful and protracted than anything he had previously faced in America.[99]

There were also persistent efforts by South African authorities to isolate King as a source of influence inside their country. South African newspapers carried articles denouncing him as a communist and a rabble-rouser.[100] Early in 1966, Bode Wegerif, an executive in a Johannesburg publishing company, and Dale White, an Anglican priest and director of the Wilgespruit Christian Fellowship and Conference Center near Johannesburg, faced the charge of "subversive ties" for distributing "more than a thousand long-playing records of a speech" by King. Acquitted "after an intensive investigation and interrogation" by South African security police, Wegerif and White described their actions:

> We have undertaken the sponsorship of this record in our individual capacities because we believe that Dr. Martin Luther King's address has direct relevance to the churches and to all men of good will in South Africa. We consider it of utmost importance that this statement of conviction by King, whose words and actions encourage and inspire millions of people throughout the world, should be heard in this country.[101]

King's belief in the potential for genuine and lasting change in both the United States and South Africa suffered severe blows in 1966. In both contexts, he saw a growing tendency among many whites and some blacks to justify racial separatism and to resort to violence as a means of settling racial conflict.[102] This sense of reality, coupled with the insensitivity and unresponsiveness of the U.S. and South African governments, left King pessimistic about the possibility of the oppressed being liberated in America and South Africa in the immediate future. Even so, he remained as dedicated as ever to the work of the SCLC, to the anti-apartheid agenda of the ACOA and the ANLCA, and to the worldwide cause of humanity for freedom, peace, and community.[103]

In 1967, King characterized the struggle against racism as being "among the moral imperatives of our time." Uppermost in his mind at that point were not only the United States and South Africa, but also Rhodesia, which he feared could "become another South Africa." "The world," King explained, "cannot stand another South Africa."[104] The fact that South Africa continued to defy the civilized world bothered him greatly. The time for dynamic speeches and paper resolutions, King felt, had ended, and concrete nonviolent action remained the only salvation for a nation already drenched in the blood of black men, women, and children. It was his hope that the ACOA and the ANLCA would do more to make this known.

In April 1967, King received a request from T. Wendell Foster, Jackie Robinson, and other ACOA representatives about pushing for the exclusion of South Africa from the 1968 Olympic Games in Mexico City. Robinson, the former baseball star and the main force behind the idea, sought to accomplish this goal by working with organizations like the U.S. Olympic Committee (USOC) and the International Olympic Committee (IOC), and by drawing on the insights and influence of internationally known activists such as King. Robinson appealed to King as "one deeply interested in sports and as a firm believer in interracialism," declaring, in a letter to the civil rights leader, that "I hope you will agree with me that it is essential for American representatives, particularly those involved in the Civil Rights struggle and concerned athletes, to speak with a clear voice on such a crucial issue."[105] Although King agreed wholeheartedly with efforts to persuade the IOC to suspend South Africa for violating Olympic rules in the selection of athletes, efforts that were ultimately successful, he was not a major participant in them. Caught up in the planning stages for the Poor People's Campaign, he limited his own involvement primarily to the signing of statements on the issue.

The plight of political prisoners in South Africa was another problem that attracted King's attention in 1967. In October of that year, the South African exile Dennis Brutus, director of the World Campaign for the Release of South African Political Prisoners, requested that King's name be "associated with our Campaign and with the work of the International Defence and Aid Fund."[106] Having kept up with Brutus's campaign through reports provided by the ACOA and the ANLCA, King consented to the request without hesitation. Brutus's request alone afforded further proof of the admiration and respect that oppressed South Africans had for King, and of their knowledge that their own quest for liberation could benefit from the magic of his name and from the spiritual and intellectual resources of the movement he led.[107]

The death of Albert J. Luthuli in July 1967 must have created a lot of uncertainty for King concerning the future of South Africa. Luthuli was struck by a train near his home in Groutville, Natal, and King was among many leaders worldwide who suspected foul play. The tragedy was not really surprising to King and his associates in the ACOA and the ANLCA, especially considering Luthuli's image as "the unbending unyielding, staunch personification" of the anti-apartheid crusade among black and white South Africans alike.[108] The South African government had had enough of Luthuli. In contrast, the loss of Luthuli for King meant that the world could no longer be as confident as it once was in a future South Africa where interracial justice would exist without resort to violence.

King and Luthuli had come to share so much by 1967. Their most prized quality as leaders had always been their ability to see human commonalities beneath human differences. This was the essence of their spirits. Luthuli's use of expressions such as "the New South Africa," "a broad South Africanism," or "a raceless South Africa" had long impressed King, providing some intellectual stimulation for King's own vision of "the New South," "the American dream," and "the world house." Indeed, Luthuli's ideal of "an authentic, comprehensive South African culture" drawing on African and European elements, an ideal that fully embodied his concept of community, clearly paralleled King's own ideal for both South Africa and America.[109] Moreover, the two men were drawn together by their constructive criticisms of the Christian Church, by their belief that religion had to be a force in overcoming racism and establishing human community, by the Christian compassion and reasonableness that undergirded their philosophies and practice of nonviolence, and by their conviction that the only meaningful freedom was that to which all Americans and South Africans had equal access.[110] Equally important is the fact that Luthuli's life of simplicity, determined spirit, and brave acts of defiance became for King examples to be imitated as King explored the dimensions of prolonged and massive civil disobedience toward the end of 1967.

Also in 1967, King's hope for some type of permanent organization linking the concerns of African Americans and oppressed South Africans was frustrated as the ANLCA began to decline sharply. At the ANLCA's 1967 conference, the last major one held by the organization, the urgency of the situation was raised again, and the "flood of resolutions" made in 1962 and 1964 were reiterated, reaffirmed, or revised on the basis of new developments in Africa. Most of these resolutions, including those on South Africa, were "eventually relegated to the dustbin of history." "In spite of its great potential," writes Milfred C. Fierce, "ANLCA faded quickly from the scene after the 1967 conference, a victim of empty coffers, a problem that has plagued Black American organizations throughout U.S. history."[111] George M. Houser claims that the ANLCA "never lived up to its potential" because, "as an elite group," it failed to build a solid foundation among the black masses:

> Gradually, the ANLCA lost momentum. Its strength was also its problem. It could function in the name of the leaders of the civil rights movement, but it was not able to establish its own base in the black community. Its leaders were primarily concerned for their own organizations and programs. African issues were appealing and important, but also secondary. Fund-raising was critical, and the ANLCA never could find a financial base apart from its constituent groups.[112]

The failure of the ANLCA to fulfill its mission presented a direct challenge to Martin Luther King Jr.'s idea, set forth clearly in 1967, that African Americans could lead the way in the liberation of oppressed South Africans and people of color the world over. Unlike leaders such as Paul Robeson and Malcolm X, who considered Africans and other so-called Third World peoples eminently capable of leading their own struggles and planning their own destinies, King argued that blacks in America, as possibly the most well educated and materially affluent among the world's peoples of color, were best suited to assume a vanguard role in liberating those tormented by high levels of poverty, illiteracy, and the subversive impact of racism, colonialism, and neocolonialism:

> The hard cold facts today indicate that the hope of the people of color in the world may well rest on the American Negro and his ability to reform the structure of racist imperialism from within and thereby turn the technology and wealth of the West to the task of liberating the world from want.[113]

It would be wrong to dismiss this perspective as merely arrogant triumphantism, despite the fact that King's views on Africa at times appeared to be distorted by an underestimation of the power of African cultures, and by assumptions of Western cultural superiority. In fact, King believed that African Americans had much to learn from the examples and the practical wisdom of black South Africans and other peoples of color who struggled against oppression. This is why he placed himself and his people permanently in debt to men like Albert Luthuli and Mohandas K. Gandhi, whose names are indelibly etched in the annals of the struggle for social justice and human equality in South Africa and the world generally.[114]

During the last year of his life, King found the ACOA to be a much more vibrant and resourceful organization than the ANLCA for applying outside pressure on the South African regime. He continued to serve on the National Committee of the ACOA, and that organization still provided the reports and other sources on which his perspective on developments in South Africa was based. However, King's views on apartheid at this time were also influenced to some extent by groups like Operation Crossroads Africa (OCA) and the Pan-African Students Organization in the Americas, Inc. (PASOA), both of which consisted of students who studied race relations in the United States and South Africa.[115]

King's final reflections on the nature of apartheid, and on possible ways of eliminating the problem, clearly conformed to positions long held by the ACOA. On these matters, time did not bring a drastic change of mind for him. He said early in 1968 that racism denied the universal parenthood of God, violated the central affirmations of the gospel, and constituted a major barrier to human community on a global scale. Furthermore, he warned that the failure of humans to respond quickly, creatively, and constructively to the challenge of overcoming racism in all forms could result in the total destruction of human life and civilization.[116]

The question of how to best dismantle apartheid steered King toward a number of important considerations. He never doubted the need for the oppressed to define and lead their struggle inside South Africa. In fact, King believed that interracial coalitions, which included South Africa's blacks, Coloreds, Asians, and well-meaning whites, were absolutely essential in the quest for a peaceful and racially inclusive South Africa. While he understood that the ANC, the PAC, and other radical groups could not logically be excluded from the quest for a new South Africa, he continued to hope for the triumph of more moderate and peaceful elements at the highest level of the anti-apartheid crusade in South Africa. This helps explain why King, in early 1968, still evoked the memory of Albert Luthuli, comparing his non-cooperation with the evil apartheid system to the civil disobedience of Socrates and the three Hebrew boys in the fiery furnace. Realizing that he stood in the same dissenting tradition as Luthuli, Gandhi, Socrates, and Shadrach, Meshach, and Abednego, King observed that

> I'm convinced that if I had lived in South Africa I would have joined Chief Luthuli, the late Chief Luthuli, as he had his campaigns, openly to disobey those laws, and to refuse to comply with the pass system, where people had to have passes and all that stuff to walk the streets.[117]

King placed a special burden for eliminating apartheid on the shoulders of white people, especially since he viewed them as the major and most consistent promoters of racism around the world. While in London in the winter of 1968, King, in a moment of stern prophecy, cautioned:

> Now if the white world does not recognize this and does not adjust to what has to be, then we can end up in the world with a kind of race war; so it depends on the spirit and the readjusting qualities of the white people of the world, and this will avoid the kind of violent confrontation between the races if it is done properly by white people.[118]

In King's view, whites would not serve as a viable force in the movement against apartheid as long as they desperately and ruthlessly sought after world power and domination—as long as they remained obsessed with racism, war, and wealth to the exclusion of higher moral and spiritual values. This is why King stressed the need for whites to overcome the "tragic ambivalence in their souls," and to develop "the spirit" and "the readjusting qualities" necessary for participation in a new humanity. He held that the very survival of whites themselves depended on their capacity for such a maturation process, especially since "three-fourths of the peoples of the world are colored." The possibility of white people reaching such a level of maturity was not totally dismissed by King, though he did wonder at times if racism had rendered many whites irredeemable.[119]

This emphasis on the importance of interracial unity, interracial alliances, and higher human values in the drive for South African liberation logically coincided with King's and the ACOA's idea that religion should be central to the struggle against racism in the world. King advanced this view on a very high level of sophistication by 1968, frequently giving religion and education equal priority in his analysis of means. His criticisms of Christians in the United States and South Africa for not engaging creatively the question of race were telling enough, to say nothing of his challenge to seminaries and other religious institutions to do a better job in race relations.[120]

Moreover, because King's vision of human community was *Christocentric* (Christ-centered) rather than *Christomonistic* (restricted to followers of Christ), he naturally felt that Jews, Muslims, Buddhists, Hindus, African traditionalists, and other religious groups also had a significant part to play in the campaign against apartheid in particular and racism in general. Indeed, King believed that strong interreligious or interfaith crusades, launched by the world's great religions against racism, were absolutely essential to the realization of the beloved community. This perspective was implied in the strongest possible terms in his use of the metaphor of "the great world house" or "the worldwide neighborhood"—a situation in which "all inhabitants of the globe are now neighbors," striving "to live with each other in peace."[121]

Correspondence with Students from South Africa

A significant aspect of Martin Luther King Jr.'s relationship to South Africa in the 1960s had to do with the many letters he exchanged with students from that country. The most fruitful time for such correspondence came in the mid-sixties, when King was increasingly and more consciously releasing the African American struggle from its domestic context and relating it to the broader human struggle. Mindful of the relevance of King's message and activism for their cause, South African students worked through various channels to meet, to associate with, and to hear him. In April 1965, Raymond Hoffenberg, a professor of medicine, wrote King on behalf of the Students Visiting Lecturers Trust Fund (SVLTF) of the University of Cape Town, inviting him to serve as the T. B. Davie Memorial Lecturer for August of that year.[122] "We feel that your acceptance would provide inspiration to many young people in South Africa," said Hoffenberg, "and would do much to enhance the concept of brotherhood amongst those dedicated to fight against racialism." While reaffirming his "deep and intense concern about and interest in the racial problems of South Africa," King did not accept the invitation "because of longstanding previous commitments."[123] In July 1965, C. W. de Kiewiet, of the American Council on Education in Washington, D.C., approached King on behalf of the SVLTF, asking him to appear as the T. B. Davie Memorial Lecturer for August 1966. Letters from Monica Wilson, chairman of the SVLTF, soon followed.[124] King accepted this second invitation, but wondered if he would be able "to get into South Africa."[125]

As King negotiated a possible appearance before the SVLTF, invitations came from another student group in South Africa. Widely known and respected as the National Union of South African Students (NUSAS), an interracial organization based at the University of Cape Town and devoted to the defense and promotion of "democracy in student affairs in the universities and in South Africa," this group requested King's services as both a writer and speaker.[126] In 1965 and 1966, King was asked to contribute articles "on any subject concerning race relations" to issues of the *NUSAS Journal*, requests he never honored because of "extremely crowded schedules of activities."[127] In the fall of 1965, the NUSAS invited King to participate in its Annual Congress, scheduled to occur at the University of Natal in Durban the following summer. The organization's letter to King stated in part:

> The invitation to you from the student assembly was made because of our concern for the issue of civil rights in all societies, our recognition of your symbolic leadership before the whole world, our respect and admiration for your integrity and courage in the face of many difficulties, and finally, our belief that you see in youth and the academy, the possibilities for a better world.[128]

Having a deep faith in interracial student groups as builders of solidarity between people in the United States and South Africa, King responded affirmatively to the invitation. In his usual spirit of humility and generosity, he asserted that

> I am extremely honored by your invitation to open the forthcoming 41st Annual Congress of the National Union of South African Students at the University of Natal in July of next year. I have long been concerned about the situation in South Africa and have developed tremendous admiration for the students, leading churchmen and African leaders who have been able to maintain a nonviolent spirit in the present situation. . . . I will begin immediately to make the necessary contacts to secure a visa from your government.[129]

Preparations for King's involvement in the NUSAS Annual Congress began on a serious note in October 1965. A copy of the address given at the previous Annual Congress was sent to King, and the NUSAS published a pamphlet praising him as a Nobel Peace Prize recipient and highlighting his views on education, religion, economic insecurity, communism, capitalism, segregation, violence and nonviolence, international relations, and a range of other issues.[130] The pamphlet, titled simply *Martin Luther King Jr.*, was widely distributed at NUSAS centers and among its overseas representatives.[131]

The South African government immediately took steps to sabotage the NUSAS's efforts and plans. Letters exchanged between the organization and King were interfered with, forcing them to communicate via the

NUSAS's London office. The same problem arose in King's communications with the SVLTF.[132] The forces of apartheid, inside and outside governmental circles, attacked King with the intensity and ferocity of lions. Peter Mansfield, the president of the NUSAS of Cape Town, sadly reported to King in a letter:

> Our invitation to you has resulted in some considerable controversy in certain South African quarters, including sections of the press and the South African Broadcasting Corporation. A number of anonymous and illegal pamphlets have been publicly circulated in an attempt to smear your name, and attacked the action of NUSAS in deciding to invite you to open its next Congress. There is of course much speculation as to whether you are likely to obtain a visa to enter South Africa should you decide to accept our invitation.[133]

The assault on King's philosophy and activities in South Africa in 1965 proved even more vehement than what he had experienced during his sponsorship of the *Declaration of Conscience* and the *Appeal for Action Against Apartheid*. At the Cape Synod of the Dutch Reformed Church in November of that year, "the Rev. J. A. Heyns and Dr. J. D. Vorster made serious accusations against Dr. Martin Luther King," claiming that he had "communist sympathies" and was "hardly Christian." They succeeded in persuading the synod "to pass a resolution expressing disappointment that the Vrye Universiteit of Amsterdam had conferred an honorary degree on Dr. King."[134]

Numerous letters with similar charges against King appeared in *Cape Times,* a South African newspaper. One letter spoke of King's "presence as a student at the Communist Highlander Folk School at Monteagle, Tennessee," referred to the "gross public indecency and debauchery" of his "nonviolent demonstrators" during "the riots in Selma and Birmingham," and echoed J. Edgar Hoover's claim that he was "the most notorious liar in America."[135] "If he is not a communist," said another of King, "there is plenty of evidence that his National Association for the Advancement of Coloured People has been infiltrated by communists." Yet another insisted that "Dr. King may be a 'nonviolent leader,' but his inflammatory speeches and 'freedom marches' certainly led to much race hatred and violence."[136] Such outrageous charges were indistinguishable from those King faced in America, suggesting to him striking similarities in the psyche of white supremacists in the United States and South Africa.

Ian Robertson, who followed Peter Mansfield as president of the NUSAS, found the hatred for King to be quite strong throughout South Africa. "There was great animosity toward Dr. King in white South Africa," he remembers, "and a lot of John Birch Society material, replete with denunciations by J. Edgar Hoover, appeared on our campuses at the time."[137] Although the attacks on King made South African students more determined to meet and listen to him, they were ill-prepared to surmount the obstacles that blocked such an opportunity. By the end of 1965, the NUSAS had concluded that King would not be allowed in South Africa. The NUSAS representative Peter Mansfield, in a letter to King, commented:

> Obviously there is a possibility that you may be refused a visa. We are extremely keen to hear you speak, and would like you to consider the possibility, in the event of a visa being refused, of tape-recording a speech for us which could be played to the delegates at the Congress. There is no need to make a decision on this now, but we would like to hear your ideas on this question.[138]

As King explored ways of possibly entering South Africa, he was contacted by yet another South African–based student group known as the Anglican Students' Federation (ASF). The ASF invited King to serve as guest speaker at its National Conference, scheduled for July 1966. "The subject we would like you to speak on," remarked the ASF publications officer, Stephen Hayes, "is 'The Role of the Christian Student in the Struggle for Social Justice.'"[139] Repeating concerns raised by the SVLTF and the NUSAS, the ASF speculated that even if King agreed "to speak at our conference, the South African Government will not grant you a visa to enter our country, as they are obviously unsympathetic to the Civil Rights Movement in the USA, of which you are regarded as one of the chief representatives."[140]

King's desire to fulfill engagements with the ASF and the other student groups led him to apply for a visa, though he remained pessimistic about his chances of ever visiting South Africa. "I have been invited to lecture in South Africa by . . . outstanding student groups of your country," said King in a letter to the South African embassy early in 1966. He continued:

> I have accepted . . . these invitations and I have a great interest in visiting South Africa in order to exchange cultural and human rights concerns. My

visit will be purely as a lecturer. My schedule here in the United States would not allow me to stay over the period involved in the lectures and one or two receptions that have been requested by the students. I would also be interested in spending a few hours talking with some of the religious leaders. In the light of this, I am herewith applying for a visa to South Africa in order to make a personal appearance for these engagements. I would appreciate all of the cooperation that you can give.[141]

The answer King received a month later was fully expected. Vice-Consul N. M. Nel, of the South African Consulate-General Office in New Orleans, put it bluntly:

> In response to your application for a visa for entry into the Republic of South Africa, submitted to the Consulate-General on the 9th February, 1966, I have to inform you with regret that after due consideration, your application has not been approved.[142]

King's inability to visit South Africa undoubtedly ranks among the most unfortunate realities of his thirteen years as an advocate for racial justice and community. As significant as his impact was on the oppressed in that country, spiritually and materially, there is reason to believe that his contributions toward the goal of a new South Africa would have been greater had he walked among the people in that land.

The Impact of King's Death on South Africans

Martin Luther King Jr.'s influence in South Africa had reached its highest point when he fell victim to an assassin's bullet on April 4, 1968. The tragedy robbed oppressed South Africans of one of their most powerful and articulate voices outside South Africa, a voice capable of attracting attention and inspiring action across the global community. King had helped sensitize the world to South African apartheid, perhaps the most racist system known to humanity. His most lasting contribution, however, consisted in the manner in which he related the problems of oppressed South Africans to those of African Americans and a larger human family that needed to come to terms with the true meaning of the beloved community. Indeed, King showed South Africans and Americans how racial and ethnic pluralism can be maintained and respected even as people engage in fruitful dialogue and the building of harmonious relationships that transcend all barriers.

Reactions to King's death on the part of South Africans varied. Blacks, Asians, and Coloreds were gripped by an overwhelming sense of sadness. The outburst of shock, grief, and anger among black South Africans was especially intense. The painful memories expressed by Joseph Louw, a black South African photographer who took the first pictures of King after he was shot, were reflective of the typical black South African response to the murder. Stunned by the tragedy, Louw recalled: "I never did photograph him full in the face. I had to keep my distance and respect." "At first," he continued, "it was just a matter of realizing the horror of the thing. Then I knew I must record it for the world to see."[143]

For the more radical elements in the ANC and the PAC, King's death served as yet another example of the futility of nonviolent resistance in a violently white racist society. On the moderate side, however, the tragedy provided ultimate proof of the need for humans to follow a peaceful course in the struggle for survival and liberation. George W. Shepherd Jr., who associated with King in the ACOA, acknowledged the power of this moderate position, but emphatically declared that the loss of King and Albert Luthuli "marked the end of an era of attempts at peaceful reform through nonviolence." "The lives of these two men joined together in their faith and common African heritage," Shepherd added, "symbolize the fate of the dream of human brotherhood in our age of violence."[144]

The assassination of King also evoked mixed responses from white South Africans. Glowing tributes came from a few whites in South Africa's Catholic, Anglican, Methodist, and Dutch Reformed churches—whites who had been genuinely challenged by King's push for unified Christian witness against apartheid. Motivated by a different spirit, Prime Minister John Vorster used the assassination to warn clerics who planned "to do the kind of thing here in South Africa that Martin Luther King did in America" to "cut it out, cut it out immediately, for the cloak you carry will not protect you if you try to do this in South Africa."[145] The Registrar of the Nederduitse Gereformeerde Kerk reiterated Vorster's point, denounced King's methods as counterproductive, and charged that the King assassination was "part of a communist plot to create chaos, civil war and disruption of the 'established order.'"[146] Interestingly enough, these harsh comments were made at a time when violence against South Africa's oppressed community reached unprecedented levels, and when an increasing number of anti-apartheid activists, inside and outside South Africa, were abandoning nonviolence and turning to what they considered more radical methods.

The loss of King was particularly painful for activists in the ANLCA and the ACOA, but they were sustained by priceless memories of what he had done as a spokesman for the otherwise unheard in the United States and South Africa. Roy Wilkins and Whitney M. Young, with whom King had worked in the ANLCA, felt that the crusade against racism in America, South Africa, and other parts of the world had taken a tragic turn with the killing of King. George Houser of the ACOA and other activists connected to the International Defence and Aid Fund (IDAF), meeting in London on April 19–21, 1968, "expressed sorrow at the tragic assassination and Martyrdom of Dr. Martin Luther King Jr., an American sponsor of the International Fund." King's "constant struggle for racial justice and equality was a momentous influence not only in the United States," the activists said further, "but also in Africa and throughout the world."[147]

For many in the United States and South Africa, nonviolence was subjected to its most difficult test with the assassination of King. Disciples of peaceful protest found themselves struggling to defend nonviolence as the greatest innovation in human relations. The choice of violent revolution no longer appeared difficult for many among the oppressed. Even ardent Christians sought biblical and theological support for the use of violence as a large-scale political weapon.[148] It was in response to such shifting moods that Colin Morris wrote *Unyoung, Uncolored, Unpoor,* a 1969 work that shattered many of the moral claims that King, Gandhi, and Luthuli had made concerning nonviolence. Written in response to a student from southern Africa, who wondered if a Christian should use weapons in the struggle against oppression, the book concluded that nothing short of violent revolution "will cauterize the stinking sores" of nations like South Africa.[149] This became a crucial consideration for many people of color in South Africa as they looked to the 1970s.

CHAPTER 3

ON DIFFERENT TERMS
King's Fading Legacy in South Africa in the 1970s

We are aware that the white man is sitting at our table. We know that he has no right to be there; we want to remove him, . . . strip the table of all trappings put on by him, decorate it in true African style, settle down and then ask him to join us on our own terms if he wishes.

Stephen Biko, 1976[1]

In South Africa the situation is such that political integration, in other words, black/white coalitions, cannot be realistically discussed.

Allan A. Boesak, 1976[2]

Can you tell me how I can commend nonviolence to blacks who say that the resistance movements in Europe during World War II were lauded to the skies and still are, but what blacks consider to be similar resistance movements are denigrated because they are black?

Bishop Desmond Tutu, 1977[3]

The extent to which Martin Luther King Jr. continued to influence anti-apartheid movements inside and outside South Africa in the 1970s is open to serious debate. For some, this period represented a continuing shift away from Kingian principles and methods, a pattern that had begun with the African National Congress (ANC), the Pan-Africanist Congress (PAC), and other radical elements in 1960.[4] For others, the 1970s signaled a time during which there occurred a reaffirmation of King's views on love, nonviolence, and community for the South African context.[5] Whatever the case, King's dream for South Africa lived through the sustained organizational activity of the Southern Christian Leadership Conference (SCLC) and the American Committee on Africa (ACOA), and through South African–based groups like the National Union of South African Students (NUSAS). Although the American Negro Leadership Conference on Africa (ANLCA), an organization that bore the marks of King's influence, died out in the early seventies, it provided the "seed for the creation of TransAfrica [the black American lobby for Africa and the Caribbean]," with its call "for the birth of a permanent organization to carry out the objectives of the conference" regarding South Africa in particular and Africa in general.[6]

This chapter highlights the relevance of King's ideas and methods for movements against South African apartheid in the 1970s. The emphasis is placed on significant challenges to King's thought and methods inside South Africa, on King's influence on the thought and praxis of Desmond Tutu and Allan Boesak, on anti-apartheid thinkers and activists in America who evoked King's memory and promoted his ideas and methods in relation to South Africa, and on the international tribute to King by anti-apartheid advocates in 1979.

Challenges to the King Legacy in South Africa

Martin Luther King Jr.'s principles and methods confronted a strong challenge in South Africa in the seventies as people of color there considered a range of strategies and tactics to dismantle the apartheid system. Nonviolent absolutism gave way to a "freedom by any means necessary" ethic in some circles, thus reviving memories of Malcolm X's challenge to African Americans a decade earlier.[7] The ANC and the PAC, already banned and forced underground because of unrest and the passage of the Unlawful Organizations Act in the 1960s, turned increasingly to political activism and armed struggle. The concept of violence in self-defense, or counterviolence, as articulated and employed by these groups, had won many converts among the oppressed in South Africa by the mid-1970s. Many black youths left South Africa seeking military training in ANC guerrilla camps in Zambia and other countries, and PAC guerrillas who had spent years in bush camps in the Congo and China attempted incursions into South Africa. This growing acceptance of armed retaliation against the forces of apartheid seemed to reflect, in the words of one newspaper columnist, "King's fading legacy" in South Africa.[8]

Several developments coalesced to account for this shift from the philosophy and methods associated with King. First among these were the South African government's "violent suppression of protests and the abundance of new martyrs."[9] The mass arrest of ANC and PAC leaders at Rivonia in the early and mid-1960s under apartheid laws such as the Terrorism Act and the Suppression of Communism Act, the detention of thousands of anti-apartheid activists without trial throughout the sixties and seventies, and the daily slaughter of defenseless people of color during these years convinced growing numbers that nonviolent action was anachronistic. This conviction found powerful reinforcement toward the end of 1976, after thousands of black South Africans had been killed or injured for protesting the compulsory use of Afrikaans and inferior educational standards in African schools.[10] The murder of Bantu Stephen Biko in 1977 and the death of the PAC's Robert Sobukwe a year later brought even more proof that the white regime was determined to maintain white domination and black subordination at all cost, and that appeals to reason and for restraint and compromise were merely an exercise in futility.[11]

The emergence of the Black Consciousness Movement (BCM) in South Africa in the late sixties and early seventies also contributed to the movement away from nonviolent protest for many. The BCM was an expression of African nationalism that gave birth to organizations such as Black Community Programmes (BCP), the Black People's Convention (BPC), the Interdenominational African Ministers' Association of South Africa (IAMASA), various black worker unions, and the South African Students' Organization (SASO).[12] Viewed in some circles as a child of the all-black SASO, the BCM's "main guiding founder and inspiration" was Stephen Biko, who filled a leadership vacuum left with the death of Albert Luthuli, the imprisonment of Nelson Mandela, and the banning of Robert Sobukwe.[13] From its origin, the BCM's "strategy toward the achievement of a non-racial egalitarian society was black solidarity," a strategy developed earlier by the ANC and the PAC.[14] The BCM addressed itself mostly to black youth, urging them "to prepare for a new phase of the struggle for freedom."[15] "The idea behind Black consciousness," writes Donald Woods, "was to break away almost entirely from past black attitudes to the liberation struggle and to set a new style of self-reliance and dignity for blacks as a psychological attitude leading to new initiatives."[16]

Biko and his associates felt that black unity was essential in meeting the enormous challenges of white power, and particularly white-on-black violence. Mokgethi Motlhabi expresses the BCM's strategy toward black unity in these terms:

> This would lead to the ability to bargain with white people on an equal basis rather than as inferiors—as according to the present state of affairs. While engaged with this immediate goal of raising consciousness and creating solidarity, they regarded whites and their government as irrelevant. Therefore, there was no need for or any attempt at direct confrontation with the government. Crisis leadership was provided when needed but, on the whole, the BCM engaged itself fully with its researches, relief projects, and education. In other words, it addressed itself critically and creatively to the black community, including the Bantustan leaders, who were regarded as "sell-outs" of their own people because of their cooperation with the government.[17]

Martin Luther King Jr. would not have unequivocally endorsed the BCM in South Africa, but its existence was inspired in some ways by the movement he led in the United States. Biko and others in the BCM were inspired by King's challenge to white power, and by his zeal for black freedom.[18] With the BCM, however, the names of Biko, Nelson Mandela, Robert Sobukwe, Kwame Nkrumah, Leopold Senghor, Marcus Garvey, Malcolm X, the Black Panthers, and other militants in Africa and the United States became more influential than that of King, especially since they "did not rule out violence in self-defense."[19] The BCM in South Africa almost paralleled, and was influenced by, the rise of black power among American blacks, and both movements symbolized King's waning influence as far as nonviolent methods and black integrationist ideology were concerned.[20]

Although the BCM drew inspiration from the black freedom struggle in the United States, it had its own roots in South African history and particularly in the experiences of black South Africans. James Leatt, Theo Kneifel, and Klaus Nurnberger have emphasized this point, noting especially those factors that they felt distinguished the struggle in America from the BCM on the levels of ideology, policy, and strategy:

> The ferment among black Americans in the sixties influenced the emergence of black consciousness as a social-political force in South Africa. In particular, the writings and activities of Stokely Carmichael, Rap Brown, George Jackson, Malcolm X, James Cone, and Albert Cleage attracted lively interest

among early exponents of black consciousness in South Africa, and helped to fan the flames already burning there. But while leading figures in the Black Consciousness Movement drew on the American experience, there were considerable differences between the two situations. Generally speaking, black Americans did not challenge the American social and political system as such. They demanded full integration, based on the already accepted principle of equality. As a minority they wanted to exercise, without any restrictions, their citizen rights guaranteed by the U.S. Constitution. In contrast, blacks in South Africa claimed they constitute the majority of the population and could no longer be denied full citizenship. Like their black American counterparts they are victims of racism. But unlike black Americans, blacks in South Africa argued that full citizenship involves a radical dismantling of the South African system because its constitution, laws, and economy favour the dominant white group. Blacks cannot appeal to an inherently non-discriminatory constitution to redress the injustices meted out to them.[21]

Despite their opposition to certain aspects of King's thought on nonviolence and black separatism, activists in the BCM agreed with his basic idea that the new South Africa had to ultimately embrace all her inhabitants without restrictions. "We are looking forward to a non-racial, just and egalitarian society in which colour, creed and race shall form no point of reference," declared Stephen Biko in 1976. In words amazingly similar to King's, Biko insisted that "tribalistic, racialistic or any form of sectional outlook" should ultimately be categorically rejected.[22] This vision stood at the core of the philosophies of the BPC, the SASO, and other elements of the BCM. However, they were abundantly clear in stating that black solidarity and liberation had to be the precondition for any reconciliation and community that might occur across racial and ethnic boundaries later, a position quite at odds with King's notion that liberation, reconciliation, and the creation of community must happen simultaneously. At times the BCM appeared far more adamant than King had been in arguing that genuine integration and/or community can take place only between equals, and that blacks and whites should share in its definition. "The concept of integration, whose virtues are often extolled in white liberal circles," wrote Biko in 1973, "is full of unquestioned assumptions that embrace white values."[23] Here Biko's argument was essentially the same as that made by Malcolm X and black power theorists in America.

The BCM leaders believed that the issues that divided black South Africans were much more enormous than those that had fragmented

African Americans during the King years. Unlike the civil rights leaders in the United States, those in the BCM had to confront tribal chiefs and leaders of homelands who put their own political agendas above the needs of the community as a whole. This is why Biko spent so much time condemning tribalism and bantustan leaders like Gatsha Buthelezi, Lucas Mangope, and Kaizer D. Matanzima, who were "leading black people to a divided struggle—to speak as Zulus, to speak as Xhosas, to speak as Pedis."[24] It is obvious, then, that the problems Biko and others in the BCM faced with the idea of coalitions extended beyond whites to blacks themselves. Because of the politics of divisiveness that characterized the black South African situation, it would have been unwise for the BCM to rely solely on the black freedom struggle in America as the blueprint for bringing a unity of purpose and action to its struggle.[25]

The sustained assault the BCM mounted against white liberalism was more reminiscent of Malcolm X than of Martin Luther King Jr. Moreover, King would not have agreed with the SASO's decision to break away from the multiracial NUSAS in the 1970s, especially since he had seen this organization as a model for the kind of interracial cooperation and harmony that had to occur on a much broader scale in South Africa. While he would have understood the BCM's distrust of multiracial coalitions to fight apartheid, especially where whites were involved, King would have found the following explanation for black separatist organizations ultimately inconsistent with the beloved community ideal:

> In essence the argument against white liberalism is that in a non-racial, non-exploitative, egalitarian society black consciousness would be irrelevant. But in South Africa racism is institutionalized, and the economy exploits blacks, so that in the face of strong white racism (including that of liberals) there must be solidarity among blacks. They reject the liberal view that what is required to oppose apartheid is the formation of non-racial groups. White liberal efforts to alleviate black oppression, it is said, are counterproductive; in fact they sugar the pill of apartheid and obscure the real fact of black/white polarization which exists in South Africa. Efforts to form non-racial alignments in effect divert black energies from the prime task of "politicisation of blacks by blacks."[26]

Considering its misgivings about any movement that challenged the established order, the South African government was not likely to separate the BCM from King's legacy. Its banning of recordings of King's "I Have a

Dream" speech in early 1971 was probably the best evidence of this tendency.[27] In 1972, South African officials took their first major actions against the BCM. They outlawed the BPC, the SASO, and some sixteen other black secular and religious groups under the BCM, and they banned, silenced, imprisoned, or eliminated key black leaders. In 1976, still other banning orders were issued under South Africa's Internal Security Act, which replaced the Suppression of Communism Act. Furthermore, the South African Government encouraged Chief Gatsha Buthelezi's more conservative *Inkatha* Movement as an alternative to the ANC, the PAC, and the BCM.[28] Although Buthelezi tended to compare himself with King, Stephen Biko and other black consciousness advocates dismissed him as a participant "in the white man's game" of containing "the political aspirations of the black people."[29]

The South African government's assault on black consciousness, marked by the politics of divide and conquer, proved largely unsuccessful. The loss of Biko, who died in detention under extremely suspicious circumstances on September 12, 1977, revitalized black consciousness in South Africa and figured prominently in the establishment of the Azanian People's Organization (AZAPO) a year later.[30] The AZAPO stressed the connection between race prejudice and economic exploitation under the apartheid system, and it reoriented black consciousness by "taking it to the broad masses of people." In its analysis of racism and economic injustice as perennial allies, the AZAPO was in line with the ideology of Martin Luther King Jr. However, on the questions of black solidarity, multiracial alliances, and means for ending oppression, it was closer to previous groups under the BCM than to King.[31]

Compounding this turn away from Kingian-Gandhian-Luthulian ideas and protest methods to more radical means in the seventies was liberation theology, which came from black Americans and from Latin America. This theology related the Christian faith and the entire biblical revelation to the liberation cause, and much of it "sanctioned violence in some cases, particularly by the oppressed."[32] Black theologians in South Africa quickly discovered that liberation theology coincided with the goals of the BCM, and that it could be adapted constructively to their struggle against apartheid.[33] This explains in part why South African theologians such as Stephen Biko, Manas Buthelezi, and Mokgethi Motlhabi collaborated with the black American theologian James H. Cone on a book called *The Challenge of Black Theology in South Africa* in 1973.

Interestingly enough, black power advocates like Malcolm X and Eldridge Cleaver were quoted in this volume, but there was hardly a reference to Martin Luther King Jr.[34] Apparently, Biko, Buthelezi, Motlhabi, Cone, Basil Moore, Mongameli Mabona, and other contributors to the work felt, perhaps unconsciously, that affirming the connection between black consciousness and black theology in the South African context had little or nothing to do with King. They must have also been mindful that King had rejected any idea of black theology as a separate intellectual discipline when it first surfaced in America in the mid and late sixties.[35]

Biko was perhaps the most ardent proponent of liberation theology in South Africa in the 1970s. His murder was a loss not only to the black theology movement, but to theologians of every background for whom human liberation was the key to the meaning of the Christian gospel.[36] Gayraud S. Wilmore, a pioneer in the development of black theology in the United States, has written the following about Biko's role as a liberation theologian, and about the link between theology and black consciousness for the oppressed black communities in South Africa, the United States, and the Caribbean:

> Biko helped to spearhead the black theology project of the students who withdrew from the 1968 University Christian Movement (UCM) Conference at Stutterheim to form the South African Student Organization (SASO). By the 1970 UCM Conference at Roodepoort, black consciousness and black theology were as inseparable in South Africa as were black power and black theology in the United States, following the publication of James H. Cone's *Black Theology and Black Power* and the statements of the National Conference of Black Churchmen in 1969 and 1970. The "parallelism of spontaneities," to use a phrase of David Martin, flowed back and forth between black theologians in the United States, South Africa and the Caribbean during the early 1970s. Steve Biko, with Sabelo Ntwasa, Mokgethi Motlhabi, and Manas Buthelezi, took the leadership in hammering out a black theology of liberation among young Christian groups in Southern Africa that paralleled developments in the U.S. initiated by NCBC and the Society for the Study of Black Religion.[37]

Biko's strong defense of "Christ as a fighting God, not a passive God who allows a lie to rest unchallenged," appeared somewhat at odds with Martin Luther King Jr.'s image of Christ as the embodiment of the spirit of nonviolence. Biko explained the thrust of black theology in ways that

King, with his more traditional approach to the faith, may have found politically inexpedient:

> It seeks to bring back God to the black man and to the truth and reality of his situation. This is an important aspect of black consciousness, for quite a large proportion of people in South Africa are Christians still swimming in a mire of confusion—the aftermath of the missionary approach. It is the duty therefore of all black priests and ministers of religion to save Christianity by adopting black theology's approach and thereby once more uniting the black man with his God.[38]

Although black theology in South Africa, as articulated by Biko and others in the BCM, appeared a bit more radical than King's, it did not escape King's influence. As was the case in the United States, black theology in South Africa was inspired to some extent by King's zeal and work for the freedom of people of African ancestry everywhere. To the extent that black theology in both South Africa and the United States was Christian, and to the degree that it centered on the liberation of the oppressed, it reflected the legacy of King. Also, black theology in both contexts was informed by King's view that any successful black revolution had to be grounded in the spirituality and emotive powers of black people, and that such a revolution had to embrace black freedom as well as the freedoms of all other oppressed peoples across the globe.[39]

King's Influence on Desmond Tutu and Allan Boesak

Whatever influence Martin Luther King Jr.'s ideas and methods had inside South Africa in the 1970s can be attributed primarily to the work of Desmond Tutu and Allan Boesak. These two black Christian ministers and theologians displayed an admiration and respect for King in this period that easily recalled Albert J. Luthuli's influence among black South Africans generally. Tutu must have been quite conscious of the importance of King's life and thought when he explored the similarities between African and black American theologies in a 1975 essay, and Boesak when he compared the ethics of King and Malcolm X in his doctoral dissertation at the Theological Academy of Kampen in the Netherlands in 1976.[40] Tutu and Boesak, black South Africans steeped in the traditions of their people, were able to connect spiritually and intellectually with King, an ability not as readily evident among more radical elements in the BCM in the seventies. While stamping their own identities on the anti-apartheid movement in South Africa, Tutu and Boesak recognized at the same time that they owed a great deal to King and the civil rights movement in America.[41]

Desmond Tutu's identification with King and the black freedom struggle in the United States began long before he became a major force in the crusade against South African apartheid. While in London in the early and mid-sixties, he was constantly exposed to media coverage of civil rights activities, an experience that would not have been possible in South Africa, and one which undoubtedly reinforced his sense of the unity of the African American and black South African struggles. Thus, it is not surprising that by the late seventies, as he rose in the ranks of leadership among his people, Tutu had begun to speak of the ways in which King's philosophy and praxis were instructive for oppressed South Africans.[42]

The Christian understanding that King brought to his rejection of apartheid influenced Tutu tremendously. Despite the different styles and traditions that separated King, the Baptist clergyman, from Tutu, the Anglican bishop, their opposition to apartheid emerged out of a basic understanding of the Christian doctrines of love and brotherhood. Tutu agreed completely with King's insistence that racial separation in all forms not only degrades human personality and denies the interrelatedness and interdependence of human beings, but it also violates the parenthood of God and the essential oneness of God's creation. Throughout the 1970s, Tutu echoed King's belief that the love of God is inseparable from the love of neighbor. For Tutu, as for King, this conviction found its strongest support in the life and ministry of Jesus Christ.[43] This became Tutu's most consistent argument as he confronted apartheid laws and customs through nonviolent action.

Tutu fully embraced King's insights into the meaning, character, and actualization of human community. In 1978, he reminded fellow South Africans of King's challenge that "together we must learn to live as brothers or together we will be forced to perish as fools."[44] As was evident with King, Tutu stressed the communitarian ideal as the organizing principle of all his thought and activities. All other important concepts that pervaded Tutu's writings and public speeches—for example, love, nonviolence, forgiveness, human dignity, morality, freedom, justice, reconciliation—were explicitly related to his understanding of community. Here the spirit and influence of King were unmistakable for Tutu.[45] King's communitarian ideal became quite significant for Tutu as he promoted, with awesome precision, his own view of "a new South Africa that is just, nonracial, and democratic, where black and white can exist amicably side by side in their home country as members of one family."[46]

But the Tutu of the seventies questioned King's notion that violence is always an immoral and impractical method for the oppressed. While sharing King's view that nonviolence is always the best and most desirable means for actualizing community, Tutu insisted, on the other hand, that a violent response to oppression can at times be justified and unavoidable. After expressing his own respect for and identification with nonviolence at the South African Missiological Conference in 1977, Tutu explained why it was irrational for the world to expect oppressed South Africans to limit themselves to nonviolence as an absolute principle:

(1) The Christian Church is not entirely pacifist;
(2) Blacks are left wondering what practical alternatives are available, given the palpable failure of nonviolent forms of protest and opposition;
(3) There is a hollow sound to white arguments for the way of nonviolence, given their at least tacit support for state and legal violence.[47]

Tutu concluded with references to the difficulties he faced in recommending nonviolence to blacks who were constantly bombarded with positive images of Europeans who used violence in redemptive ways during World War II. For Tutu, it was virtually impossible to overcome the moral dilemma involved in advocating absolute nonviolence for blacks on the one hand, while condoning the use of violence by whites on the other.[48]

Allan Boesak, a minister in the Dutch Reformed Mission Church and president of the World Alliance of Reformed Churches, wrote and said far more about King than any other black South African in the seventies. In 1976, he devoted half of his doctoral dissertation to a serious discussion of King's ethics in the American context. Although Boesak made no effort to seriously relate King's ethics specifically to the South African situation in this work, much of what he wrote about King's communitarian ethic had significant implications for addressing issues of race in any setting at that particular time.[49] Boesak's purpose was to provide "a theological interpretation of the ethics" of King and Malcolm X, a work that was important in its own right, and important also because the philosophies and methods of King and Malcolm were the subject of considerable debate in some circles in South Africa in the seventies.[50]

Like Tutu, Boesak was impacted by the prophetic posture King exemplified in attacking systems of oppression. For Boesak, King's use of the language and symbols of Amos and other ancient Hebrew prophets, who denounced idolatry and the mistreatment of the poor by the privileged, made his message especially powerful and relevant for black Americans, oppressed South Africans, and other peoples who suffered on grounds of race and class. Influenced by King, both Boesak and Tutu accepted the tradition of the poor in the Hebrew Scriptures as one source that provided the primary themes and the hermeneutical norms for confronting patterns of injustice in South Africa in the seventies.[51] To be sure, King's prophetic model of leadership proved useful to the two South African leaders as they seriously pondered the role of the minister and the church in an unjust society.

In 1977, Boesak published a book in which he discussed King in relation to the socio-ethical dimensions of black theology and power. In that study, he contended that King helped create "a new consciousness" that "influenced black people in South Africa and all over the world."[52] Such a contention obviously set Boesak at variance with some of the more radical elements in the BCM, who were not as inclined to think of King in this manner. First, said Boesak, King urged his people to develop "an unassailable and majestic sense of their own value," a "Black self-love," that could serve as "the creative precondition for a new black/white relationship." Second, King analyzed and interpreted the black condition in light of the harsh realities of white power. Finally, continued Boesak, King pointed to "the relation between racism and capitalism," a connection so evident in the oppression of blacks and other people of color in the United States, South Africa, and elsewhere.[53]

Boesak's book is most interesting at those points where he treats King within the context of black power. While admitting that King had a "role in preparing the way for black power" in its most contemporary expressions, Boesak declared that black power and black consciousness had a history in the United States and Africa that extended far beyond the civil rights leader:

> Black power found expression in Henry Garnet's step-by-step plan for resistance; in Frederick Douglass's reminder to blacks that "there is no progress without struggle"; in Marcus Garvey's "Back to Africa Movement." It found expression in Enoch Mgijima's struggle when he and his people preferred to die rather than give up the freedom they had found in the Bulhoek Community; in Chief Gonnema and his Hottentot people when they fought their hopeless war against the colonists in the Cape, trying to regain

their cattle and their land and with it their dignity as a people. Black people must come to respect this proud tradition, a tradition which produced Kimpa Vita, the African prophetess who was burned to death for preaching the Black Messiah in the Congo of the eighteenth century; a tradition which produced Albert Luthuli, Malcolm X, and Martin Luther King Jr.[54]

Boesak portrayed King as a perceptive critic of black power, as one who analyzed that phenomenon in terms of its positive and negative features. King's interpretation of black power as "a cry of disappointment," as "a psychological call to manhood," and "as a call to black people to amass their political and economic strength," had, according to Boesak, meaning and significance for black Americans and black South Africans alike. The problem for King, Boesak added, was "not the concept of power, or even black power; it was how this concept was understood that caused the problem."[55] In other words, King felt that the slogan *black power* would be equated by the opposition with violence and racial separatism, and not as black people's efforts to transform their powerlessness into "creative and positive power." Although sympathetic to concerns raised by King along these lines, Boesak denied that violence and racial separatism were issues to be considered in dialogues concerning black power. For Boesak, only after a sharing of power between blacks and whites would such issues become important in discussions and debates between the races.[56]

It was virtually impossible for Boesak to agree wholeheartedly with King's positions on the questions of racial separatism and violence in the seventies, especially since he moved in an atmosphere charged with an uncompromising spirit of black power and black consciousness. While sharing King's view that a new South Africa should ultimately be characterized by a spirit of community and democracy between peoples of color and whites, Boesak insisted that such an ideal could not be logically discussed between the races as long as apartheid existed. "In South Africa," he lamented in 1977, "the situation is such that political integration," or "black/white coalitions cannot be realistically discussed." On the question of methods preferred to win freedom, Boesak, though hopeful of a nonviolent solution, argued nonetheless that "retaliatory violence is necessary for the affirmation, the self-respect, the manhood of black people."[57] Boesak refused to defend nonviolence as an absolute principle, even as he employed it as a mode of practical action through prayer vigils and acts of civil disobedience.

Much of King's importance for Boesak rested in the fact that he contributed to a black theological tradition for the oppressed in the United States and South Africa. Put another way, King reflected the essence of black theology in affirming, in word and deed, that God sides with the oppressed in their struggle for justice and community. In noting the importance of King's legacy for black theology, Boesak clearly separated himself from Stephen Biko, who showed less of a tendency to associate King with such a radical development. In any event, Boesak concluded that the black theological tradition constituted an important bridge between King and black people in American and South African history:

> This relation between the black struggle for liberation and Black Theology has only seldom been severed. It has been kept alive by the black church movement which was begun in South Africa by Nehemiah Tile and in America by Richard Allen. It has been kept alive in the struggle for sociopolitical freedom from Mangena Mokone to Albert Luthuli; from Hendrik Witbooi in Namibia to Martin Luther King Jr. in America. Basically today, this fact has not yet changed.[58]

In the seventies, Boesak protested "very strongly against the total division (and contrast) some make between Black Theology in South Africa and Black Theology in the United States."[59] Furthermore, Boesak was ever quick to acknowledge his personal indebtedness to Martin Luther King Jr. and the black theology movement as advanced by James H. Cone and others in America. The black ethicist Peter J. Paris has shared the following about the combined influences of these sources on Boesak's thinking:

> His book *Farewell to Innocence: A Socio-Ethical Study on Black Theology and Power* (Orbis, 1977) claims a close alliance among all liberation theologies but especially between black theology in the United States and South African theology. Further, he argues that human liberation from oppression is political activity justified by God and the awareness of this marks the end of innocence. No longer will black South African Christians need to accept their plight and believe the myths aimed at keeping them in subjugation. In brief, Boesak's theology synthesizes the nonviolent philosophy of Martin Luther King Jr., and the self-determining initiative of black theology.[60]

It would be problematic to refer to Desmond Tutu and Allan Boesak as merely disciples of King in the seventies. Neither of these men confined himself to a particular school of thought. Although they agreed with King on certain principles, as the foregoing discussion shows, Tutu and Boesak also subjected elements of King's thought to serious, critical scrutiny. They were merely admirers of King; solid thinkers who confronted white South Africans with what they perceived to be a final chance to respond positively to the challenge of nonviolence and community. Indeed the concept of racial reconciliation in Tutu's and Boesak's writings and speeches in the seventies, a concept quite similar to King's, confronted *all* South Africans with a new sense of moral obligation, much like that emphasized in the poems of the brilliant South African exile Dennis Brutus and the stories of the South African exile Peter Abrahams.[61] To some extent, Tutu and Boesak were living examples of how King's legacy of ideas and activism continued to challenge and motivate some oppressed South Africans in the seventies, even as his general influence in South Africa declined.

Keeping King's Dream for South Africa Alive in America

Martin Luther King Jr.'s fading legacy in parts of South Africa in the seventies did not in any way reflect what he meant for anti-apartheid activists in other parts of the world. In the United States, King's vision of a more open and just South Africa was promoted by black Americans who had either worked with or had been inspired by him, and who also built on his earlier efforts to bring the civil rights and anti-apartheid movements into full cooperation with one another. King's former aides and associates in the SCLC, the ACOA, and the ANLCA were particularly important in this respect. Bayard Rustin, the brilliant civil rights activist who served the SCLC in numerous capacities in the fifties and sixties, advocated a nonviolent solution to the apartheid problem in the seventies. Jesse Jackson, the Baptist preacher who headed the Operation Breadbasket arm of the SCLC under King in the late sixties, and who started People United to Save Humanity (PUSH) in the early seventies, took a similar position.[62] The same can be said of Ralph D. Abernathy, King's closest friend and confidant, who presided over the SCLC throughout most of the seventies. Jackson and Abernathy joined other former King aides and associates in the SCLC—among them Joseph Lowery, Walter Fauntroy, and Bernard Lee—in echoing King's earlier call for the international community to utilize nonviolence completely through strong diplomatic and economic sanctions against South Africa.[63]

In the tradition of King, representatives of the SCLC seemed convinced that pressure from the nations of the world was the key to effective nonviolent protest inside South Africa. In September 1976, Bernard Lee, the Executive Vice President of the SCLC, sent a strongly worded letter to the UN Secretary-General, Kurt Waldheim, arguing that the indiscriminate killing of South African blacks made it impossible for them "to continue the nonviolent tactics they learned from the late Dr. Martin Luther King Jr." Lee recommended that the United Nations dispatch a peacekeeping force to South Africa, a suggestion widely supported among civil rights activists in this period following the Soweto uprising, and one with which King would hardly have taken issue.[64]

George M. Houser and others in the ACOA kept King's dream for South Africa alive in many ways through their work in the seventies. Their efforts occurred mainly through fund raising and appeals to governments and heads of state on behalf of a free and inclusive South Africa. ACOA leaders also occasionally invited South Africans to meet with and to address them on issues and concerns pertinent to their country. Of particular importance to Houser and others in the ACOA in the seventies was South Africa's stubborn persistence in frustrating Namibia's independence. The organization supported the UN's 1976 *Resolution 385,* which condemned South Africa's "illegal occupation of Namibia, its growing domination, and its oppressive rule," and which also called for "elections under UN supervision and control leading to independence."[65] The ACOA's position on Namibian independence at this juncture clearly stirred recollections of Martin Luther King Jr., who had consistently expressed an interest in the status of South West Africa.

King's former associates in the ANLCA entered the seventies determined to remain a voice in U.S. policy toward South Africa and Africa as a whole. James Farmer, Dorothy Height, A. Philip Randolph, and Roy Wilkins continued to attack apartheid in public speeches and through appeal letters and other documents, but not as a strong united body of the ANLCA. The ANLCA actually ceased to exist in the early seventies, at the very time that the South African governments's repression of black rights and activism was most intense.[66] The disintegration of the ANLCA dashed hopes, raised by King and others in the 1960s, for a permanent organization that would merge the concerns of the black freedom movement in America with those of oppressed South Africans.

The U.S. Congressman Charles Diggs and the preacher-activist Leon Sullivan of Opportunities Industrialization Centers (IOC), both of whom were inspired by King, were probably the most active African American leaders in the struggle against apartheid in the seventies. Diggs had served on the National Committee of the ACOA with King. As chairman of the House African Subcommittee, he pushed for UN economic sanctions against South Africa, for the denial of visas to South African government representatives wishing to visit the United States, for a revocation of South Africa's sugar quota to the United States, for the removal of the U.S. tracking station from South African soil, and for the breaking of U.S. business ties with South Africa.[67] King had recommended most of these same policies in the sixties.

After visiting South Africa in 1971, Diggs became a strong critic of policies adopted by the Richard Nixon and Gerald Ford administrations toward South Africa.[68] Like other civil rights activists, he refused to separate the United States' weak stand against South Africa from its lack of a strong commitment to African Americans. This was only logical during a time when civil rights gains shrank drastically before war-fed inflation, resurgent racism, and repressive government policies. In any event, efforts to oppose Diggs in U.S. government circles intensified, and his access to South Africa had been virtually cut off by the late seventies.

Leon Sullivan's contribution to the anti-apartheid cause assumed a somewhat different character. In 1977, Sullivan, a member of the board of General Motors, introduced the "Sullivan Principles," a voluntary code of conduct for U.S. companies with affiliates in South Africa. This document advocated a policy of nondiscrimination in employment practices, in quarters designed for eating and comfort, in work facilities, and in employment benefits. The Sullivan Principles, imbued with the spirit of Martin Luther King Jr. and the civil rights movement, were eventually adopted by churches, universities, and other organizations as a minimal standard of conduct for South Africa–related U.S. companies in which they owned stock.[69]

Also in 1977, the concern of African American leaders for a liberated South Africa became evident in the founding of TransAfrica under Randall Robinson. Based in Washington, D.C., this organization, from its origin, reflected King's legacy on two levels. First, in its drive to influence a more positive and aggressive U.S. policy toward South Africa and other parts of the black world. Second, in the fact that some of its original sponsors were organizations with which King had worked closely:

> The plans for TransAfrica, percolating for at least a decade, got the final boost it needed at the Black Caucus sponsored by the Black Leadership Conference on Southern Africa in September 1976. The better known

Black organizations were all there to endorse the "African-American Manifesto on Southern Africa"—NAACP, Operation PUSH, National Council of Negro Women, Association of Black Foundation Executives, Southern Christian Leadership Conference, and a host of others with and without portfolio. The Manifesto condoned armed struggle in southern Africa, and delivered a fusillade of criticism against U.S. private and government "hypocrisy" in South Africa. When the dust settled and the smoke cleared however, the most promising development at the conference was the removal of the swaddling clothes from TransAfrica—the Black American lobby for Africa and the Caribbean.[70]

TransAfrica soon caught the attention of opponents of apartheid throughout the United States and worldwide. The effectiveness of this new organization, realized to the fullest in the 1980s, resulted from the fact that "most other Africa-oriented Black-American organizations" deferred to it and threw the weight of their resources behind its agenda and activities.[71]

Some of the most conscious efforts to pursue King's dream with respect to South Africa occurred with the Martin Luther King Jr. Center for Nonviolent Social Change in Atlanta, Georgia. In the seventies, the leading figures in this multimillion-dollar building-crypt-park complex challenged the morality and legitimacy of South African apartheid in ways consistent with King's philosophy and methods. Coretta Scott King, King's widow, frequently stated that nonviolence afforded the best path to a truly free, peaceful, and racially inclusive South Africa. In December 1975, Mrs. King, after returning from South Africa, proudly recalled the "serious efforts to resolve problems nonviolently" there in spite of "the dangers of greater warfare."[72] Two years later, in a speech in Washington, D.C., Mrs. King encouraged President Jimmy Carter "to find nonviolent answers to this growing and disturbing situation" in South Africa.[73]

Because Martin Luther King Jr.'s impact on the American churches and culture in general was so profound and evident in the seventies, one wonders why American religious institutions did so little to address the South African apartheid problem. The black church in its national institutional form remained preoccupied with survival issues in the United States, and was more of a spectator than a participant in anti-apartheid activities. However, there were notable exceptions. In 1975, the Bishop's Council of the African Methodist Episcopal Church (AME) pledged its support for majority rule in South Africa and Rhodesia. The council was led by

Bishop H. H. Brookins, who had previously been expelled from South Africa and Rhodesia because of his attacks on their racial policies and practices, and because of his support for Rhodesia's African National Council, a black nationalist group.[74] In 1978 the AME Church, the African Methodist Episcopal Zion Church (AMEZ), the National Baptist Convention of America, the National Baptist Convention USA, and the Progressive National Baptist Convention united under the auspices of the National Council of Churches and asked major banks in the United States "to establish a policy that no new loans will be made nor existing loans renewed to the Pretoria, South Africa government."[75] Actions along these lines were not only in conformity with positions expressed a decade earlier by King, but also reflective of the black church's historic interest in strengthening ties with Africa.[76]

White American churches responded to apartheid in much the same way they responded to racism in their own country. Most engaged in a conspiracy of silence around the issue. A few participated in the adoption of resolutions urging government action and vigorous activity on the part of banks and South African–based U.S. companies against apartheid. These actions took place mostly with liberal churches that functioned in connection with bodies like the National Council of Churches (NCC) and the World Council of Churches (WCC). In contrast, American fundamentalists completely ignored the apartheid problem, and only rarely did the more moderate evangelicals address it. Speaking in Durban, South Africa, to a mixed crowd of some 45,000 in 1973, the internationally known evangelist Billy Graham warned, "If we don't become brothers— and become brothers fast—we will destroy ourselves in a worldwide racial conflagration." Continuing his appeal to the whites and persons of color present at the crusade, Graham, in a statement powerfully reminiscent of Martin Luther King Jr., observed:

> This is not just a South African problem. This is a worldwide problem. America today has the finest civil rights laws the world has known, but the problem is deeper than the law. The problem is the human heart. We all need a new heart.[77]

This statement appears all the more interesting when compared to comments Graham made while touring the African continent in 1960. At that time, the evangelist described "the U.S. racial problem as an embarrassment to Americans in Africa," and resolved that he would plan "no crusade in South Africa as long as apartheid, or segregation of the races, is the practice."[78] These remarks came weeks before Graham and King "shared an experience of ethnic and cultural understanding at the Tenth Baptist World Congress of the Baptist World Alliance."[79] While not always in agreement with King's approach to the problem of racism, Graham insisted nevertheless that the problem would end only when more ministers "set an example of Christian love . . . as Martin Luther King has done."[80] Under King's influence and inspiration, Graham became more mindful of the social implications of the Christian faith, particularly as related to southern Jim Crow and South African apartheid. Significantly, Graham has never publicly acknowledged his debt to King at this level of his consciousness. Even evangelical scholars, who have traced Graham's mounting public commitment to social concerns, and especially to improved race relations, have ignored the tremendous challenge and inspiration he received from King and other African Americans who risked their lives to make America better.[81]

This has not been the case with Jimmy Carter, another self-proclaimed evangelical, who became president of the United States in 1976. Carter said repeatedly in the seventies that King and the black freedom movement of the fifties and sixties made him more sensitive to racism as a barrier to human community. This explains in part why Carter made "human rights" the primary focus of his administration. But Carter's call for a new and more democratic South Africa did not find expression in what King would have regarded as well-defined, concrete proposals and actions. While deploring the violence and repression of the South African Government, its assistance to the Ian Smith regime in Rhodesia (Zimbabwe), and its actions in Namibia, Carter failed nevertheless to devise initiatives strong enough to break the patterns of white power and black oppression in South Africa.

George W. Shepherd Jr. reported that "Vice-President Walter Mondale stood up strongly" to the South African prime minister, John Vorster, in May 1977, demanding "nothing less than full participation for all of South Africa's citizens in its government and economic life."[82] The Carter administration remained unconvinced that the interests of black South Africans were best protected in the bantustans, or the homeland system, but it still opposed a strengthened arms embargo against South Africa.[83] Such an approach was evidently at odds with priorities set forth by King more than a decade earlier. The Carter initiative was undermined in a sub-

tle way by UN ambassador Andrew Young, a former King aide, who compared "the situation in South Africa with the civil rights situation in the
American South."[84]

An International Tribute to King in 1979

Perhaps the most interesting assessments of King's legacy for South Africa
came from world leaders who met at the King Center in Atlanta in
January 1979. An international tribute to King on his fiftieth birthday
marked the occasion. Arranged in part by Enuga S. Reddy, a longtime
anti-apartheid activist and admirer of Mohandas K. Gandhi, the tribute
was part of a special meeting of the UN Special Committee Against
Apartheid (UNSCAA).[85] Reddy, Director of the UN Centre Against
Apartheid (UNCAA) at the time, spoke for people worldwide in declaring
that the time had come for the global community to honor King "for his
contribution to the struggle against apartheid."[86] Stirring tributes to King
were offered by dignitaries from various parts of North America, South
and Central America, Europe, the West Indies, Asia, and Africa. A greater
recognition of King's significance for South Africa would not have been
possible, especially since the event was held on the grounds of the greatest
landmark bearing King's name, and also because tributes to both the King
legacy and the work of the UNSCAA echoed simultaneously through the
many speeches and songs heard on that occasion.[87]

Tributes given by American representatives established the tone of the
event. In the opening speech, Governor George Busbee of Georgia praised
King for "being one of the first respondents" to the founding of the UN-
SCAA in 1963. "Rev. King abhorred *apartheid* and racial inequality in any
form," he exclaimed, "likening the American civil rights struggle of blacks
to other such struggles in South Africa, Asia and Latin America." Busbee's
speech ended on a cautionary note, warning that "unless this Special
Committee against *apartheid,* the King Center and others concerned with
human rights continue to press" King's dream "for the basic rights of all,"
people in South Africa and other countries "can only expect terror,
hunger, illiteracy, and disease."[88] Busbee's remarks struck a responsive
chord in Mayor Maynard H. Jackson of Atlanta, who asserted that
"*apartheid* must be stricken from the face of this earth, and from the
awareness of those who carry its hydra-headed evil from day to day."[89]
Andrew Young, the U.S. representative to the UN, commended the King
Center and the UNSCAA for "helping this nation become more acutely

aware of the situation in southern Africa, and of our responses to the problem of *apartheid.*" Young went on to remind his listeners that King's legacy, as far as the struggles in South Africa and America were concerned, could not be divorced from that of Gandhi and Albert J. Luthuli:

> Nonviolence came to us from Africa. It was Mahatma Gandhi who in his early protest used nonviolence against *apartheid.* It moved on to India. It was reborn again under the leadership of Chief Albert Luthuli. . . . We have seen it develop in such a way in the United States of America that is quite different from the experiences which occurred in other parts of the world. That is as it should be. But one of the things that concerns me is that we in the United Nations and those of us who come out of this nonviolent tradition have always tended to think of nonviolence as it was last demonstrated in our town. I would like to contend that what we see happening across the world today is very much influenced by a nonviolent understanding of how change can occur.[90]

A fitting footnote to the aforementioned tributes was added by Herschell Challenor, a representative of the United Nations' Educational, Scientific and Cultural Organization (UNESCO) in Washington. "In proclaiming forcefully that his struggle for the freedom of the black man in America could not be separated from that of his brothers in southern Africa," she proclaimed, "Martin Luther King renewed the basic tie linking the African diaspora to the mother continent." "The voice of Martin Luther King has swelled into an anthem of freedom," Challenor continued, "rising above the muffled groans from the holds of the slave ships, the cries of revolt of the children of Soweto and of the Sharpeville martyrs, and the murmur of the numberless voices of the Montgomery, Washington and Selma marchers." With a powerful sense of how King's struggle transcended American racism and South African apartheid to embrace racism as a world phenomenon, Challenor concluded:

> Let us in the international community pledge ourselves to renew and fulfill Martin Luther King's dream of a time when the world would see itself as one great family of nations where "no man would be an island unto himself" and "where man would not be judged by the colour of his skin but by the content of his character."[91]

Representatives from parts of Europe, the most ever to appear at a single event at the King Center, gave tributes that were equally moving and challenging. Kurt Waldheim, Secretary-General of the United Nations, characterized King as one who invoked "reason over force," and as one whose "name today is synonymous with freedom" in South Africa and the world over. "His overriding belief in world community," stated Waldheim concerning King, "coincided with the steadfast position taken by the United Nations, which rejects the illegal practice of *apartheid* in South Africa and holds it to be a grave danger to international peace and security."[92] Prime Minister Olla Ullsten of Sweden concurred, noting that those persons and nations that admired and respected King "are always under the obligation to use all peaceful means available to fight the evils of *apartheid*." The Swedish leader ended his tribute with a statement that captured in full measure the meaning of King and the civil rights movement for whites and blacks in South Africa:

> We hope and pray that the white minority of South Africa will also finally understand the message of love that Martin Luther King Jr. so desperately tried to make his compatriots understand and accept. We hope and pray that it is not yet too late to get rid of the fear/hate and violence that *apartheid* breeds, that there is still time to heal the wounds of distrust and dissension, inflicted to divide and rule the people of South Africa. . . . We hope and pray that one day all the children of South Africa will be part of a nation where people are judged by what they are, and where they will be able to sit down together as brothers, join hands in freedom and sing "Free at last, Free at last, Great God Almighty we are free at last."[93]

Kurt Frydenlund, the Minister for Foreign Affairs of Norway, pointed to the unfortunate but inevitable shift away from Kingian nonviolence in South Africa in the seventies. "All these leaders know the costs of a violent solution to the racial problems of southern Africa," he explained. "Immense human suffering, material destruction, possible civil wars, most probably big power involvement. Nevertheless, they see a resort to armed struggle as the only alternative open to them."[94] And, further on, Frydenlund argued that the proper course for the world community was not to castigate oppressed South Africans who turned to violence, but to impose sanctions and other "non-armed pressure" that would make King's methods more acceptable and workable in their context:

> We cannot blame them. We cannot ask them to be patient, for patient they have been for decades. . . . We cannot recommend to them the strategy of nonviolence, because that has been applied since the days of Albert

Luthuli. . . . What we can do, however, and in fact must do, is to ask what
we ourselves can contribute to bringing about a negotiated settlement. This
is a most essential question for us to deal with. Because the prospects for
achieving negotiated settlements are closely linked with the attitude taken
by the outside world to the white minority regimes in southern Africa.[95]

While unable to appear in Atlanta for the international tribute to King,
Pope John Paul II sent "greetings together with the assurance of his prayers
that the evocation of this outstanding figure will advance the establishment everywhere of peaceful, just, and friendly relations between people
of different races."[96] This statement was reinforced in the tribute of
Vladimir N. Martynenko, the representative of the Ukrainian Soviet
Socialist Republic to the UN, who quoted King on the need for the "complete isolation and boycott of the racist regime of South Africa." "The best
tribute to Martin Luther King Jr., to all fighters against racism, *apartheid,*
and colonialism," Martynenko observed, "will be a growing unity of actions of all peoples of goodwill, and the fight for the final elimination of
racism, *apartheid* and colonialism from our earth."[97] Similar comments
came from Hugo Scheltema, the representative of the Netherlands to the
UN, who suggested that King provided the principles that inspired UN
action against apartheid.[98] The call for sanctions against South Africa was
further advanced by Romesh Chandra, president of the World Peace
Council (WPC), who emphasized that "this is what Martin Luther King
Jr. would have wished for."[99]

An appropriate climax to European tributes to King came in the words
of Jan Kulakowsi and the Reverend Canon L. John Collins. Kulakowsi,
general secretary of the World Confederation of Labour in Brussels, declared that "the person and the action of Martin Luther King are and always will be a source of inspiration and a stimulus for those fighting
against all forms of racism, discrimination and injustice, and especially
against apartheid, the most flagrant and odious expression of racism of our
times."[100] Collins, president of the London-based International Defence
and Aid Fund for Southern Africa, which King supported more than a
decade earlier, reported that King never abandoned hope in the possibility
of a triumph of nonviolence in South Africa:

> Martin Luther King Jr. was always deeply sympathetic to and supportive of
> the African liberation struggle of southern Africa. Even in this difficult con-
> text he never lost his belief in the rightness and efficiency of the attempt of

nonviolence. To this end he pledged constantly for effective international action against South Africa in order to bring about peaceful change.[101]

In an emotional moment, Collins suggested that King was one of a very few world leaders who demonstrated through praxis what should be the moral responsibility of every human being regarding apartheid:

> When the history of this century comes to be written, it is men like Martin Luther King Jr., like Albert Luthuli, Mahatma Gandhi and such who will be remembered. These are the people that we ought to be regarding as those who we just don't honour, but we do everything in our power to follow and meet with their great ideals and demands upon themselves.[102]

The Asian Group of the UN was strongly represented at the 1979 meeting in Atlanta, and it, too, presented rich statements that highlighted King's meaning and significance for South Africa. Isao Abe, the representative of Japan to the UN, expressed the conviction that the UNSCAA, in its quest to eliminate apartheid, was simply standing in the tradition of King, whose struggle "transcended national boundaries." Abe pointed specifically to the civil rights leader's sponsorship of the *Appeal for Action Against Apartheid* in 1962, claiming that "it is actions of this sort that form part of the reason for which the Special Committee against Apartheid has chosen to join today in honouring the memory of Dr. Martin Luther King Jr." Dismissing apartheid as "an affront to the memory of a man like Dr. King," Abe added: "Let *apartheid* be abolished, let all men enjoy the peace, freedom, and prosperity to which they are entitled, and let the vision of Martin Luther King Jr. be realized at last."[103] This challenge also coursed through the tribute of Rikhi Jaipal, the representative of the prime minister of India, who stated that "while the obstacles in our path may be many, there cannot be a more fitting tribute to Martin Luther King Jr. than to march on in the belief that 'We shall overcome.'"[104] A proper benediction to the Asian tributes came from Tayyab Siddiqui, the UN representative from Pakistan, who renewed his country's commitment to the total eradication of apartheid, "the cause to which Dr. Martin Luther King Jr. dedicated his life."[105]

The Africans who participated in the international tribute spoke out of a profound sense of identification with King and African Americans in general, and with the values that had long impelled their movement toward freedom. "We in Africa share" King's vision of "a world free of racial injustice, poverty, and war," said Representative Mohamed Osman of the Sudan, "because large parts in our continent are still dominated by racist regimes, foremost amongst which is the *apartheid* regime in South Africa." Osman went on to explain that

> The struggle which was waged by Dr. King for the elimination of racial discrimination against the black community in the United States, is a clear demonstration of the close relationship between the struggle of the Afro-Americans and that of the indigenous South Africans, in terms of sharing a common heritage and a common enemy. The advances made in this country in alleviating discriminatory practices against the black community have led in turn to a more active participation by the American Administration in resolving the problems of racial discrimination and colonization in the southern part of our continent.[106]

Osman's reflections found support from Ahmed Esmat Abdel Meguid, the Egyptian representative to the UN. Meguid recalled King's involvement in 1962 in the *Appeal for Action Against Apartheid,* a campaign that symbolized the bonds and obligations between black Americans and black South Africans, and insisted that the civil rights leader "is regarded, until the present moment, by the freedom fighters in southern Africa as their spiritual leader who guides and inspires them in their struggle for freedom, independence and dignity."[107] Leslie O. Harriman of Nigeria, the Chairman of the Special Committee Against Apartheid, repeated Meguid's claims concerning King's role in the *Appeal for Action Against Apartheid,* and added that

> when Dr. King led the civil rights movement, he did not merely send reverberations throughout this land. Millions of peoples in Africa and the Third World saw instantly that the struggle in Montgomery and Birmingham, in Selma and Albany, was the same as the struggle in Johannesburg and Accra, in Algiers and Kingston.[108]

The tributes shared by black South African leaders vividly reflected the nature of the debate that was raging inside their country concerning the relevance of King's ideas and methods. While expressing a personal admiration for King, Gabriel Setiloane, a representative of the ANC, complained that the method King had learned from great men like Gandhi and Luthuli simply had not worked in South Africa. "The question that must be put to you today," Setiloane maintained, "is why is it that this thing that has been learned from South Africa and has been successful in other parts of the world is not in the place of its birth, where Mahatma Gandhi," and "Albert Luthuli did it with others?" Acknowledging that "I can't say that I have dreams like Martin Luther King Jr.," Setiloane asserted that experience had amply demonstrated the inapplicability of Kingian and Gandhian principles of love and nonviolence to the South African context:

> Those who are often so very much taken by these philosophies; very good indeed. However, we who have been trying to put them into practice, have come to a realization that the success of a strategy is not only in the strategy itself; it is not intrinsic in the strategy. The success or failure of a strategy really often depends on the adversary with whom or against whom the strategy is being put. It is high time that diplomats and world leaders are quite clear of the fact that the adversary that we are dealing with in South Africa is not the same as the adversary that Martin Luther King Jr. dealt with here; or that Mahatma Gandhi dealt with in India when he was dealing with the British colonial regime. These men were dealing with adversaries perhaps who had certain principles in them and therefore who could respond to the kind of principle and the kind of strategy to which they were devoted.[109]

Essentially the same sentiments came from Erett Radebe, a representative of the PAC of Azania (South Africa). After pledging "ourselves anew to go beyond the mountain top and retrieve King's dream," Radebe defended the PAC's choice of armed struggle over Kingian nonviolence as both honorable and pragmatic:

> It has been a simple decision to choose methods different to those advocated by Dr. King in our struggle in Azania. . . . The choice to take up arms to meet the repressive violence with revolutionary violence is not only a merit of honour but as far as our experience is concerned, it is the only way to eliminate the centres of incendiary violence to which the oppressed masses of Azania have been subjected for more than three centuries.[110]

For Radebe, the PAC's method of armed resistance in no way violated King's special meaning for black South Africans. "The support we enjoy from all over the world for this just cause is thanks to the sacrifices from men like King, Biko, and Sobukwe," he observed, who "have drawn attention to the glorious struggle for liberation in Azania." Radebe closed his tribute with words that underscored for many the sense of urgency implied in King's dream for South Africans and humanity as a whole. "Until mankind is free, not only from the vulgarity of racial discrimination, apartheid, and all systems denying us fundamental human rights, but from the equally vulgar exploitation of man by man, Martin Luther King Jr.'s dream will remain unfulfilled."[111]

All of the Africans involved in the 1979 international tribute to King seemed genuinely interested in how the world community could best pursue King's ideal of a new South Africa. Paul Bomani, the ambassador of Tanzania to the United States, held that it was frustrating to see that the world had done so little to end apartheid since King's death. "We still have to ask ourselves in 1979," he noted, "how many more have to fall before the world can have the will to jointly marshal the vast resources we command, for the noble purpose of eliminating *apartheid* from mankind's agenda?"[112] Abdirizak Haji Hussen, Somalia's UN representative, advanced the point further, suggesting that the world's toleration of apartheid could not be rationalized since the "fundamentals championed by Dr. Martin Luther King Jr. are also cornerstones of the Charter of the United Nations and of the Universal Declaration of Human rights."[113] Alex Ouaison-Sackey, the ambassador of Ghana to the U.S., reaffirmed this feeling, and reminded those present that the involvement of the UNSCAA "in the sponsorship of this homage should remind" all nations that support South Africa "of their guilt and of the judgment that awaits them." While commending both the King Center and the UNSCAA for joining "hands in this historic act of commemoration," the Ghanaian leader scolded the international community for the tragic ambivalence revealed in its need to honor King while, at the same time, refusing "to break with that terrible 'crime against humanity' which bears the name '*apartheid.*' "[114]

The impact of the Atlanta meeting on the policies of nations toward South Africa is difficult to assess. The policies of some nations remained essentially unchanged. Others imposed diplomatic and economic sanctions against the apartheid regime, thus bringing their policies more in line with the King legacy. It became clear in time, however, that the subsequent relationships of nations to South Africa would be determined more by the realities of the 1980s than by any conscious need to actualize Martin Luther King Jr.'s dream.

CHAPTER 4

A QUESTION OF OPTIONS
King and Anti-Apartheid Activism in the 1980s

*We are determined to fight to the bitter end for the libera-
tion of our people. I am afraid that the white regime will
have to decide whether to give in, when they realize they
are fighting a futile battle. It is their decision whether they
want to give in violently or sensibly and save our country.*

Winnie Mandela, 1984[1]

*[I]t is one of those things that you have to do, as there is no
other alternative. I don't think I am peculiar in this respect.
I think that many people in the A.N.C. would be glad if
there was no need for violence. But the need is there, and
we have got to go ahead with it, bitter as it is.*

Oliver Tambo, 1985[2]

*The crucial question for leaders and ordinary people in
South Africa who admire Martin Luther King Jr. and his
philosophy of nonviolence, is what relevance does that philosophy have for their situation? Is it possible to use nonviolence, or is counter-violence the only option left?*

C. F. Beyers Naudé, 1986[3]

artin Luther King Jr.'s philosophy and methods met perhaps their
greatest test in South Africa in the 1980s. The obstacles to change
in that country remained as formidable as ever. Polarization
reached unprecedented levels along both tribal and racial lines, as

the forces of the African National Congress (ANC) and Inkatha clashed, and as frightened whites moved increasingly to the right. Debates concerning violence and nonviolence raged in the streets, in churches, and in the halls of academia, and a final, fatal confrontation between the races appeared more possible than at any time in the past.[4] Frustrated with the lack of sufficient international pressure against South Africa, even proponents of nonviolence became less hopeful of a peaceful end to apartheid. In this "critical, quite traumatic period in the history of our land," as one black South African put it, the search for alternatives to a possible race war intensified, a search that involved not only a serious assault on classical Christian attitudes toward war and peace, but also an intense critical re-examination of Kingian-Gandhian-Luthulian principles.[5]

This chapter establishes a context for understanding Martin Luther King Jr.'s continuing influence on the South African freedom struggle in the 1980s. Of particular interest are King's impact on the increasing search for alternatives to violence and racial separatism in South Africa, his importance as a role model for black South African leaders, his symbolic significance for elements in the UN Special Committee Against Apartheid (UNSCAA), and the ways in which his spirit was reflected in reactions to apartheid in America and elsewhere.

King and the Continuing Search for Options in South Africa

The South African government took numerous steps in the eighties to destroy anti-apartheid activism in both its violent and nonviolent forms. Control of black movements into towns tightened, and states of emergency were declared at various times. Police arrests and detentions without charges rose, particularly in the case of black trade union leaders, and so did reports of torture and deaths in detention.[6] Several massacres occurred, conjuring up images of Sharpeville two decades earlier. In November 1984, an estimated 150 persons were killed at Sebokeng; 18 were killed and 225 were wounded at Crossroads in February 1985; and about 43 lost their lives at Langa on March 21, 1985.[7] Millions of blacks lost their so-called South African citizenship, and some were given a false status of "independence" in the so-called homelands of Transkei, Bophuthatswana, Venda, and Ciskei. New laws significantly expanded the South African armed forces, allowing for attacks against ANC exiles in Lesotho. In a move obviously designed to divide black opinion and to co-opt Colored and Indian voters, the white minority government set in motion a new constitution allowing limited rights to Coloreds and Indians under white control in a tricameral parliament.[8] Moreover, the apartheid regime interfered with progress toward Namibian independence, and continued its military and economic destabilization of neighboring Mozambique, Angola, and Zimbabwe.[9]

Some oppressed South Africans greeted these government crackdowns with protest methods similar to those employed and advocated earlier by Martin Luther King Jr. Blacks staged protests and strikes against apartheid education, wages, and bus and rent increases. The August 1984 elections for the new tricameral parliament were heavily boycotted by Coloreds and Asians, and community, worker, and student protests continued through the fall of that year.[10]

In the late eighties, black South African clergymen led prayer vigils and marches against parliament and the apartheid system as a whole, and black South African women organized for anti-apartheid campaigns.[11] Despite the continuing efforts to dismantle apartheid through organized, peaceful means, serious doubts about the relevance of King's ideas and methods remained evident in many quarters. Touched by the South African regime's continued repression and stubborn resistance to change, and inspired by the continuing vitality of the Black Consciousness Movement (BCM) and liberation theology, scores of black South Africans refused to even consider nonviolence as a viable and potent method in their struggle.[12]

This attitude found powerful symbolic expression during the violence of the summer of 1985, when black South African youths smashed the small building that stood as a shrine to Mohandas K. Gandhi near an Indian township called Phoenix.[13] The desecration was a clear sign of the waves of violence that would follow. This move toward counterviolent means resulted primarily from a sense of what was actually practical in the South African context, and was not in any way a harsh judgment on the morality of nonviolence as articulated and practiced by men such as King, Gandhi, and Luthuli. "I know many peace-loving people who have been forced into violence," said Motlalepula Chabaku, a black female pastor in exile from South Africa. "They have suffered violence and in desperation they turn to counter-violence."[14] In an essay on South Africa in the mid-eighties, Thomas G. Karis of the Ralph Bunche Institute on the UN in New York reported that

> According to recent opinion surveys, a growing number of South African blacks have come to accept violence as unavoidable if there is to be basic change. And, encouraged by the increasing legitimacy of "armed struggle"

as a tool against the regime, young blacks have begun to use guns and throw grenades as well as rocks and stones. At mass meetings, young blacks frequently shout slogans urging the ANC to supply them with Soviet-made AK-47 assault rifles and sometimes are to be seen carrying wooden replicas of the rifle.[15]

The continuing trend toward violent resistance to apartheid helps explain why the issue of violence versus nonviolence was such a major topic of discussion in books and other sources in South Africa and throughout the world in the 1980s.[16] The white South African church leader Beyers Naudé pointed to one of the central questions in this discussion in a 1986 interview. "Given the support of the major Western powers for apartheid, and the lacking unity of peace-loving forces," he remarked, "the crucial question" for South Africans "who admire Martin Luther King Jr." is "what relevance does" his philosophy "have for their situation?"[17]

The former King aides Walter Fauntroy and Andrew Young discovered the declining significance of King for some black South Africans while addressing a meeting of African political leaders in Gaborone, Botswana, in January 1987. Fauntroy, the congressman from Washington, D.C., briefly referred to King's birthday on that occasion, "but purposely avoided the mention of King's philosophy of nonviolent protest because he decided 'it is not relevant for the situation.'" Fauntroy actually said that "the violence of the South African government has suspended the moral obligation of pacifism."[18] When asked if King would approve a violent response to apartheid at that point, Fauntroy quickly responded: "He would not. He would have said that if the entire world turned violent, I would not."[19]

Mayor Andrew Young of Atlanta, Georgia, was much more forceful in expressing King's views at the Botswana meeting. He lectured to African politicians and students on the peaceful destruction of American apartheid under King's leadership, and advocated tolerance, patience, and quiet perseverance on the part of South African freedom fighters. "Chucks of skepticism from five hundred students greeted the unfamiliar theory," wrote the newspaper columnist Jim Galloway, and "one man on crutches hotly declared himself unlikely to believe a call for nonviolence from an American such as Young." "You are already violent, you have Star Wars, you have enough arms to do the job," cried the man. Young found himself grasping for words when the man noted the hypocrisy of an American government that encouraged pacifism among South African freedom fighters while supplying weapons to rebels in Angola.[20] "The audience was suspicious of a theory apparently endorsing docility," reported Galloway, "coming from a representative of a country they blamed almost entirely for South Africa's white regime."[21] "The expression for patience is about four years too late," declared one of the politicians in response to Young's challenge. The editor of a liberal South African journal agreed, noting that "King was *okay* for his time in his country, but the glamour and his time are gone." The white American historian George Fredrickson, who published a comparative study of racism in South Africa and the United States in 1981, echoed these remarks, and suggested that "The big lesson . . . learned by the ANC and other groups was that nonviolence doesn't work here." After the meeting, Jim Galloway concluded that "in Gaborone, Botswana, twelve miles from the South African border, the Rev. Martin Luther King Jr. is a hard sell."[22]

The rejection of King's nonviolent methods was most evident within the ranks of major political movements and mass organizations inside South Africa in the 1980s. The Zulu chief Gatsha Buthelezi of the Inkatha movement accepted the necessity of violence to achieve change shortly after the 1977 crackdown of the South African government, but he consistently claimed in the eighties that "the time is not ripe."[23] The Pan-Africanist Congress (PAC) never ceased to prepare for what it saw as an inevitable violent confrontation with whites. The ANC continued to combine political and armed actions in its encounters with the apartheid system. By 1980, more than 4,000 refugees had undergone training in ANC guerrilla camps "while some 2,500 had been brought to trial for sabotage." In that year, ANC attacks on police stations and government-linked economic targets escalated fourfold.[24] In 1982, at least twenty-nine sabotage attacks, two assassinations, and "an armed operation could be attributed to the ANC."[25] By 1985, the ANC resistance campaigns were escalated to the stage of "a people's war." According to the ANC president Oliver Tambo, "this new policy represented a necessary response to the regime's own escalation of violence, since South African security forces were killing children and perpetrating 'massacres . . . inside and outside the country.'"[26]

The ANC's emphasis on violence as "a necessary response" to oppression seemed consistent with the idea of war as "a negative good," or as a tool "to block the surge of an evil force in history," an idea Martin Luther King Jr. held before embracing nonviolence as a way of life.[27] The ANC leaders actually accepted nonviolence as a matter of principle in the eighties, a position that brought them closer to King than one would imagine at first glance. Armed resistance was always viewed by them as unavoidable in the South African context. And even when the ANC employed this tactic, it did not wantonly attack nonmilitary targets or noncombatants, such as women, children, and the aged.[28] Oliver Tambo said in a 1985 interview that "I think many people in the ANC would be glad if there was no need for violence. But the need is there, and we have got to go ahead with it."[29] In its stress on avoiding unnecessary and excessive violence, and on employing armed resistance to achieve justice, the ANC appeared very much in line with important aspects of classical just war theory.[30]

The ANC's position on the necessity and inevitability of violence as a response to apartheid was shared in the 1980s by leaders of groups such as the PAC, the BCM, the Azanian People's Organization (AZAPO), and the Azanian Students' Organization (AZASO). Despite internal struggles over leadership, created by the death of Robert Sobukwe in 1978, the PAC continued to train guerrillas for violent revolt against apartheid. While devoted primarily to raising the consciousness of black South Africans regarding white racism and capitalist exploitation, the BCM remained open to violent resistance on the grounds that conflict of a violent nature already existed between the interests of peoples of color and those of whites. The same can be said of the AZAPO and the AZASO, a student organization committed to political radicalism from its founding in the late seventies.[31] Elements in all of these organizations remained hopeful for peaceful, fundamental change in South Africa, even as they doubted the relevance of Martin Luther King Jr.'s tactics for their situation.

Several other organized movements originated in South Africa in the 1980s as questions concerning the best possible means for ending apartheid dominated discussions. One such organization was the United Democratic Front (UDF), described in some circles as "a nonracial, nonviolent and legally constituted movement."[32] Launched in 1983, it devoted its energies to bus and rent boycotts, anti-constitutional reforms, anti-sports-tour campaigns, operations for the unbanning of the ANC, and movements for national unity against government-imposed states of emergency.[33] The UDF accepted nonviolence in practical rather than absolute terms, a position not fully identical with King's. Its refusal to embrace nonviolence as an absolute principle, coupled with its sympathies for and ties with the ANC, led Gatsha Buthelezi to characterize it as "an advocate of violence," as "the terror wing of the ANC," characterizations which probably said more about the Zulu chief himself than about the UDF.[34]

Also in 1983, the National Forum (NF) was launched by the AZAPO "to oppose the Nationalist government's constitutional proposals." Rooted in an "Africanist ideology," the NF adopted as its policy statement the socialist manifesto of the AZAPO, a document that upheld the principles of antiracism, anti-imperialism, noncooperation with the oppressor, independent working-class organizations, and opposition to all ruling-class parties.[35] While attaching some significance to boycotts, strikes, civil disobedience, street demonstrations, and other nonviolent forms of anti-apartheid agitation, the NF's stand on Kingian nonviolence was no different from that of the AZAPO, the AZASO, and other black consciousness groups.

The BCM gave birth to black trade union groups in the mid-eighties that would affect "the future course of black resistance." The Congress of South African Trade Unions (COSATU) was organized in December 1985 by some 650,000 black South African workers. The Azanian Confederation of Trade Unions (AZACTU) also emerged. These and other trade union groups signaled the coming of age of workers in the anti-apartheid crusade, and they united working-class interests with a determination to end white political domination.[36] Although respectful of the nonviolent traditions shaped by King, Gandhi, and Luthuli, these organizations were open to any methods that promised radical changes along class and race lines in South Africa. In the summer of 1987, Elijah Barayi, president of the COSATU, spoke for millions of black South African workers when he urged blacks to utilize any means necessary to "seize power from the intransigent government." Daring the South African president, Pieter W. Botha, to arrest him, Barayi went on to laud members of the ANC as "freedom fighters" who represented hope for a new South Africa.[37]

Despite the outright rejection of Martin Luther King Jr.'s nonviolent absolutism in many sectors of South African society, his views on nonviolence and violence remained relevant to the continuous debate on the subject in South Africa throughout the eighties. Much of this debate occurred among educators, church leaders, and theologians, some of whom did not agree wholeheartedly with King's methods nor the armed resistance embraced by elements of the ANC and the PAC. At the center of the debate stood Mokgethi Motlhabi, the director of the Educational Opportunities Council (EOC) in Johannesburg. In his writings, Motlhabi made important distinctions between the tradition of nonviolence in South Africa and the traditions associated with King and Gandhi. In 1988, he questioned the relevancy of King's and Gandhi's perspective on redemptive suffering for the South African context, suggesting that violence was the only language whites truly understood:

> King believed that unearned suffering is redemptive. In South Africa, though, self-suffering, rather than move the heart of the oppressor as both King and Gandhi thought was finally possible, seems to be an indication of weakness to him and thus something to be exploited to the full to drive home the point that it is a waste of time. . . . It seems . . . that people must first be exterminated before the oppressor's heart can be moved, if at all.[38]

Theologians and church persons were the dominant figures in this growing debate concerning violence and nonviolence, a development not surprising in view of the moral and ethical issues involved. The subject surfaced in a powerful way in September 1985, with the appearance of *The Kairos Document,* a statement framed by theologians of various racial and religious backgrounds in South Africa. The document criticized the church for its "tacit support" of "the growing militarization of the South African State," and for defining nonviolence and violence in ways that benefited the government over those genuinely struggling for a new South Africa:

> The stance of "Church Theology" on nonviolence, expressed as a blanket condemnation of all that is called violence, has not only been unable to curb the violence of our situation, it has actually, although unwittingly, been a major contributing factor in the recent escalation of State violence. . . . The problem for the Church here is the way the word violence is being used in the propaganda of the State. The State and the media have chosen to call violence what some people do in the townships as they struggle for their liberation, that is, throwing stones, burning cars and buildings and sometimes killing collaborators. But this excludes the structural, institutional and unrepentant violence of the State and especially the oppressive and naked violence of the police and the army. These things are not counted as violence. And even when they are acknowledged to be "excessive," they are called "misconduct" or even "atrocities" but never violence. Thus the phrase "violence in the townships" comes to mean what young people are doing and not what the police are doing or what apartheid in general is doing to people. If one calls for nonviolence in such circumstances one appears to be criticizing the resistance of the people while justi-

fying or at least overlooking the violence of the police and the State. . . . Violence, especially, in our circumstances, is a loaded word.[39]

In 1987, Charles Villa-Vicencio, a professor in the Department of Religious Studies at the University of Cape Town, published a major work drawing together the pivotal figures and issues in the debate.[40] White and black theologians from the academy and the church grappled not only with the traditional willingness of South African churches to bless the use of state violence while opposing violence on the part of the oppressed, but also with the cogency of King's, Gandhi's, and Luthuli's ideas concerning nonviolence as a mode of practical action.[41] The positions taken by white theologians and churchmen, such as Beyers Naudé, John de Gruchy, and Charles Villa-Vicencio, were intriguing to say the least, particularly in light of the views held by most whites on these matters in the eighties. Naudé, de Gruchy, and Villa-Vicencio chided the dominant church traditions in South Africa for their long-standing hypocrisy on the question of violence versus nonviolence. Although hopeful for a peaceful transition toward nonracial democracy in South Africa, they also acknowledged that such a development was probably impossible without violence.[42] Villa-Vicencio clearly identified the problems involved in achieving a nonviolent revolution in South Africa, problems that, in his view, were not encountered by Gandhi and King:

> Nonviolent ways to radical peaceful change appear to be effective only against regimes which find their authority in a commitment to justice and tolerance, rather than in ruthless tyranny. Such ways are also only likely to succeed where the hegemony and self-determination of the rulers are not about to be wrested totally from them. In India, only Britain's colonial power was at stake, while home-rule was never in question when Gandhi's nonviolent resistance achieved its aim; and in the United States the black population constituted only ten percent of the entire American population when Martin Luther King's passive resistance campaign achieved its desired effect. It would also be naive not to recognize that other "violent" factors, including the presence of more militant revolutionary leaders, contributed significantly to the nonviolent means employed by Gandhi and King. Above all, it would be naive not to recognize the cost in lives which such "nonviolent" struggles exacted. In South Africa more than colonial power is at stake, with whites recognizing that their privileged "way of life" cannot survive in a new South Africa. It is "home-rule" that is threatened. In fact, there is no obvious historical evidence of a privileged ruling class ever hav-

ing surrendered power without blood being spilled in armed revolution. South Africa is involved in more than a civil rights struggle; the very socio-economic identity of the country is at stake.[43]

Black South African theologians brought the full weight of their intellectual and experiential sources to their discussions of violence and nonviolence. They were largely responsible for keeping Martin Luther King Jr.'s name at the center of these discussions. In his treatment of "a Black Theology of self-defence or self-affirmation" in 1986, the Soweto priest Buti Tlhagale declared that King's "peace at all costs doctrine"—rooted in the assumption that nonviolence finally "reaches the opponent and so stirs his conscience that reconciliation becomes a reality"—was not borne out by the black South African experience. "For almost a century now," Tlhagale complained, "the inherently violent apartheid system has simply entrenched itself with all the viciousness imaginable. There are no signs of reconciliation on the horizon."[44]

The views of Allan Boesak and Desmond Tutu demand special consideration because of their boundless admiration for King. Both men had become more radical and perhaps less hopeful of a nonviolent solution to apartheid by the 1980s. Some discussion of how each theologian viewed King is in order. Boesak, the president of the World Alliance of Reformed Churches and a founder of the UDF, leaned more toward nonviolence than violence. However, he did not accept nonviolence to the same degree as King, a point that undermines any suggestion that the two men be called "nonviolent leaders" in the same sense.[45] While praising King and Albert Luthuli for their "theology of refusal," for refusing to surrender to the violence of the status quo, Boesak contended that the incredible "hypocrisy of white Christians on the issue of violence" made it particularly difficult for oppressed South Africans to subscribe to nonviolence in absolute terms. "You can hardly expect blacks to believe the gospel of nonviolence coming from those who, all through their history," argued Boesak, "have relied upon violence and military action to get what they wanted and to maintain unjust systems."[46] In view of the South African situation, Boesak's pacifism, which did not completely dismiss the possible need for violence, seemed far more "realistic" or "practical" than what King desired for South African freedom fighters two decades earlier.[47]

The views of the Anglican bishop Desmond Tutu were critically important in the South African discussion concerning nonviolence and violence, especially since he won the Nobel Peace Prize in 1984. Like Albert Luthuli, a fellow black South African who received the award in 1961, the Tutu of the eighties emphasized the need for nonviolent change in South Africa. His insistence on resistance to unjust laws as a moral imperative was, as Charles Villa-Vicencio has suggested, essentially the same as Martin Luther King Jr.'s, but Tutu did not share the depth of King's commitment to nonviolent resistance.[48] Therefore, Sheila Brigg's assertion that "Bishop Desmond Tutu, like Martin Luther King Jr. before him here in the United States, espouses nonviolence," must be made with some qualification. The differences in the nature of King's and Tutu's commitments to nonviolence must be assessed and understood before one can grasp the meaning of Brigg's contention that

> The nonviolence of Martin Luther King Jr. or Bishop Tutu has the liberation of the oppressed as its highest goal; it recognizes evil as evil and rejects it as such. It also clearly envisages the kind of society that it desires to emerge from the struggle for liberation which is—in Martin Luther King Jr.'s words—"the beloved community."[49]

Tutu wrote extensively in the eighties about how the subject of violence helped further polarize an already deeply divided South Africa. "White South Africa regards violence and terrorism as that which normally emanates from the oppressed black community either internally or externally," he complained. "They refuse to accept that the South African situation is inherently violent, and that the primary violence is the apartheid system."[50] It was the structural, institutionalized, unprovoked violence of apartheid that, according to Tutu, made possible and necessary outbursts of counterviolence among black South Africans. "Black South Africans have tried nonviolent protest," Tutu added, but "white South Africa remained relatively unmoved," and "the Sharpeville paradigm has been repeated again and again."[51] While insisting that "We regard all violence as evil (the violence of an unjust system such as apartheid and the violence of those who seek to overthrow it)," Tutu went on to indicate in 1987 why he found it impossible to accept nonviolence as an absolute principle:

> There are some remarkable people who believe that no one is ever justified in using violence, even against the most horrendous evil. Such absolute pacifists believe that the Gospel of the Cross effectively rules out anyone taking up the sword, however just the cause. I admire such persons deeply, but sadly I confess that I am made of less noble stuff. I am a lover of peace

and I try to work for justice because only thus do I believe we could ever hope to establish durable peace. It is self-defeating to justify a truce based on unstable foundations of oppression. Such a truce can only be inherently unstable, requiring that it be maintained by institutional violence. . . . Nonviolence as a means toward ending an unjust system, presupposes that the oppressors show a minimum level of morality. Even in such a situation the nonviolence path is a hazardous one requiring considerable courage and moral fortitude. It was possible for Gandhi to arouse moral indignation and thus support for his cause against the British Raj; perhaps only because there were those in England whose sensitivities were such that they were outraged by the treatment meted out by the army to peaceful demonstrators. I doubt, however, that such a Gandhian campaign would have saved the Jews from the Nazi holocaust.[52]

Tutu also argued in 1987 that sometimes violence is "justifiable to topple an unjust system," a view clearly different from Martin Luther King Jr.'s. Noting that "international action and international pressure are among the few nonviolent options left," a point made by King in reference to South Africa in the 1960s, Tutu explained:

Should the West fail to impose economic sanctions it would, in my view, be justifiable for blacks to try to overthrow an unjust system violently. But I must continue to work to bring an end to the present tyranny by nonviolent means. Should this option fail, the low-intensity civil war . . . will escalate into full-scale war. When that happens, heaven help us all. The Armageddon will have come.[53]

Given Tutu's openness to the possibility of violent revolution as a final option in South Africa, one wonders about Father Buti Tlhagale's claim that "Tutu's stance" on violence was "reminiscent of the position that was taken by Martin Luther King, Jnr., a position that cost him his life."[54] From all indications, both King and Gandhi were more thoroughgoing in their pacifism than the Tutu of the 1980s. Like Boesak, Tutu stood more in that tradition of pragmatic pacifism associated with Albert Luthuli and the ANC before the Sharpeville massacre. While refusing to embrace the thoroughgoing pacifism of King and Gandhi, Tutu shared their hope that the revolution in South Africa would ultimately be peaceful:

I continue to believe that we do have an outside chance that a negotiated settlement could be reached reasonably peacefully if the international community intervened decisively with effective pressure on the South African government to lift the State of Emergency, to remove the troops from the black townships, to release all detainees and political prisoners, and to un-ban black political organizations.[55]

Black South African women were not completely divorced from the discussions concerning methods. They simply conducted in a lower key the debate that raged among black and white men in the church and the academy. Winnie Mandela, the wife of the political prisoner Nelson Mandela, spoke and wrote at some length on violence and nonviolence. Evoking the memory of Albert Luthuli on one occasion, she insisted that "it was never the policy of the ANC to be violent." "Terrorism was in fact introduced by the white man in this land in 1652," she continued. "We used our spears and shields. We, the indigenous races of this country, lived harmoniously. The first acts of terrorism were when they shot our grand-fathers and grabbed their land."[56] Winnie Mandela's openness to the pos-sibility of the need for violent revolution in South Africa seemed to find support from the black clergywoman Motlalepula Chabaku. In an inter-view in the late eighties, she noted that David's family situation on the battlefield did not improve until he dealt with Goliath, "the main source of terror and violence," a point that had important implications for black-white relations in South Africa. While refusing to condemn "my brothers and sisters" who "go for an armed struggle," Chabaku explained that "I belong to those who still hope for peaceful change in the midst of escalat-ing violence." She further observed, in a statement that revealed her tie to African American women in matters of spirit, that black South African women had much to contribute to a peaceful revolution in South Africa:

> We women have the special role of working for peace and liberation be-cause we have a great power for peace. It was a woman like Harriet Tubman who was able to liberate men, women, and children. It was a woman like Rosa Parks who turned the tide of history. Women can be a source of hope and peace, if we rise and play the responsible role to which we are called. Jesus called us specially, specially.[57]

Black and white South African leaders and thinkers were quite con-cerned in the eighties about the need for the church to engage in the prac-tical application of nonviolent principles, thus calling to mind Martin Luther King Jr. two decades earlier. In words reminiscent of King, Boesak raised the critical questions that occupied the minds of Christians across church and denominational boundaries in his country: "How does the Christian church react to the violence inherent in apartheid society, and how can the church react to the violence of the police or the military in South Africa?"[58] In a statement that obviously contains words borrowed from King, Boesak urged black South African Christians to challenge both white Christians and the state on the necessity for nonviolent action and "conscientious disobedience" as a response to apartheid:

> The church must initiate and support meaningful pressure on the en-trenched system, as a nonviolent way of bringing about change. The church must initiate and support programs of civil disobedience on a massive scale and challenge white Christians especially on this issue. It no longer suffices to make statements condemning unjust laws and then tomorrow to obey those laws as if nothing were amiss. The time has come for the black church to tell the government and its supporters: we can not in all good conscience obey your unjust laws, because noncooperation with evil is as much a moral obligation as is cooperation with good.[59]

This challenge to the church, made in 1984, was repeated in many cir-cles. In September 1985, *The Kairos Document* critiqued biblical and the-ological models that encouraged Christians to follow policies of nonaction and nonresistance in relation to apartheid.[60] Frank Chikane, General Secretary of the South African Council of Churches (SACC), strongly criticized the church in 1988 for its failure to set the kind of example rep-resented by Martin Luther King Jr. and other theorists and practitioners of nonviolence:

> History damns the Church for not having put the nonviolent method to the test itself. It was left to Martin Luther King Jr., Mahatma Gandhi, and Don Helder Camara to engage in concrete nonviolent action, to force those in power to redress the grievances of the underdogs in society. The history of nonviolence in the ANC and UDF, following the path of these classic disciples of nonviolent action, must come as an indictment of us in the Church. It exposes our failure and omissions.[61]

One hears in this statement echoes of the same critique King made of the American churches. In similar terms, Desmond Tutu asserted in 1989 that the church's willingness to move beyond the mere advocacy of nonvi-olence to the practical employment of that principle could inspire millions of blacks and whites to seek alternatives to violence:

One of the things we need to do is take up seriously this whole question of nonviolence. We are amateurs at nonviolent action. All we've been doing really is preaching it, and it's not been a truly viable alternative to violence. We've spoken as if just to exhort people is enough; whereas if they were to see that we're serious about this, then people would begin to think that it is a credible program that we are suggesting.[62]

The kind of posture exemplified by African American churches under the leadership of King in the fifties and sixties remained important for Tutu, Chikane, and Boesak as they set the parameters of prophetic witness for South African Christians. The same can be said of white church leaders such as Charles Villa-Vicencio, John W. de Gruchy, and Beyers Naudé. Throughout the 1980s, these and other South African church leaders were saying with increasingly loud voices that planned boycotts, strikes, acts of civil disobedience, sanctions, and divestment were "the last nonviolent means left to break the evil of apartheid."[63]

Churches inside South Africa found it virtually impossible to ignore these challenges, especially since they claimed to be moral forces in the society. In 1981, Methodist leaders in South Africa publicly recited a solemn oath to nonviolently oppose the apartheid system and "to bring about a free and just southern Africa," and the Presbyterian church urged "civil disobedience and instructed its ministers to break certain apartheid laws."[64] Meeting during a state of emergency in South Africa in September 1985, a group of South African evangelicals decided that their theology, heavily influenced by European and American missionaries, had avoided the problems of racism and oppression while lending support, directly and indirectly, to the violence of the status quo.[65] Although the group, inspired largely by *The Kairos Document,* drafted a statement in a spirit of confession and repentance, and called for redemptive change or renewal, it did not deal sufficiently with questions of violence and nonviolence in light of the radical demands of the scriptures.[66] Also in 1985, the SACC declared that "disinvestment and similar economic pressure are called for as a peaceful and effective means of putting pressure on the South African government to bring about those fundamental changes this country needs," but this declaration did not translate into major, concrete action on the part of the council itself.[67] Many churches in South Africa, black and white, appeared content to simply verbalize what Martin Luther King Jr. called "pious irrelevancies" and "sanctimonious trivialities."[68]

In the late eighties, South African churches sought to advance their practical use of nonviolent means to a new stage. In 1986 and 1987, hundreds of clergy, disturbed by the image of the church in South Africa, broke apartheid laws and defied new government regulations against the oppressed, and many were arrested for "threatening the security of the state" through their demonstrations and calls for international sanctions against South Africa.[69] On February 19, 1988, Archbishop Stephen Naidoo, Desmond Tutu, Allan Boesak, Frank Chikane, "and scores of other church leaders led hundreds in a prayer service and march on the South African Parliament, to demand the restoration of the right of peaceful protest." Referring to the spiritual significance and the moral tone of this event, one writer recounted: "In the spirit of nonviolent civil disobedience, as exemplified by Gandhi and Martin Luther King Jr., they refused to disperse and retreat when confronted by a menacing line of riot police, but calmly knelt in prayer."[70] More than two hundred church leaders of the SACC convened in May 1988, and voted "to launch a new campaign of nonviolent action to remove the system of apartheid."[71] At the forefront of this mounting activism, this "Standing for Truth" campaign, were black South African clergymen, a development quite similar to what happened with King and other black church leaders in the United States in the fifties and sixties.

King's ethical reflections on community caused almost as much discussion and debate among South Africans as his nonviolent absolutism. King's vision of the beloved community—a vision of a completely integrated society based on love and justice—proved enormously significant for South African churchpersons, theologians, and other anti-apartheid activists as they drew their own portraits of a new South Africa. Throughout the eighties, Desmond Tutu, in his writings and speeches, warned South Africans that "We will die as fools, if we cannot learn to live together as brothers—to paraphrase Martin Luther King."[72] "We would like to have a South Africa," Tutu maintained, "where black and white will live amicably together as members of one family."[73] As was evident with King, the concepts of the *imago Dei* (all persons are created in God's image and are therefore reflections of the divine), of the social nature of human existence, and of the interrelated structure of reality became essential components of Tutu's vision of community.[74]

The same was true of Allan Boesak and Frank Chikane, both of whom shared King's concept of the church as the symbol of community. In

1984, Boesak contended that King's work for human understanding and community was consistent with the reconciling function of the true church of Jesus Christ. Boesak asked: "Was not Martin Luther King Jr., the true image of the church when he dared to dream of love, peace, justice, and human understanding, even as the authors of hatred and bigotry were plotting to kill the dreamer?" Boesak went on to state that authentic community would occur in South Africa only after "love between black and white" has been "translated into terms of political, social, and economic justice."[75] Chikane, who followed Tutu as General Secretary of the SACC, advanced essentially the same arguments. Chikane was as persistent as Boesak and Tutu in claiming that the building of genuine community in South Africa had to begin with the church, a position that explains his devotion to breaking "the apartheid structures which divide the church into white, colored, Indian and African churches."[76]

This communitarian ethic found expression in the actions of some South African churches. In 1981, the Methodist church, the second largest church in South Africa at that time, formally condemned the enforced social, economic, and political segregation of the races as "sinful, the work of the devil."[77] A short time later, the South African Catholic Bishops' Conference took a similar position, denouncing apartheid as antithetical to community as established by divine principles. White South African religious leaders and thinkers, such as Andrew Parang, Beyers Naudé, and John de Gruchy, stressed the communitarian ideal in their teachings and work with black clergymen in the SACC. Anti-apartheid documents resulting from such efforts included pastoral letters, synodical resolutions, declarations by various churches and denominations, and confessional statements such as *The Belhar Confession of Faith* issued by the Dutch Reformed Mission Church, all of which defined the struggle for community and peace in South Africa as a moral imperative.[78] Sentiments of this nature coincided with positions Martin Luther King Jr. took in interviews and speeches on South Africa a generation earlier.

Interracial and all-black political organizations never reached full agreement on how community could be actualized in South Africa in the 1980s. Embracing a communitarian ideal similar to King's, the UDF "welcomed the participation of whites," and "a few whites" became "prominent in its leadership."[79] Much of this was inspired through the leadership of Allan Boesak. Frank Chikane apparently saw the UDF as something of a microcosm of the new South Africa, mainly because it drew together "a variety of groups—churches and church groups, sports associations, community, labor, student's, women's, youth and political organizations."[80]

The ANC shared this approach to community, despite its rejection of King's belief that nonviolence is the only means for actualizing the communitarian ideal. This organization, which accepted its first non-African members in 1969, elected two Indians, two Coloreds, and one white to its National Executive Committee in 1985.[81] Its vision of "a non-racial socialist" South Africa squared with the beloved community concept as defined by King.[82] Winnie Mandela expressed the ANC's official position when she observed: "Our future South Africa will be multiracial. It will accommodate all of us. The wealth is enough for everybody."[83] In 1985, the ANC President Oliver R. Tambo emphatically denied reports that the ANC envisioned an all-black South Africa as its aim:

> All of us in the ANC have always considered that whites, like ourselves, belong to our country. We took the earliest opportunity to dispel the notion that we are fighting to drive the whites out. We have asked whites to join us in the struggle to get rid of the tensions that come with the apartheid system. We have hoped that together we could build a non-racial South Africa—and by non-racial we really do mean non-racial. Our charter says that South Africa belongs to all who live in it, and we say that people who have chosen South Africa as their home are welcome here. There is plenty of room for them. We don't really see our white compatriots as white in the first instance. We see them as fellow South Africans. We were all born in that country. We live on that continent. It is our country. Let's move away from these distinctions between Europeans and non-Europeans, whites and non-whites.[84]

The AZASO's stand on interracial community was essentially the same as that of the ANC, suggesting a shift from its 1979 position as a black consciousness group. Other black consciousness and Africanist organizations in South Africa appeared more ambivalent in their conceptions of community. The BCM stressed black solidarity while discouraging alliances between blacks and whites, though it taught that "its own existence would" become "irrelevant and unnecessary in a non-racial, non-exploitative society." As one source put it, "In black consciousness thinking, the history of South Africa can be interpreted according to a dialectical process. From the thesis of white racism and the antithesis of black solidarity a synthesis will emerge: true humanity without regard to race or colour."[85] While pursuing as an ultimate goal a nonracial, "democratic socialist state of Azania," the BCM, in contrast to Martin Luther King Jr., did not feel that alliances between the races were primary in achieving this end. For the BCM, black South Africans, as an initial step, had "to develop a sense of solidarity through the concept of group power, and in this way build a broad base from which to counter the divide-and-rule strategies of whites."[86]

This conception of community applied in the case of other black consciousness groups as well. The AZAPO, the principal black consciousness organization in South Africa, criticized the participation of whites in the UDF and ANC, "seeing them as representatives of the ruling class."[87] This group also tended to separate its primary goal of black solidarity from its ultimate goal of a society that transcended classism and racial capitalism:

> In political terms, AZAPO envisages a future state in which all persons shall have the right to property and to participate freely in the political machinery of the country. As a strategy AZAPO nevertheless advocates exclusion of whites from its organization and activities, since whites are "part and parcel of the oppressive system." There can be "no meaningful integration between unequals."[88]

Viewing racial capitalism as the root problem, the NF also emphasized noncollaboration with whites while promoting "the establishment of a democratic, antiracist worker republic in Azania, where the interests of the workers shall be paramount through worker control of the means of production, distribution and exchange."[89] Black South African trade unions, such as the COSATU and the AZACTU, followed a similar philosophy in the 1980s. In terms of the communitarian ethic, black consciousness groups in general in South Africa found more affinity with Malcolm X and black power advocates than with Martin Luther King Jr., mainly because of their view that integration as commonly defined could only result in continued white dominance.[90]

The PAC's idea of community clearly set it apart from King's views. In the eighties, this group continued to oppose the involvement of whites in the liberation struggle. Its philosophy centered on the kind of black unity that would eventually lead to the overthrow of white domination and the building of an African nation.[91] The PAC took a stronger position than any other Africanist organization in South Africa against the type of integration that King and Albert Luthuli had previously envisioned for their countries.

The Inkatha movement's philosophy paralleled King's in the value it attached to persons irrespective of race, sex, or ancestry. Its vision "of a non-ethnic, democratic, unitary state forged within a multiracial framework" embodied some of the elements of King's communitarian ideal. But Inkatha's tendency to organize along ethnic or tribal lines, and to define itself exclusively in terms of a drive for national cultural liberation, seemed to demonstrate that its final goal was not the beloved community as articulated by King and Desmond Tutu.[92]

South Africa remained a bitterly divided country in the eighties. The different philosophies and methods embraced by various persons and organizations loomed as a contributing factor. The unpleasant and even violent confrontations between the UDF and the AZAPO followers, between the ASAPO and the PAC, and between the ANC and Inkatha, graphically highlighted the problem from this angle. Tribalism and the more devastating policy of racial separation continued unabated. Tensions between blacks and whites remained high. Although the Asians and Coloreds massively boycotted the August 1984 elections for a new tricameral parliament, thereby demonstrating unity with Africans in some measure, the relations between these groups were also fraught with tensions and suspicion.[93] Martin Luther King Jr.'s earlier description of a South Africa tragically plunging into the quagmire of fragmentation and violence remained as true as ever.

King as a Role Model for Black South African Leaders

Martin Luther King Jr. remained an important role model for black South African leaders in the 1980s, a function not surprising in view of his historic contributions as an African American who struggled against white oppression. For some, he represented the best in terms of black aspirations and achievement. Others viewed King as a symbol of hope and community for people of African descent everywhere. Still others copied his style and used his words as they described their pain under apartheid and their vision of a South Africa free of racial oppression, economic exploitation, and wars of aggression.[94]

Desmond Tutu frequently evoked King's name in the midst of struggle. During a speech at the Partners in Ecumenism Conference of the National Council of Churches in Washington, D.C., in September 1984, Tutu paid tribute to King and black Americans in general for the impact of the civil rights movement on the South African liberation crusade:

What you have done during the years has had very crucial repercussions for those of us in South Africa. . . . A part of the whole of your mission has been helping us to recover the sense that we, too, have a share in this wonderful heritage which St. Paul calls "the glorious liberty of the children of God."[95]

Tutu was known to use King's name and words when analyzing concepts such as love, nonviolence, community, and the response of the Christian to laws that contradict God's sovereign will and plan for humanity.[96] This led many of his admirers worldwide to compare him with King. Recognizing this tendency, one of Tutu's biographers wrote in 1988:

To his own embarrassment and to the irritation of many of his friends (who see it as irrelevant), Tutu finds himself being likened to the civil rights leader Martin Luther King. Though King was a Baptist, Tutu an Anglican, though King's reserve is in contrast to Tutu's sparkle and wit, with both men being black ministers, both speaking out of a sense of moral outrage, both passionately affirming the humanity of every individual person, both advocates of nonviolence—the comparison is inevitable. The minister and politician Jesse Jackson, who feels Desmond Tutu's stature is such that he should be seen in the prophetic tradition with Jesus Christ and Mahatma Gandhi, came back from a visit to South Africa in 1979 claiming to have met 'the Martin Luther King of South Africa . . . his manner, his steadfastness, his blend of the infrastructure of the Church on the one hand and his calling beyond the Church on the other' recalling the civil rights leader. The journalist Allister Sparks pointed out that both men were Christians with a mission, rather than politicians with a strategy, both have a streak of militancy within their moderation, both have a way with words, though Tutu 'in a style with more of a cutting edge than King's rolling rhetoric.' Dr. William Howard feels that Tutu has Martin Luther King's ability to hew a stone of hope from a mountain of despair.[97]

The tendency to draw comparisons between Tutu and King was probably more typical of Americans than of peoples elsewhere in the world. Coretta Scott King's awarding of the Martin Luther King Jr. Nonviolent Peace Prize to Tutu at an ecumenical service in Atlanta on January 20, 1986, was certainly one indication of this tendency.[98]

Allan Boesak's frequent references to King led many in the eighties to view him as something of a disciple of the civil rights leader. In a 1985 review of Boesak's book, *Black and Reformed* (1984), the Harvard University scholar Preston N. Williams referred to the South African leader's "many borrowings acknowledged and unacknowledged from Martin Luther King Jr."[99] In another review of this same book, Paul R. Spickard noted, perhaps with some misreading of the sources, that "like one of his models, Martin Luther King, and to the consternation of those who would dismiss black militants as communists, Boesak declares that Marx has no place in his work toward South African liberation."[100]

Boesak was more apt than Tutu to quote extensively from King in his writings, speeches, and interviews in the eighties. In *Black and Reformed,* he made frequent mention of King in his discussion of God, love, peace, justice, theology and the church, and human understanding and community, though direct references to the civil rights leader are far more extensive in Boesak's *Farewell to Innocence* (1977). In a 1988 interview, Boesak, as on numerous other occasions, shared perhaps his favorite quotation from King, one that underscored the essence and importance of the committed life: "There are some things so dear and so precious and so eternally true that they are worth dying for. And if you are not willing to die for those things, then you are really not fit to live."[101] On April 3, 1988, Boesak "preached to the memory of Martin Luther King Jr.," an event which, along with other evidence, revealed the extent to which he regarded the civil rights leader as a role model:

> He spoke passionately about what the martyred American prophet meant to him and South Africa. King is everywhere around Allan Boesak—his home and office are full of pictures, books, tapes, and mementos. Boesak is self-consciously a disciple of King, and makes regular reference to him and the freedom movement he led. Now more than ever, Allan Boesak and other South African church leaders are reflecting on King and the relevance of his radical nonviolence for the next phase of South Africa's history.[102]

Jim Wallis recounted a profound experience he had with Boesak and other black South African clergymen at a special service of the SACC, where memories of King and the civil rights struggle connected with the deep emotions and determination of people undaunted and undiminished by apartheid:

> During the service we sang a beautiful but sad song in Zulu, the words of which meant, "What have we done to deserve all this suffering? Our only sin is the color of our skin." We joined hands at the close of the service and sang "We Shall Overcome." One could feel the strength and suffering of a freedom struggle that transcends time and place and imagine how pleased

Martin Luther King Jr. would have been. The worshipers danced and sang their way out of the chapel, feet stomping, fingers pointed upward, and offering one last Zulu song whose words meant, "Don't worry. We have the victory."[103]

What a splendid affirmation of the hopes and dreams of King and Albert Luthuli. Here was an occasion when the traditional worship experience served to solidify oppressed South Africans with the spirit of King and the civil rights movement in the United States, despite the spatial divisions imposed by time and geography. "We Shall Overcome," the theme song of the civil rights struggle, united in melody and meaning with Zulu song, and the dancing, foot-stomping, and the raising of hands created rhythms that attested to the underlying unity of certain essentials of African American and black South African cultures. To be sure, the experience, in which suffering and sadness found ironic oneness with hope and affirmation, testified to the inseparable link between black art, spirituality, and the quest for freedom.[104]

It was primarily through Boesak that King's ideas impacted the broad contours of black South African theology in the 1980s. Describing King as "a co-worker with God," Boesak regarded the civil rights leader as a principal progenitor of the black theology that reached its fullest maturity in both America and South Africa in the eighties.[105] Louise Kretzschmar, in her slim volume on black South African theology, concurred, noting in 1986 that "it was not only from post-colonial Africa that South Africans drew inspiration," but "the civil rights movement in the USA and the leadership of people such as Martin Luther King also served as models for study and adaptation."[106] Unfortunately, some of the best available treatments of black South African theology in this period failed to make this connection.[107]

This tendency to identify with King, and to see him as an example to be followed, was not simply confined to theologians like Boesak and Desmond Tutu. The established writer Mark Mathabane, who wrote the internationally popular book, *Kaffir Boy: The True Story of a Black Youth's Coming of Age in Apartheid South Africa,* spoke in 1986 about the sense of identification he and so many of his people felt with King, "a God-fearing man who died fighting to set his people free."[108] Franklin Sonn, "a coloured leader of distinction" who headed a "modern training school for young coloureds" near Cape Town, acknowledged that "his model is Martin Luther King Jr."[109]

When asked if it was "accurate to see his role as being similar to that of Martin Luther King Jr., during the late sixties when King's leadership was challenged by 'black power' advocates," the controversial Zulu leader Gatsha Buthelezi said in 1986 that "it is very accurate indeed." Richard J. Neuhaus reports that it was typical of Buthelezi to evoke "the memory of Martin Luther King Jr., for whom he has unbounded admiration, when he speaks about martyrdom. He does not seek it, he does not want it, but he does not fear it."[110]

King's mystical authority as a kind of black messiah was almost as evident in parts of South Africa as in the United States. This was only natural for black people who had had limited opportunities to acclaim truly great leaders who influenced liberation struggles worldwide.[111] This does not mean that black South Africans pressed King's symbolic significance to the exclusion of heroes and martyrs in their own country. More specifically, King was accepted into their pantheon of heroes and martyrs. This was King's meaning throughout southern Africa in the eighties, a period during which blacks in that part of the world were clamoring for freedom with a new sense of urgency. Samora Machel, the marxist president of Mozambique, spoke for blacks throughout southern Africa on this matter. While visiting King's resting place in Atlanta, Georgia, in 1985, Machel declared: "In the struggle against apartheid we are continuing the spirit and example of Martin Luther King. And we shall win." The same message echoed through the words of Shun P. Govender, the South African anti-apartheid activist. "We thank you for telling us, in the life and death of Martin Luther King Jr.," he asserted, "that peace and justice are possible. History is not fate. We shall not be humiliated and suffer forever. . . . We have King as our tomorrow."[112]

Remembering King's Work Against Apartheid in 1982

Martin Luther King Jr.'s contributions to South African freedom received special recognition from world leaders in 1982. At the invitation of Coretta Scott King, a delegation of the UN Special Committee Against Apartheid (UNSCAA) participated in the observance of the slain civil rights leader's fifty-third birthday at the Martin Luther King Jr. Center for Nonviolent Social Change in Atlanta, Georgia. Meeting in January 1982, the delegation consisted of Alhaji Yusuff Maitama-Sule of Nigeria, the chairman of the Special Committee; Vladimir A. Kravets of the Ukraine, the vice chairman; Ibrahim Noor, the secretary; and the ambassadors of

India, Somalia, and Trinidad and Tobago. Seminars and other events commemorating Martin Luther King Jr.'s birthday were held, and possible actions "against *apartheid* during the International Year of Mobilization for Sanctions against South Africa" were discussed with Atlanta's mayor Andrew Young and other U.S. civil rights activists.[113] The UN delegation also laid a wreath on behalf of the Special Committee at King's grave, attended an ecumenical service at the Ebenezer Baptist Church, and took part in the official dedication of the King Center's Freedom Hall Complex.[114]

This King birthday observance marked the first of several major anti-apartheid events staged in 1982 by the UNSCAA. Considerable attention centered on "ways and means of promoting public action against apartheid." The spirit of the observance carried throughout the year, as leaders of the Special Committee held consultations with representatives of governmental and nongovernmental organizations around the apartheid problem. The need for more youth and student activities against apartheid remained high on the agenda of the UNSCAA, triggering reminders of concerns raised by King two decades earlier.[115]

The appearance of members of the UNSCAA in Atlanta also connected well with the King Center's broadening sense of mission regarding South African liberation. In a letter to Enuga S. Reddy, the Director of the UNSCAA, Coretta Scott King insisted that "the presence of this distinguished delegation gave witness to the universality of Martin's work and Dream of a world-wide Beloved Community with peace and social justice for all people."[116] The widow of King went on to rededicate herself to the spreading of "Martin's message of love and nonviolence throughout the world," noting the pressing need to confront "nations and peoples in such a way that Martin's nonviolence will be universally embraced as our only viable alternative to world chaos."[117]

On November 5, 1982, the UN General Assembly evoked King's memory during a special meeting "devoted to the International Year for Sanctions against South Africa." The event commemorated the twentieth anniversary of the first General Assembly resolution urging sanctions against South Africa (*Resolution 1761* of November 6, 1962), a resolution fully backed by King and his colleagues in the American Committee on Africa (ACOA) and the American Negro Leadership Conference on Africa (ANLCA). In its official records, the Assembly stated: "This solemn meeting is a reaffirmation of our unshakable opposition to *apartheid*. On behalf of the people of South Africa, we say here that comprehensive and mandatory sanctions against the Pretoria regime are imperative."[118]

After reaffirming its "solidarity with the national liberation movement of South Africa," the UN General Assembly awarded gold medals to world leaders who had impacted the anti-apartheid struggle since the middle of the century. They included the late Houari Boumedienne, the former president of Algeria; Romesh Chandra, president of the World Peace Council (WPC); Madame Jeanne Martin-Cisse of Guinea, president of the International Committee of Solidarity with the Struggle of the Women of South Africa and Namibia; Archbishop Trevor Huddleston, president of the British Anti-Apartheid Movement; Chief Abraham Ordia, president of the Supreme Council for Sports in Africa; Jan Nico Scholten, member of the Netherlands parliament and later chairman of the Association of West European Parliamentarians for Action Against Apartheid; and the late Martin Luther King Jr.[119]

The Assembly noted the irony of honoring King, one who "shall always belong to that same United States whose government is responsible for collaboration with the *apartheid* regime."[120] Bernice King, the youngest daughter of the civil rights leader, accepted the award on behalf of her father. "Martin Luther King Jr. was profoundly concerned about the tragic suffering inflicted on his black brothers and sisters in southern Africa," she asserted with the dynamism that would characterize her own style as a minister. Remembering that her father "was one of the very first American leaders to call for sanctions against apartheid," Bernice King concluded her acceptance speech with words that drew a stirring round of applause from her listeners:

> My father's words and the challenge he laid before us are as relevant today as they were in 1965. The day is fast approaching when people of goodwill all over the world will rise up in nonviolent solidarity with freedom fighters in Africa. With this unshakable commitment, we will forge a glorious new era of justice, peace and equality for freedom-loving people everywhere.[121]

The spirit of the 1982 tributes to King clearly matched those paid to him by world leaders in 1979. Indeed, such tributes offered proof of King's continuing significance for the anti-apartheid struggle, even as growing numbers of oppressed South Africans questioned the relevance of his philosophy and methods for their cause.

King, Black America, and the Mounting Crusade Against Apartheid

Black leaders in the United States continued to exemplify Martin Luther King Jr.'s spirit and example in the worldwide campaign against South African apartheid in the 1980s. Among such leaders were U.S. representatives William H. Gray III of Pennsylvania and Walter Fauntroy of Washington, D.C.; the Congressional Black Caucus chairman Mickey Leland of Texas; President John E. Jacob of the National Urban League; Benjamin Hooks of the NAACP; Jesse Jackson of the National Rainbow Coalition (NRC) and People United to Save Humanity (PUSH); Joseph E. Lowery of the SCLC; Leon Sullivan of the Opportunities Industrialization Centers of America (OIC); Franklin Thomas of the Ford Foundation; and Mary Berry of the U.S. Civil Rights Commission.[122] While largely unmindful of the nature and breadth of King's activities on behalf of South African liberation in the 1950s and 1960s, these leaders must have felt nonetheless that in struggling for a free South Africa they were somehow keeping alive the late civil rights leader's commitment to racial justice. This was quite evident in the manner in which they combined their anti-apartheid activities with persistent efforts to solidify civil rights gains and black political power in America.

Several of these leaders had been a part of King's SCLC team in the sixties, and their anti-apartheid involvements in the eighties tended to reflect in a special way King's inspiration and influence. Walter Fauntroy, a liaison between federal agencies and the SCLC when King died, participated in street demonstrations against apartheid, invited black South African anti-apartheid activists to speak at his church in Washington, D.C., and used his influence as a member of Congress to push for sanctions against South Africa. As pastor of the New Bethel Baptist Church, Fauntroy made his pulpit a vehicle for the creation of opposition among black churchpersons to apartheid.[123] The same can be said of Joseph Lowery, who pastored a United Methodist congregation in Atlanta, Georgia, and who succeeded Ralph D. Abernathy as president of the SCLC in 1977. In a speech delivered on December 10, 1983, "Human Rights Day," Lowery alluded to the failure of the American government, churches, corporations, and citizens in general to respond appropriately to the evils of apartheid:

> I am painfully aware of the failure of my own nation to act with courage and moral sensitivity in efforts to eliminate apartheid and express moral

outrage through sanctions and other diplomatic means. It is indeed ironic, as it is sad, that a nation born out of the hunger for liberty and self-determination would defend or cooperate in any manner with such a tyrannical regime as the government of South Africa. We must urge support and co-operation of the artists and athletes ban. Churches must refuse to do business with South Africa. And we must organize nationally to address the issue of doing business with corporations that do business with South Africa, individually as well as institutionally.[124]

Also on this occasion, the SCLC circulated pamphlets containing Lowery's remarks along with Martin Luther King Jr.'s and Chief Albert Luthuli's joint appeal for sanctions against South Africa, issued December 10, 1962, and with King's entire speech on South Africa, given at New York's Hunter College on December 10, 1965.[125] At this point, the SCLC clearly saw itself acting in the tradition of King.

In 1988, Lowery attacked conservative Republicans in Ronald Reagan's administration for ignoring the moral concerns emanating from apartheid. The SCLC leader joined an interdenominational group of clergy in calling upon President Ronald Reagan to "show the same concern for human rights in South Africa that he showed for human rights in the Soviet Union during the recent Moscow summit," noting that "we don't want to see Mr. Reagan segregate his concern for human rights." Lowery argued that the challenge to Reagan was quite appropriate, since the American leader had "assumed 'global leadership' in the fight for peace."[126] Lowery had already repeatedly confronted churches, seminaries, colleges, and universities in the United States with a similar challenge.[127] His challenge to Reagan grew partly out of a general dissatisfaction with the president's domestic agenda, which involved a retreat from civil rights and especially the erosion of affirmative action guidelines.

The Jesse Jackson of the 1980s agreed wholeheartedly with Lowery's contention that African Americans, and particularly black leadership, should assume a special role in the movement against South African apartheid, a view that reached perhaps its fullest expression with Martin Luther King Jr. two decades earlier. Jackson carried his prophetic witness against apartheid to various corners of the world. In September 1979, after a seventeen-day visit to South Africa, Jackson testified before the U.S. House of Representatives' Subcommittee on Africa, Committee on International Relations, expressing views that became a vital part of his campaign rhetoric as a presidential candidate in the eighties. In referring to

America's relationship to South Africa, Jackson told the committee: "We have reached the countdown stage in the long struggle between the forces of freedom and institutionalized racism. It would be unwise, to say the least, for our country to be on the side of supporting moral bankruptcy and institutionalized racism."[128] In terms remarkably suggestive of King, Jackson recommended United States leadership in imposing "world economic sanctions" against South Africa, declaring that "the human community cannot co-exist with apartheid. It is a moral illegitimacy that we must fight."[129]

Early in 1985, Jackson toured Europe and joined demonstrations against South African apartheid. In Bonn, West Germany, he locked arms with 100 protesters representing the Christian Initiative to Free South Africa and Namibia Movement outside the South African embassy there. In words similar to those spoken by King in the 1960s, Jackson reminded the protesters that apartheid was essentially a continuation of the Nazism which murdered six million Jews during World War II:

> Forty years ago, we declared the end to a reign of terror that tore at the soul and seam of the human family with such devastation that we still tremble. Forty years ago this continent lay in waste and blood and ashes. Forty years later the Phoenix has emerged from rubble with a new lease on life. The stench of blood has given way to the fragrance of life. . . . Though the Nazi troops surrendered officially forty years ago, Nazism has not yet surrendered. It has simply shifted. The same ethical grounds (that were used) for rejecting the Third Reich in Germany must be employed to stop the Fourth Reich in South Africa. So many of the SS troops went from Germany to South Africa. Thus, in some measure, the germ of genocide was not buried in Bitburg, it was transferred to Johannesburg. Shifting the site of the cancer is inadequate. We must root the death germ out of our body politics. If it simply shifts or remains dormant in the right climate or temperature, it will rise again.[130]

At Plotzensee, Jackson laid a wreath at the point where 2,500 Jewish men, women, and children had been either hanged or beheaded, and he explained that the very salvation of the human race demanded that apartheid be destroyed. "With all of our passion and with all of our pain we cannot resurrect the dead," he proclaimed. "But if we learn from their deaths, and behave differently, we can rob death of its sting and add immeasurably to the worth of their lives."[131]

Because of the frightening similarities between the Nazi regime of Hitler and the apartheid regime in South Africa, Jackson deemed it unconscionable that Israel provided military support to the P. W. Botha government. Thus, he insisted that Jews in Israel and in the diaspora should resist the "unbridled fascism" and "fanatical racism and classism" that "precipitated such a human scourge" as the holocaust:

> And that is why people who were victims of that and those who were survivors of that situation should staunchly resist the Fourth Reich, which is South Africa. I mean every moral and ethical imperative that made us say *no* to Hitler and the Third Reich should make us say *no* to Botha and the Fourth Reich. One difference in the Third Reich is that so much of Hitler's dirt was in the dark. Many people found out very late just what was happening. In the case of Botha, he is bold, public, has nuclear power, an open relationship with America, an open relationship with Israel, is receiving arms from Israel, and even some of the Jews in South Africa who were victims of Nazi camps are operating within the context of that system. It is that entanglement that makes a very complicated and yet a morally challenging situation.[132]

Jackson's assault on apartheid continued in the late eighties. He traveled to various parts of southern Africa, an experience that deepened his understanding of and opposition to apartheid. The most memorable of his trips occurred in 1986, when he spent seventeen days in southern Africa's front-line states, attempting "to seize the moral offensive against apartheid" and to rebuild the spiritual bridges between blacks there and blacks in the United States. In conversations with the leaders of Angola, Botswana, Mozambique, Tanzania, Zambia, and Zimbabwe, Jackson emphasized the need for black unity in ending South Africa's racist system and her aggression toward surrounding African states.[133] He promised these leaders that he would urge the United States to "impose tougher economic sanctions against South Africa," and to implement "a Marshall Plan" for the "respect, aid, trade, development, and defense of the southern region of Africa."[134] These same concerns had been raised by Martin Luther King Jr. some twenty years earlier.[135]

Coretta Scott King's anti-apartheid activities in the 1980s, like those of Jackson and her late husband, covered a broad spectrum of involvements. She saw herself as building on King's persistent efforts to bring the African American and black South African struggles into full cooperation with one another. In December 1981, she explained her own activities "as further testament to the growing international recognition of my husband's work and of our efforts here" at the Martin Luther King Jr. Center "to become the forum for which new advances can be made in (the) long campaign to eliminate the indignities and inhumanities of apartheid."[136] Between 1979 and 1990, Coretta King and her staff at the King Center in Atlanta held numerous symposia, seminars, and workshops on South Africa, inviting in such notable figures as Joseph Lowery of the SCLC, Randall Robinson of TransAfrica, Congressmen Charles Diggs and William Gray, A. W. Clausen of the World Bank, Allan Boesak and Bishop Desmond Tutu of South Africa, UN Secretary-General Kurt Waldheim, and President Kenneth D. Kaunda of Zambia. All of these men strongly evoked the memory of Martin Luther King Jr. as they addressed the intensity and urgency of the South African situation during their visits.

This was especially true of Boesak and Tutu, both of whom described themselves as admirers of King. On January 20, 1986, at the King Center's international conference on apartheid, and during its activities in connection with the first national celebration of King's birthday, Coretta King presented the King Nonviolent Peace Award to Tutu, a gesture quite appropriate for the occasion. After receiving the award, Tutu vowed that the forces of justice would ultimately win in South Africa as they did under King in the United States. The South African leader was honored for his dedication to overthrowing apartheid by peaceful means.[137]

In the mid-eighties, Coretta King supported the anti-apartheid activities of Randall Robinson, and she also worked to some degree with the Free South Africa Movement in the United States. She and other members of the King family staged protests outside the South African embassy in Washington, D.C., and willingly went to jail for their activities.[138] In the fall of 1985, Mrs. King joined Mrs. Desmond Tutu and Tandi Luthuli Gcabashe at Morehouse College in Atlanta, Dr. King's alma mater, in urging blacks and whites throughout the country to register their strongest protests against apartheid through demonstrations and other acts of defiance.[139]

As was the case in the 1970s, Coretta King visited South Africa in the eighties to personally assess the gravity of the situation there, a privilege her husband wanted but never had. Her September 1986 visit to the racially divided country received wide attention in the media. "I went to South Africa as a peacemaker," she reported, "trying to bring people together for greater dialogue in a nonviolent manner." Her initial decision to meet with P. W. Botha and other high-ranking officials of the South

African government was canceled because of the strong disapproval of Allan Boesak, Winnie Mandela, and other black South African leaders. However, Coretta King's peacemaking mission, which resulted in meetings with Boesak, Winnie Mandela, and others, was clearly in the tradition of Martin Luther King Jr. and his vision of a working relationship between black Americans and black South Africans to eliminate racism.[140] Indeed, the very nature of Mrs. King's relationship to Bishop and Mrs. Desmond Tutu, Allan Boesak, and Winnie Mandela, in dealing with the apartheid problem, was in some ways reminiscent of Dr. King's relationship to Albert Luthuli.

Coretta King's anti-apartheid statements were among the strongest offered by an African American leader in the eighties. In August 1985, she referred to institutionalized violence as the worst aspect of the apartheid system, a point with which her husband would have wholeheartedly agreed:

> There is the more massive institutional violence of apartheid. There's the forced separation of thousands of families. There's the violence of poverty and exploitation forced on the black majority. . . . And there is the violence to the human spirit and human dignity that comes with legalized racism and the lack of political representation.[141]

Mrs. King went on to attack the South African government for its consistent attempts to confuse the issue and to deceive the world about its true intentions:

> It also intensifies its external aggression by claiming that it is trying to stop expansionism. The South African government is trying to convince the world of its role as a Western ally, a bulwark against Communism. In this way, it hopes to portray the issue in Southern Africa as Soviet expansionism—instead of the apartheid terrorism it really is.[142]

The courageous black leadership in South Africa, Coretta King said in 1985, was the country's best hope for becoming a truly civilized and respectable society. She was particularly impressed with leaders like Allan Boesak, Desmond Tutu, and Nelson Mandela. She saw in Boesak images of her husband. The same can be said of her view of Tutu, whom she felt embodied the dreams of all freedom-loving South Africans "in his relentless fight against the barbarous system of apartheid."[143] Mrs. King praised Tutu as one who "works at the center of the violent political climate," but who "calls for radical change through peaceful and nonviolent means, believing that all men and women regardless of race are brothers and sisters."[144] She called Nelson Mandela "a living legend and the embodiment of an alternative political order," and joined other black leaders in clamoring for his release from prison, a concern expressed by her husband twenty years earlier. "In his proven courage, uncorrupt ability, and his willingness to suffer for the liberation of his people," Mrs. King added, "Mandela has become a powerful symbol of freedom throughout Africa and around the world."[145]

Coretta King was generous in her praise for black South African female leaders as well. She was quite familiar with the courageous grass-roots leadership of women like Winnie Mandela and Albertina Sisulu, who stood as "mothers in the community" of the oppressed. One of the most touching moments of Mrs. King's 1986 visit to South Africa occurred when she and Winnie Mandela embraced, with tears flowing down their cheeks. Coretta King's struggles during her own husband's jail-going, and her role in the civil rights movement in the United States in the 1950s and 1960s, made it quite easy for her to identify with the wife of Nelson Mandela. She saw in Mrs. Mandela and Albertina Sisulu examples of the kinds of roles women should play worldwide in addressing the problem of racism. Thus, Coretta King insisted that "the women of every nation, particularly the United States and Great Britain, should begin to organize selective patronage campaigns in support of freedom and justice in Namibia and South Africa." "Let us make no mistake about it," she continued, "apartheid, like starvation in Africa, is very much a women's issue. . . . Freedom, self-determination and world peace are nothing if not women's issues, and they cannot be achieved without the active involvement of women."[146] Here Mrs. King proved much more progressive-minded than her husband, who was never completely free of the concept of female subordination, and who almost always thought in terms of male leadership in the black South African struggle.[147]

The failure of Americans to take seriously their moral responsibility with respect to apartheid bothered Coretta King. "Although most of us are aware of the South African government's systematic abuse of the black majority under the policy of apartheid," she observed in 1983, "too many Americans have not honestly faced the issue of our responsibility for this continuing tragedy. There's no escaping the fact that American dollars subsidize apartheid and the economic exploitation of black workers."[148] Two years later, Mrs. King asserted that "we mourn for the United States because our government and many American businesses are supporting apartheid."[149] Such practices were for her inconsistent with the dream of Martin Luther King Jr.:

> Like Martin, we must reach out to help our brothers and sisters in South Africa. Martin Luther King in the midst of his struggle for black civil rights in this country, was one of the very first American leaders to call for sanctions against apartheid. Why? Because he understood the necessity and importance of linking our struggle for human rights, dignity and freedom with the on-going struggle in South Africa. He knew the danger of waging an isolated struggle and understood the strength of joining forces against a powerful foe.[150]

Coretta King challenged all Americans to follow the example set by the King Center on the apartheid problem. "We understand that the leadership of the anti-apartheid movement must come from within South Africa," she explained, but "we are determined to do our part."[151] She further noted: "We pledge our wholehearted recommitment to the mammoth undertaking of educating the American people about the crisis in South Africa and avenues for citizen action." She went on to state in 1986:

> The Martin Luther King Jr. Center for Nonviolent Social Change is dedicated to the struggle for freedom and justice in South Africa. Since the King Center was founded in 1968 we have sponsored a number of conferences and workshops on challenging apartheid, and on two occasions the Center has served as the official host for Atlanta meetings of the United Nations Special Committee on Apartheid. As the President of the King Center, I have recently traveled to Africa and met with a number of African leaders to discuss common approaches to this struggle. All said that the most effective thing Americans could do to end apartheid is to withdraw our economic support.[152]

Convinced that "the successful use of nonviolent tactics in South Africa remains our last chance to prevent a bloodbath of unprecedented proportions," Coretta King admonished black South Africans to hold firmly to the methods of her husband. She held that such methods could work "but good faith on the part of many people would have to be exhibited." "Many of the South Africans are Christians and they understand the Christian faith," she observed, "but the people must begin to understand the whole process of nonviolent resolution of conflict." Mrs. King further contended in 1986 that the ultimate success of the nonviolent approach inside South Africa depended on the extent of nonviolent pressure applied from outside South Africa, a view her husband consistently advanced in the 1960s.[153] Therefore, she urged the U.S. Congress to pass strong sanctions against South Africa, and called upon "all American corporations" to "withdraw their support of the vicious apartheid regime."[154] In the meantime, declared Mrs. King,

> [W]e are going to keep organizing against apartheid. We're going to keep marching and demonstrating. We're going to keep lobbying and registering voters and educating our fellow citizens. We're going to keep pushing for divestment. We're going to keep knocking on the doors of the embassies and consulates of the apartheid regime, and we're going to fill the jails for as long as it takes, and we shall overcome![155]

Coretta King believed that the eventual destruction of apartheid would require a unified effort on the part of people across the world. She constantly advanced this view in the 1980s. In words identical to those used by Martin Luther King Jr. in 1965, she insisted in 1984 that "the time has come for an international alliance of peoples of all nations against racism." "No nation that calls itself a democracy," she maintained, "should support the most brutally racist dictatorship on earth."[156]

Leon Sullivan of the OIC shared this conviction. The author of the widely celebrated "Sullivan Principles," Sullivan followed Martin Luther King Jr.'s earlier efforts to increase anti-apartheid activities on the part of the American churches, colleges, universities, seminaries, and corporations. Many of these institutions used Sullivan's code of conduct, which called for fair and equal employment practices for businesses with South African affiliates, as guidelines for their investments throughout the 1980s. Others rejected the code because of an unwillingness to become directly involved in anti-apartheid campaigns, and still others opposed it because of its perceived lack of militancy.[157]

It became clear toward the end of the decade that the Sullivan Principles, inspired in part by the vision of King and the civil rights movement in America, would not lead to the destruction of apartheid. Recognizing this, Sullivan joined Coretta King, Jesse Jackson, and other African American leaders in calling for a total withdrawal of U.S. businesses from South Africa in 1987. He "urged universities, pension funds, and labor unions to sell their estimated $80 billion in holdings in companies that continue their South African operations." In explaining this shift to a more radical stand, Sullivan said: "I'm taking a step beyond the 'Sullivan Principles' and attempting to use whatever abilities I have to bring every moral and economic and governmental force to bear for the cause of justice and freedom in the country."[158]

Interestingly enough, Sullivan's call for disinvestment (U.S. corporations should remove their investments from South Africa until certain types of reforms are implemented) and divestment (foundations, churches, pension funds, universities, seminaries, and other institutions with stock in U.S. corporations that have business dealings in South Africa should sell the stock), a call similar to that made by King in the 1960s, came only after many American businesses had already taken such steps. By the end of the eighties, some 200 American corporations had followed either a policy of disinvestment or divestment with respect to their operations in South Africa. Campaigns for disinvestment and divestment on many college and university campuses were suspect for reasons underscored by David Riesman, a Harvard University professor who strongly supported Martin Luther King Jr.'s work with both the *Declaration of Conscience* (1957) and the *Appeal for Action Against Apartheid* (1962):

> I saw them as distractions by which uneasy and guilt-prone whites could think of themselves as "doing something" on a racial issue, without getting involved in the much more troubling and intricate American domestic issues, including those of the campus itself. Moreover, I saw University trustees as charged with maintaining the fiscal stability of institutions, and not giving in to relatively easy shows of virtue by divestment.[159]

The Pennsylvania congressman William Gray III approached the apartheid problem from a slightly different angle, though he, too, found merit in the push for disinvestment and divestment. Like the former King aide Walter Fauntroy, Gray, a clergyman as well as a politician, used both the pulpit and the halls of Congress as forums for discussing and shaping public opinion around apartheid. In 1986, Gray—along with Congressmen Walter Fauntroy, Mickey Leland, and Ronald Dellums of California—led the way in sensitizing Congress to the evils of apartheid, a contribution that led to the congressional vote in favor of sanctions against South Africa in that year.[160] Gray also joined the Free South Africa Movement along with Coretta King and others, and he sent letters to Americans throughout the country soliciting support for the movement.

In one letter he commented: "I sincerely hope that you will join me in the Free South Africa Movement today, and help us lift the cruel and inhumane yoke of apartheid's oppression from the black majority, before all hope for peaceful change fades."[161] Gray's view that outside pressure was necessary to effect nonviolent change inside South Africa, a view constantly promoted throughout the 1980s, was yet another indication of how African American leaders continued to advance the ideas and methods of Martin Luther King Jr. with regard to South African apartheid.

Though never closely associated with King, Randall Robinson and TransAfrica employed tactics used by the civil rights leader in their anti-apartheid campaigns. In November 1984, Robinson, Walter Fauntroy, and Mary Berry of the U.S. Civil Rights Commission staged 1960s-style protests and sit-ins outside the South African Embassy in Washington, D.C. This led to "daily protests lasting 53 consecutive weeks in Washington and at South African consulates in 26 cities across the U.S." More than four thousand persons were arrested, among whom were twenty-three members of the U.S. Congress, and a number of mayors, civil rights activists, actors and actresses, entertainers, and presidents of fraternities, sororities, and other black organizations. TransAfrica and its spin-off organization, the Free South Africa Movement, secured a national stage on which to make their case against South Africa's racial policies and practices. Through persistent protest and lobbying for global economic sanctions against South Africa, TransAfrica played a vital role in forcing Congress to pass sanctions in 1986.[162] Furthermore, Randall Robinson frequently joined Jesse Jackson, Joseph Lowery, Coretta King, Walter Fauntroy, William Gray, and other black leaders in demanding the release of Nelson Mandela in the 1980s, thus echoing a concern voiced by Martin Luther King Jr. as early as 1964.[163]

Randall Robinson's and TransAfrica's part in maintaining a strong black American movement against apartheid in the eighties was in some ways more important than that of Coretta King and the King Center in Atlanta. Desmond Tutu attested to this when he asserted that "it is because of Randall Robinson's untiring efforts and the fine organizing work of TransAfrica that the anti-apartheid groundswell is gaining such dynamic momentum in America."[164] "TransAfrica is playing a decisive leadership role in building the Free South Africa Movement throughout America," declared Walter Fauntroy. In a similar vein, Lane Kirkland, president of the AFL-CIO, noted that "the Free South Africa Movement has acted as the conscience of America and has taken the lead in urging the U.S. government to act responsibly."[165] Randall Robinson's and TransAfrica's view that black Americans have a special responsibility in the struggle to free their brothers and sisters in South Africa, a view that undergirded their activities throughout the eighties, was very much in the tradition of King and of leaders like W. E. B. Du Bois and Paul Robeson.

Some black churches and their leadership made a conscious effort in the 1980s to contribute to the anti-apartheid fervor generated by African American congressmen and groups like TransAfrica and the Free South Africa Movement. They, too, were inspired to a great extent by the spirit and legacy of King and the civil rights movement. Under the leadership of the Reverend Theodore J. Jemison, a friend and confidant of King in the 1950s, the National Baptist Convention, U.S.A., one of the largest black church organizations in the world, pledged the resources of its seven million members for the support of black South Africans in 1985.[166] In 1989, "The Final Statement of the Black Church Summit on South Africa" was published, bringing together anti-apartheid sentiments held for more than a decade by the AME Church, the AME Zion Church, the CME Church, the Church of God in Christ, the National Baptist Convention of America, the National Baptist Convention, U.S.A., and the Progressive National Baptist Convention. The statement expressed the churches' intention to "work for total, comprehensive new U.S. sanctions," to "keep the Southern African struggle before the U.S. public," to "pray without ceasing for all the peoples of the region of South Africa," and to take other steps consistent with Judeo-Christian values.[167]

But black American churches as a collectivity did not perform to the level of their capabilities as a force in the anti-apartheid struggle. Much of this resulted from a preoccupation with their own institutional maintenance, and also the ever present need to address a multitude of problems in the African American community caused by Reaganomics and growing attacks on affirmative action. Survival and liberation concerns for blacks in America alone proved too enormous for black churches to solve, a fact that helps explain the inadequate attention to problems facing black South Africans. Yet the black church community's sense of a special relationship with black South Africans remained strong, as had been the case with black churches and their leadership during the King era.[168]

This sense of a special relationship with and responsibility toward the victims of South African apartheid was not as strong in the churches of white America, despite the challenges presented by Jesse Jackson, Walter Fauntroy, William Gray III, Joseph Lowery, and other African American leaders. A few white churches called upon the U.S. government to end all military-related and nuclear exports to South Africa, and some withdrew their stock from companies involved in that country, but most of these actions occurred in connection with ecumenical bodies in which black church persons consistently stressed such concerns while presenting a special challenge to white Christians on the question of racism in general. In 1986, for example, the governing board of the National Council of the Churches of Christ in the USA, under the AME bishop Philip R. Cousin, its first black president, condemned South Africa's racism and its destabilization of its neighboring African states, and encouraged the Christian community in the United States to push for strong economic sanctions against South Africa. This statement was an addendum to the 1977 Policy Statement of the Churches of Christ on Southern Africa.[169]

The presence of vocal black minorities in predominantly white denominations such as the United Methodist Church and the United Presbyterian Church in the U.S.A. accounted in large measure for those bodies' sensitivity to and actions against South African apartheid.[170] The average white church in this country in the eighties adopted essentially a laissez-faire approach to South Africa, and many actually supported President Ronald Reagan's "Constructive Engagement" policy, a policy that advocated stronger economic links between the United States and the South African regime.[171] Hence, the typical white church's stance on apartheid was virtually the same as it had been regarding Jim Crow in the King years.[172]

It was the moral laxity of white American churches in addressing apartheid that led to an interesting and provocative debate between Jesse Jackson and the fundamentalist preacher Jerry Falwell in 1985. Falwell, after a five-day fact-finding mission to South Africa, which involved a meeting with P. W. Botha, concluded that reinvestment in the South African economy was the best route to the elimination of apartheid, an approach that he claimed had the support of most black South Africans.[173] Disturbed by Falwell's position, Jackson declared that "To reinvest in a system that is economically collapsing is not feasible. The use of economic sanctions to get the attention of the government is where you can get the cancer out of apartheid and reserve an industrial democracy which is appealing." Jackson charged that it was unreasonable for Falwell to advocate investments in

South Africa while claiming to be an opponent of apartheid. "That's like being against prostitution but investing in a whore house," Jackson maintained, "like being against liquor and investing in a distillery, like being against smoking and investing in a tobacco company."[174] Jackson called Falwell's friendly meeting with Botha "a disservice," and his reference to Bishop Desmond Tutu as "a phony" "unfortunate." "Anyone who would choose Botha over Tutu would choose Bull Connor over Martin Luther King," Jackson argued; "would choose Hitler over the Jews; would choose Herod over Jesus; and would choose Pharaoh over Moses."[175]

The Jackson-Falwell debate concerning South Africa occurred on ABC-TV's *Nightline* and at the Thomas Road Baptist Church in Lynchburg, Virginia, a congregation of some 18,000 pastored by Falwell. The tone of the debate was reminiscent of King's dialogue with conservative white clergymen in Birmingham in 1963. Indeed, the Falwell who challenged Jackson in 1985 appeared no different from the Falwell who attacked King and other black ministers in the civil rights movement, in a sermon called "Ministers and Marches," in 1965.[176]

A similar exchange of ideas regarding South Africa took place in 1988 between Joseph E. Lowery of the SCLC and Pat Robertson, the evangelical minister and ultraconservative Republican presidential candidate. Robertson provoked the exchange by criticizing black Americans' efforts to influence South Africa's racial policies, contending that "they don't understand what they're dealing with, really, in this South African thing." Robertson went on to say that

> The blacks in this country have made this whole matter (apartheid) into an extension of the United States Civil Rights Movement. . . . And so it becomes an American political issue to say, if you want support among American Blacks for American political office you have to bash South Africa. I think that's bad![177]

Incensed by these comments, Lowery responded with words that struck at the heart of Robertson's naive, insensitive, and condescending attitude, asserting that "Robertson doesn't understand that Blacks have an affinity to their brothers and sisters in Africa just as others in this country have an affinity to people in Poland, Italy, or England. And we don't apologize for that."[178]

In Jesse Jackson's and Joseph Lowery's challenge to white American churches in the 1980s, there were echoes of the same concerns Martin

Luther King Jr. had when he attacked the racism of the Southern Baptist Convention in America and of the Dutch Reformed Protestant Church of South Africa in the 1960s. The central issue was how white churches might overcome racial barriers to become truly the body of Christ. King had targeted this as the most loaded and pressing issue confronting white churches worldwide, and this is why he criticized American churches, European churches, and other religious institutions for their moral failures in dealing with apartheid. Leaders like Jesse Jackson, Joseph Lowery, and Leon Sullivan agreed, and this explains why they extended their moral challenges concerning apartheid to white Christians across the globe. Lowery constantly denounced conservative American and European churches for opposing strong, punitive sanctions against South Africa, and for dismissing Christian activists against apartheid as quasi-marxist disciples of the World Council of Churches. While touring Europe in May 1985, Jackson urged European churches and synagogues to increase pressure against their governments to sever commercial dealings with South Africa, a challenge he had repeatedly put before the American churches and synagogues.[179] In a more compelling manner, Sullivan attacked white Christians throughout the world in December 1986 for "not being forceful enough in criticizing the racist apartheid government of South Africa." "I'd like to see the Pope say something to Botha about apartheid," he lamented. "I'd like to see the American churches doing something. I am deeply disappointed by the World Council of Churches. Where is the church?"[180]

The global Christian community reacted to Lowery's, Jackson's, and Sullivan's challenges in much the same way it responded to King's in the 1950s and 1960s. The World Council of Churches (WCC) contributed financially to the anti-apartheid activism of the UDF, the South African Council of Churches (SACC), and other organizations inside South Africa, and drafted and signed numerous resolutions encouraging all Christians to oppose apartheid on moral grounds, but these actions alone were insufficient for an ecumenical body with such massive resources. King's prediction that the World Council of Churches would become a vanguard in the struggle to banish racism from the global community, a prediction made as early as 1957, did not find fulfillment in the eighties.[181] In 1986, the World Methodist Conference on South Africa echoed the sentiments of the WCC in urging "all Methodist Churches around the globe to divest their funds immediately from corporations and banks that have direct or indirect ties to South Africa," and "to advocate to their governments a policy of mandatory economic sanctions, in order to make possible a less violent resolution of the South African tragedy." This body also expressed solidarity with those suffering in South Africa, and requested the South African government to abolish all apartheid policies and to "unconditionally release Nelson Mandela and other political prisoners and detainees."[182] These actions were very much in line with King's view of the roles the world Christian community could play in forcing a trend toward nonracial democratic rule in South Africa.

Catholics around the world did very little to change the situation in South Africa. In 1987, Pope John Paul II blasted all forms of racism, and "urged the church to speak out against injustices against blacks," but he offered no concrete ways of dismantling apartheid.[183] The failure of millions of Catholics to adequately respond to the moral challenge of apartheid remained one of the greatest threats to the realization of King's dream for South Africa.

The same applied in the case of non-Christian religions. Moslems, Hindus, Buddhists, Jews, and other groups remained virtually silent on the apartheid problem. Preoccupied with their own rituals and concerns, most lived as if the oppression of people of color in South Africa was totally unrelated to them. Even in South Africa—where Hindus, Buddhists, African Traditionalists, Christians, and Jews graced the religious scene—strong interreligious coalitions against apartheid were virtually nonexistent. Thus, King's vision of a global religious community, living together in peace and working to overcome racism and other divisive forces, did not come to fruition.[184]

The 1980s also witnessed the failure of nations of the world to adequately confront the urgency of the South African situation. King had often declared that the international community had the economic and diplomatic resources to force the process of peaceful change in South Africa, and he felt that the United States should assume the lead in such a venture. The election of Ronald Reagan as U.S. president in 1980, and the rise of Great Britain's Margaret Thatcher and other conservative voices on the world stage, made the fulfillment of that vision virtually impossible. The conservative leadership of many of the major Western powers held the view that the interests of the oppressed in South Africa could be better served through stronger economic and cultural links with that country, a view diametrically opposed to the position held by King. Reagan's so-called Constructive Engagement policy, implemented during his two terms in office, strongly opposed sanctions against South Africa, insisting that such a move would only increase the suffering of the oppressed in that country. Black leaders such as Jesse Jackson in America and Desmond Tutu in South Africa denounced the Reagan policy as "destructive engagement," an assessment with which King would hardly have taken issue.[185]

The election of George Bush in 1988 offered essentially no new hope of a change in policy. Bush continued to follow Reagan's approach in dealing with South Africa, though he did make greater use of diplomatic channels on this issue. He repeatedly rejected tougher economic sanctions against South Africa, arguing that "any further measures to weaken the South African economy threaten the strategic importance of having a stable, pro-Western government in Pretoria."[186] By the end of the 1980s, South Africa's military budget had grown 860 percent, and her efforts to destabilize and terrorize her neighboring African states had escalated, developments that in effect proved the moral failure of policies adopted by Reagan, Bush, and other conservative world leaders. Consequently, the United States did not emerge as a moral leader of the world in addressing apartheid, and such was also the case with Great Britain, Germany, Japan, and other powerful so-called developed nations. Countries like Canada, France, Australia, Sweden, India, Zambia, and Zimbabwe supported stiff sanctions against the South African regime, but the lack of unified and sustained economic and diplomatic pressure against South Africa on the part of the entire international community made these efforts seem weak and futile. Martin Luther King Jr.'s earlier call for the international potential of nonviolence to be employed against South Africa, through a massive boycott, did not materialize.[187]

Toward the end of 1989, however, the winds of change began to blow with greater force inside South Africa. F. W. de Klerk replaced P. W. Botha as South Africa's president in September 1989, and the new leader, from the day of his election, admitted that the long battle to exclude the oppressed from power had failed. Proclaiming the need for black–white reconciliation, de Klerk felt compelled to take action advocated by anti-apartheid activists worldwide since the time of King. In October 1989, he released unconditionally Walter Sisulu and four colleagues of the ANC. Initial plans to uproot *de jure* apartheid were set in motion, as South Africa's business community turned increasingly against that system.[188] If, as Africans believe, the souls of the dead continue to show interest in the doings of the living, surely these developments brought some satisfaction to King's soul. More importantly, they gave oppressed South Africans reasons to face the future with renewed hope.

CHAPTER 5

ENVISIONING A NEW ORDER
King and South Africa in the 1990s

*I will seek common cause with the ANC wherever that
common cause is justified. . . . In the interest of the black
struggle, where we can synchronize our strategies, we certainly intend doing so.*

Mangosuthu Gatsha Buthelezi, 1991[1]

*Our goal is a new South Africa. We can today even set the
dates when all humanity will join together to celebrate one
of the outstanding victories of our century.*

Frederik W. de Klerk, 1993[2]

*We place our vision of a new constitutional order for South
Africa on the table not as conquerors, prescribing to the
conquered. . . . We speak as fellow citizens to heal the
wounds of the past with the intent of constructing a new
order based on justice for all.*

President Nelson Mandela, 1994[3]

The 1990s began on an optimistic note as anti-apartheid forces in
South Africa took significant steps to avoid what Martin Luther
King Jr. often termed "tragic self-destruction in the quagmire of
racial hate."[4] Bowing to pressure from inside and outside South
Africa, President F. W. de Klerk released political prisoners, lifted the ban
on anti-apartheid organizations, and moved against apartheid laws.[5] The
African National Congress (ANC) began to shift from armed struggle to-

ward a negotiating posture. New calls for government action against white right-wing death squads reverberated throughout South Africa, and efforts to curb the violence and bloodshed between warring factions in the black community increased.[6] Many South African clergymen assumed roles as "agents of reconciliation" and called for "peace talks" between the black South African community and de Klerk's National Party, thus recalling King's insistence that the emphasis in South Africa should be on radical reconciliation between the races.[7] Namibia established its first sovereign black government, freeing itself of shackles imposed by the South African government. With these important developments, numerous political analysts and social critics announced prematurely the death of South African racism, using terms like "post-apartheid," "the new South Africa," "South Africa's transition," and "the former land of apartheid."[8] Few seemed to understand that the greatest challenges confronting South Africa around questions of race, freedom, and community stood ahead.

This chapter explores the relevance and implications of Martin Luther King Jr.'s nonviolent ethic and beloved community ideal for South Africans in the 1990s. First, it explains how King's ideas and methods related to the decline of *de jure* apartheid in the early nineties. Second, it underscores King's importance as an idealist and a symbol in sustained efforts to bring peace and community to South Africa in the period from 1990 up to the 1994 all-race elections. The discussion concludes with President Nelson Mandela's effort to promote peace and community in the new South Africa through the creation of a power-sharing Government of National Unity.

King and the Decline of De Jure Apartheid in South Africa

Apartheid was still very much alive in South Africa at the beginning of 1990. It remained symptomatic of a greater and more intense world problem. In other words, it was part of a vicious global system that involved persistent hate crimes against blacks and Jews in the United States, interethnic conflict in the former Yugoslavia and Soviet Union, violent clashes between African and Chinese students at Chinese institutions of higher learning, confrontations between black urban youth and the police in Britain, right-wing assaults against Arabs and Africans in France, blatant incidents of racial discrimination and violence promoted by neo-Nazis in Germany, and tensions between whites and peoples of color in other parts of Europe. Equally disturbing were the working coalitions and support systems developing between neo-Nazis, the Ku Klux Klan, and other racist elements in the United States, South Africa, and Germany.[9] These frightening developments suggested a need for the ongoing appropriation of Martin Luther King Jr.'s thought for ethical resources. Indeed, humans everywhere were still challenged with King's ideal of a global community in which every person is treated with dignity and respect, and where individuals pursue their own personal good insofar as it contributes to the collective good of the whole.

As "the preeminent moral issue of international relations," South African apartheid could not long endure on its shaky legal foundations. The exact point at which *de jure* apartheid began to decline is debatable. One view is that the process started with de Klerk's rise as president of South Africa in September 1989. From the day of his election, de Klerk declared that it was time to enfranchise blacks and to share power with them.[10] His unconditional release of several ANC leaders in October 1989 was certainly one important step in the direction of substantive change. On February 2, 1990, de Klerk ended restrictions on 374 anti-apartheid activists and lifted the ban on the ANC, the Pan-Africanist Congress (PAC), the South African Communist Party (SACP), and some forty-eight other organizations previously considered a threat to national security.[11] Sebastian Mallaby contends that the transition from the old toward a new order in South Africa did not actually begin until eleven days later, when Nelson Mandela, the greatest black symbol of national unity since Martin Luther King Jr., was set free after twenty-seven years in prison:

> That Sunday, February 11, 1990, ended the old South Africa and set the tone for the new. For years the release of Nelson Mandela had seemed the key to peace among South Africans, black, brown and white. In the dark days of the mid-1980s, when policemen shot at black protesters almost every month, many blacks longed for Mandela, the one leader who might talk sense into the white government and restraint into radical blacks. By the end of the decade, whites were pinning their hopes on Mandela too. After so much bitterness, the freeing of the world's most famous prisoner would demonstrate the government's openness to change. It would give South Africa a leader whose mythical status hoisted him above the dogmas that had bathed the country in violence. . . . Nelson Mandela would emerge from prison to reconcile South Africans, like a priest absolving sins.[12]

Millions throughout the world seemed to equate Mandela's release with the death of apartheid. Africans from various parts of the continent danced and sang freedom songs. People of African descent worldwide celebrated in many ways. Sermons were preached from the pulpits of African American churches, comparing Mandela's emergence from prison to some of King's triumphs in the United States years earlier. Talk of ending sanctions against South Africa grew louder among world leaders. Few appeared mindful that the freeing of Mandela had little to do with actually dismantling a racist system that still had deep roots in South Africa.[13] The state of emergency there had been only partially lifted, many political prisoners remained in jail, and legislation upholding segregation in education, housing, and other areas persisted. In short, the long campaign to free South Africa of the crippling legacy of bigotry and racial separatism—a campaign imbued with memories of Gandhi, Luthuli, King, and many who followed them—had not come to fruition.

The decline of apartheid began when the de Klerk government struck at its legal foundations. The Separate Amenities Act was revoked in 1990, eliminating the legal basis for segregated parks, buses, swimming pools, and other facilities. In time, whites-only state schools and hospitals were opened to black South Africans, and the Land Acts were repealed to allow them to farm outside the homelands.[14] *De jure* apartheid suffered powerful blows, but *de facto* apartheid continued and became in some cases more sophisticated and insidious. This change in the nature of South Africa's racism in the early nineties demonstrated the validity of King's assertion that while the breaking down of legal barriers is important and necessary, genuine peace and community must permeate the hearts of people before finding expression in a social order.[15] Even so, many political analysts concluded that de Klerk's initial moves toward reform were "clearly a turning point from which there is no return for South Africa."[16]

De Klerk's decision to forge ahead with unprecedented reform had little to do with moral considerations. Political exigencies and considerations played a larger role in this case. The impact of international sanctions on South Africa's business community and economy forced its government to come to terms with change as the only alternative, as King and many after him had predicted.[17] Furthermore, continuous black protest undermined white security and embodied the possibility of civil war. Remarkably, black protests had assumed nonviolent and violent forms, calling to mind the civil rights movement in the United States. Boycotts, strikes, freedom marches, and other nonviolent tactics had been employed almost daily in the late 1980s, and had not proven suicidal, a point that cannot be made concerning the South Africa that King knew.[18] Violent resistance had been fairly spasmodic by both the ANC and street gangs, but it, too, encouraged the initiative for change.[19]

The de Klerk government's initial moves toward reform elicited fury and apprehension in some quarters and jubilation and hope in others. When de Klerk freed Nelson Mandela, unbanned the ANC, and moved to scrap the Land Acts, South Africa's Conservative Party and other right-wing extremists threatened to derail the initiatives and predicted a white uprising that would possibly lead to the overthrow of the government.[20] Conservative town councils throughout South Africa refused to open many all-white facilities to blacks, and white thugs occasionally attacked blacks who used newly desegregated parks and swimming pools. Conservatives also fought to delay reform through foot-dragging and other tactics.[21] Southern Dixiecrats and other segregationists had responded in a similar fashion to civil rights initiatives in the United States.

White liberals and moderate National Party supporters of de Klerk looked on with cautious optimism. They shared much of the fear and uneasiness of white conservatives regarding the loss of power and privilege.[22] Some white liberals were prone to prefer planned and institutionalized tokenism for black South Africans, rather than revolutionary social progress. Consequently, Mandela, Desmond Tutu, and other black South African leaders found themselves facing essentially the same problems Martin Luther King Jr. confronted with liberal and moderate whites in America decades earlier.

Black South Africans found renewed hope in de Klerk's early reforms. Initially, the ANC was understandably wary of the new president, and Mandela, in his first public statement as a free man, declared that "there was no option but to continue the armed struggle." At the same time, Mandela "expressed the hope that the climate for negotiations could be created so that the armed struggle would no longer be necessary."[23] Mandela's openness to the possibility of negotiations with the South African government, a spirit shared by the ANC leader Oliver Tambo, was obviously in line with hopes expressed by King twenty-five years earlier. King had held that negotiation would be a crucial step in any peaceful campaign to end tension and strife between the races in South Africa.[24]

In conformity with views held by King and later by Desmond Tutu and Allan Boesak, the ANC had completely switched from the politics of confrontation to a policy of peace and negotiation by 1991. In doing so, it established itself as the de Klerk administration's principal negotiating partner in talks aimed at the ultimate creation of a new constitution and a nonracial political system. Productive talks between the two parties were threatened in July 1991, when leaks compelled senior government ministers to acknowledge that they had financed large Inkatha rallies and encouraged violence between Inkatha and the ANC. Substantive negotiations did not begin until December 1991, after months of prenegotiation discussion between de Klerk's National Party and black political organizations. The major figure in this development was Mandela, who had replaced Oliver Tambo as the ANC's president, and who defined his organization's position as "readiness to make compromises."[25] Mandela's emergence as "a man of peace" evoked memories of the role King played in the racially torn United States.[26]

Mandela's and the ANC's politics of compromise set them at odds with more militant streams of the black movement in South Africa, a problem reminiscent of King's conflicts with Malcolm X and black power advocates in America. Representatives of the PAC remained unconvinced that the time had come for peaceful and meaningful negotiations, especially since, as they saw it, "the white community has not yet come under sufficient pressure to give up the idea that white political control can be maintained indefinitely."[27] But the ANC's efforts at negotiation did have some merit, a fact readily admitted by all major black South African leaders and movements except some of the Pan-Africanists. ANC pressure had provided much of the incentive for de Klerk's early reforms. It was a force behind de Klerk's efforts to pass a "whites-only referendum." Won by a surprising 2-to-1 margin in March 1992, that measure endorsed negotiation toward "a non-racial democratic constitution."[28]

Historic negotiations between South Africa's white minority government and a wide spectrum of black political forces carried through 1992. "General constitutional principles" and a "constitutional-making body/process" remained high on the agenda. Another major setback came in June 1992, when government security forces participated in the massacre of forty-two black South Africans at Boipatong. This tragedy brought stern reminders of Sharpeville, Sebokeng, Crossroads, and Langa, forcing the ANC to temporarily suspend all talks with the de Klerk government.[29] The massacre at Boipatong raised serious doubts worldwide about the ultimate outcome of a negotiation process that once seemed so promising. "The slaughter of human beings with government connivance," as Mandela put it, made it impossible for the ANC and the black community in general to completely trust de klerk and his government in the early 1990s.[30] The Black South African community encountered the stark reality of what can happen when the oppressor refuses to engage in what Martin Luther King Jr. called "good-faith negotiations."[31]

The fall of apartheid as a legislated system of racial oppression depended in large measure on negotiations between de Klerk and Mandela. The two men were not very fond of each other. A common view was that the two men "'were delivered to each other by history,'" and neither one seemed "grateful for the gift of the other." De Klerk's paternalism and determination to dictate the terms of negotiation often conflicted with Mandela's firmness of conviction and insistence on being treated as an equal in the process. The two men severed all personal contacts at one point, "communicating only through letters and public statements."[32] Their talks were further hampered by violence between Inkatha and the ANC, a problem which interfered with de Klerk's efforts to convince whites to accept power-sharing with blacks and ultimately black majority rule.[33] But de Klerk's and Mandela's burgeoning image as "peacemakers" compelled them to sustain the negotiation process despite obstacles.[34]

The new South Africa that King and Albert Luthuli had envisioned seemed very much in sight by the end of 1993. In September 1993, the South African parliament approved a bill giving the black majority a voice in the government. The racially segregated parliament disbanded and a multiracial executive council was created to prepare for the first all-races election in April 1994. These developments led Mandela, Desmond Tutu, and other leaders to call for the lifting of the sanctions embargo against South Africa.[35] The ANC and the de Klerk government also agreed to establish a government of national unity for five years after the April 1994 elections, with the hope that all South Africans would get used to "full-scale-majority-rule democracy."[36] These advances were significant indeed, but South Africa remained essentially an apartheid state. Much more progress would have to be made before King's ideal of the beloved community could be realized for all South Africans.

Be that as it may, de Klerk's and Mandela's importance as symbols of peace and community had approached King's in the minds of people worldwide. The splitting of the Nobel Peace Prize between the two leaders in December 1993 resulted from this perception. The responses of black South Africans to this gesture of world recognition varied. Desmond Tutu, in explaining the sheer symbolism of the award as it related to South

Africa's future, acknowledged that "it's a wonderful thing that Black and White should be given this extraordinary accolade together." Winnie Mandela called the joint Nobel Prize an insult because de Klerk remained "an angel of death" with the "blood of innocent Blacks" on his hands.[37] To be sure, the choice of Mandela for the award made sense, but the selection of de Klerk, the head of the apartheid state, appeared problematic in the least. Government complicity in the continued subjugation of blacks, and the National Party's shrewd search for ways to maintain white power in the new South Africa, were clearly at variance with the spirit of community as exemplified by Luthuli, King, Tutu, Mandela, and other recipients of the Nobel Peace Prize.[38]

Even so, de Klerk and Mandela did play leading roles in starting South Africa on a new course in the early nineties. Facing heavy odds, they successfully challenged many of the legal barriers that separated whites and peoples of color. However, millions of South Africans still refused to embrace each other across racial, ethnic, and tribal categories.

King, Mandela, and the Major Barriers to Peaceful Community

Martin Luther King Jr. identified racism, poverty, and war as the greatest barriers to human community. These "giant triplets," as he labeled them, were probably more characteristic of South Africa than of most other parts of the world in the early 1990s. Organized and institutionalized racism immediately came to mind when one thought of South Africa. The country remained bitterly divided between those who desired continued racial segregation and those who preferred what King termed "an integrated society." As whites trembled at the thought of change, black South Africans called for "a free, democratic and non-racial South Africa."[39] These irreconcilable forces added to the significance and dramatic tension of discussions about what form the new South Africa should take.

Undoubtedly, racism remained the greatest barrier to peace and community. Viewing apartheid as essential to their survival and prosperity, white supremacists in both South Africa's Conservative Party and the Afrikaner Resistance Movement (ARM) reaffirmed their belief in black inferiority and vehemently opposed basic structural changes in the system. As *de jure* apartheid collapsed, elements in both turned to more drastic forms of resistance. In 1992, the Conservative Party pushed for "a white homeland" that "would demand the choicest lands" in South Africa.[40] Extremists in the ARM raised their acts of violence and terrorism to a new stage, targeting even black children and particularly black South African leaders. Chris Hani, the chief of staff of *uMkhonto weSizwe,* the ANC's military wing, was gunned down in April 1993, and plots against the lives of Nelson Mandela and other leaders were discovered.[41] Such acts appeared to be connected to a larger government scheme, which involved attacks on the credibility of Allan Boesak and Winnie Mandela, a pattern that Coretta Scott King, the widow of Martin Luther King Jr., strongly denounced.[42]

The racism of white liberals and moderates in South Africa appeared less destructive in character than that of die-hard white supremacists and extremists. However, the racism of all of these segments was rooted in guilt and fear of the future. White South Africans in general were very fearful of any kind of basic structural changes that would result in the sharing of political power and the redistribution of wealth. Even President de Klerk gave serious consideration to a system of "grand apartheid" that would have involved the voluntary acceptance of geographic separation on the part of South Africa's diverse ethnic and tribal groups, an idea he ceased to pursue by the end of 1993.[43] White South Africans commonly viewed themselves in opposition to and in competition with blacks, Coloreds, and Indians, a kind of "us-them" dichotomy that undermined community and reinforced apartheid as a social reality. But white liberals and moderates generally realized that the time had come for South Africa to move beyond the old colonial paradigm to a communitarian ideal that embraced all her people, and many subscribed to de Klerk's view of a participatory democracy based on the model of the United States Constitution.[44] Such whites were clearly more apt than right-wing extremists to see Martin Luther King Jr.'s relevance for their situation.

With few exceptions, black South Africans tended to see racism as the major obstacle to a unified South Africa. King's beloved community ideal still had meaning and significance for them, especially since they recognized certain affinities between his context and their own. The essentials of King's communitarian ethic continued to find acceptance in the thought of leaders like Allan Boesak and Desmond Tutu, and in the mission statements of organizations such as the SACP, the United Democratic Front (UDF), and the South African Council of Churches (SACC). The ANC's preference for "a multi-racial socialist state" devoid of racism, totalitarianism, and tribalism still conformed to ideas set forth by King, a point quite significant, since that organization appeared most likely to head South Africa's first black majority government. David J. Garrow suggested in 1990 that the future South Africa Mandela envisioned was essentially no different from the America King struggled to achieve:

> Like King, Mandela has a firm and clear vision of a multi-racial democratic society, a vision that is in no way communistic but that instead reflects the values of democratic or Christian socialism. King would refer to his ideal of a democratic, egalitarian society as "the beloved community," and he rejected both the economic excesses of laissez-faire capitalism and the controls of leftist and rightist totalitarianism. Mandela, in "The Struggle of My Life," has articulated a similarly humanitarian worldview, criticizing societies where "individuals . . . are but tiny organisms with private lives that lead to private deaths: personal power, success and fame are the absolute measure of values, the things to live for." Instead, Mandela says, in an ideal society individuals view themselves as "interdependent aspects of one whole, realizing their fullest life . . . where communal contentment is the absolute measure of values."[45]

Mandela frequently insisted in the early nineties that the new South Africa should result from and develop on the creative potential of the masses. In his view, the people, not government, would ultimately shape South Africa's destiny. This idea grew out of black thought traditions that influenced Mandela as well as King.[46] Mandela's belief in a people-oriented society helps explain why he, like King, rejected the "Messiah-like faith" and images many of his people sought to impose upon him. "It is not correct to elevate any human being to the position of a god," Mandela declared in an interview in 1990. He added:

> We are an organization which believes in a collective effort. I was brought up under that tradition. I think it is right that it should be preserved. I would even add that without this tradition, we would all have found it very difficult indeed to survive the years of suffering.[47]

Black South Africans' devotion to a multiracial, democratic society suggested that they were essentially in agreement with King's conviction that humans are "caught in an inescapable network of mutuality" and "tied in a single garment of destiny."[48] This was perhaps the one conviction that united parties as varied as Gatsha Buthelezi and the ANC in the early nineties. However, in a society where the issue of race kept whites, blacks, Coloreds, and Asians apart and suspicious of each other, many South Africans struggled with what such a communitarian ethic might mean socially, politically, and otherwise in their unique context.

Economic injustice and poverty further frustrated the search for peace and community in South Africa in the early nineties. As was the case with King, black South Africans viewed racism and economic exploitation as perennial allies, a view borne out by the fact that whites controlled the economy and the land.[49] This is why anti-apartheid groups like the Azanian People's Organization (AZAPO) and the National Forum (NF) identified the fundamental problem in South Africa as racial capitalism rather than racism as commonly understood.[50] The low-income projects for black South Africans stirred recollections of the ghettoes in the United States. King's description of American ghettoes as "a domestic colony" or "a system of internal colonialism" coincided with the analysis the AZAPO, the NF, and the ANC gave of the black economic situation under South African apartheid.[51]

Blacks knew that the beloved community would remain impossible under South Africa's existing capitalistic system. This explains why one found in leaders like Nelson Mandela that same rejection of the evils of Western capitalism that was evident with King. In the thought of both, the selfish ambition, cutthroat competition, and unrestrained individualism at the heart of capitalism militated against human community. This is why Mandela, like King in America in the late 1960s, advocated basic structural changes in South Africa's capitalistic system: the nationalization of basic industries, a guaranteed income for every adult citizen, and massive government expenditures to revive black residential areas and to provide education, health care, and better job opportunities for the poor.[52] Mandela argued in 1990 that there could be no positive economic change apart from the ANC's stated policy of nationalizing South Africa's mines, financial institutions, and monopolies.[53] This democratic socialism, the political and economic ideology most congenial with King's beloved community concept, was generally accepted by the AZAPO, the SACP, and other organizations. Mandela seemed most interested in restructuring his country's economic system, not in overthrowing it. As he saw it, an ANC government "would be as committed to economic growth and productivity as any free market captain of industry," a view that white and black capitalists in South Africa found difficult to believe.[54]

Black South African leaders and organizations regarded economic exploitation as a product of class privilege as well as racism, a view also quite similar to King's. This explains why the AZAPO and the ANC were as adamant in their expressions of concern for black workers as the Azanian

Confederation of Trade Unions (AZACTU), the Congress of South African Trade Unions (COSATU), and other black trade union federations. The AZAPO never wavered in its push for "a democratic, anti-racist worker republic," where the interests of workers would be paramount through worker control of the means of production, distribution, and exchange.[55] Speaking for the ANC in 1990, Nelson Mandela observed: "South Africa is a wealthy country. It is the labor of black workers that has built the cities, roads, and factories we see. They cannot be excluded from sharing this wealth."[56] Leaders in both the AZAPO and the ANC clearly saw how race served as a means of dividing the working-class people by giving poor whites, Coloreds, and Asians marginal economic advantages while encouraging their false sense of superiority over blacks. It was therefore necessary, as Mandela consistently explained in the early nineties, for both racism and classism to be abolished in order to close the gap between the "haves" and "have nots," a struggle essentially identical to that waged by King and his people in America decades earlier.[57]

Such a struggle appeared far more complicated for black South Africans than for African Americans, especially since the former faced problems more analogous to that of a colony fighting against the restraints of a colonizer. Indeed, the movement of black South Africans in the early 1990s and before was much like that of the early American colonists seeking to overthrow British domination. Furthermore, interference from certain parts of the international community complicated the problem. In 1992, the ANC experienced pressure from international businesses and agencies like the World Bank to embrace a "redistribution through growth" economic philosophy for the future of South Africa, a philosophy that seemed unlikely to radically change the economic aspects of the old colonial paradigm in a reasonably short time frame.[58] Such dynamics had to be seriously considered in any careful examination of Martin Luther King Jr.'s relevance for South Africa.

The history of South Africa suggested that King's proposed Poor People's Campaign (1967–68), a movement designed to unite poor Americans across racial and ethnic lines to dramatize and eventually eliminate the problem of poverty, afforded an appropriate and useful model for South Africans who were interested in a society devoid of privileges based on both race and class.[59] Black South African leaders knew that once political democracy came, such a model would be needed to ensure acceptable levels of economic justice and equity. Although most black South Africans in the early nineties did not discount the assistance that whites could give in such a campaign, they realized at the same time that the number of whites likely to identify completely with poor people of color was small. They knew that they could not depend solely on the moral sense of their white oppressors to free them from their menial economic condition. Determined to maintain their standard of living in the midst of economic recession and the worst drought for thirty years, most of South Africa's 4.5 million white citizens, as Mandela reported in 1990, did not even think of apartheid as an economic system that required eradication before the common good, the good of the total society, could be promoted.[60]

Developing class divisions within the ranks of black South Africans themselves posed difficulties of almost the same magnitude. Tensions and problems stemming from class differences between black South Africans surfaced in new ways in the early nineties, resulting in a pattern as disturbing as that seen by King among black Americans in the 1960s. Occupational, income, and housing discrimination, fueled by economic and political uncertainties, became more evident in South Africa's townships, where unemployment exceeded 50 percent, than among more privileged blacks. While organizations like the AZAPO and the PAC remained in the townships, the ANC and leaders like Allan Boesak and Desmond Tutu did not. Nelson Mandela accepted limousine service and access to a wider variety of resources, actions that many blacks viewed as inconsistent with his words. There was the growing belief in the townships that Mandela, Boesak, Tutu, and other established leaders were into opportunism and power, and that their increasing middle-class status was making it more and more difficult for them to speak for the masses. King encountered the same problem among African Americans, a problem that becomes unavoidable for oppressed people scrambling for power. Although leaders like Mandela, Boesak, and Tutu still commanded great respect, due in part to traditions that stress reverence for elders, they faced the same challenges from poverty-stricken young militants that King confronted. This explained much of the tension between the ANC and groups like Inkatha and the PAC. The possibility of a revolution from the grass roots mounted, adding to the uncertainty regarding South Africa's future.[61]

The problem of war and human destruction proved equally divisive and troubling. The South Africa of the early 1990s was still a society at war with itself. Violence tore at the seams of that society even as it remained a threat to neighboring states. Criminal violence reached unprecedented levels. "Crime has assumed unacceptable proportions," said Mandela in a 1994 interview, and "has turned South Africa into one of the most violent countries in the world."[62] An estimated 20,000 South Africans were victims of homicide in 1993. Much of this violence was attributed to young black South Africans. Mandela identified the institutionalized violence of apartheid as the source of the problem, thus reiterating King's claim that "violence begets violence."[63] "The system of apartheid has destroyed the future of our people," he declared. "We need the opportunities for self-assertion and self-development." Pointing to the 50 percent unemployment in his country, Mandela noted that violence was all black South Africans had ever known. This assessment of the situation was generally accepted among anti-apartheid activists, despite differences in philosophy and method.[64]

The most publicized violence occurred between black factions, highlighting tribalism as yet another barrier to peace and community in South Africa. Aided and abetted by the white minority government, the bloody rivalry between Inkatha and the ANC resulted in more than 10,000 deaths, in injuries to hundreds of thousands, and in the burning of the homes and belongings of countless families in the early 1990s.[65] Despite the historic meetings between Nelson Mandela and the Inkatha leader Gatsha Buthelezi in January 1991 and June 1993, prophets of doom predicted that the violence would probably get worse if the ANC emerged victorious in South Africa's first one-person, one-vote elections, scheduled for April 1994. Many believed that Buthelezi would create a civil war situation, especially if he implemented his threat to secede. The prognosis was that as a homeland leader, rather than a national leader, Buthelezi would push for his own separate state if excluded from national political leadership.[66] The tensions between Inkatha and the ANC, between the AZAPO and the PAC, and between other parties obviously undermined the conviction, expressed by King and numerous black leaders before and after him, that the overthrow of white domination necessarily required a strong, black united front.[67]

Debate concerning the best means of eliminating apartheid continued into the early nineties. People of various backgrounds were still asking, "Can peaceful change occur in South Africa?" King's nonviolent philosophy still appealed to many South Africans, and particularly to those who spoke of "the Leipzig option," or the advancement of peaceful protest to new and more militant levels. Leaders like Desmond Tutu and Allan

Boesak would have agreed with George Fredrickson's admission in 1990 that "government repression has eased up to the extent that nonviolent protest is now possible," and that "the situation now makes the U.S. civil rights movement more relevant," but many South African blacks recognized that the problems at hand still demanded a movement beyond a mere Kingian approach.[68]

After years of nonviolent demonstrations and civil disobedience, many militant Pan-Africanists prepared for the race war that would drive the whites out of South Africa. While asserting that the ANC "has no vested interest in violence," Nelson Mandela insisted that armed resistance should remain "a legitimate form of self-defense against a morally repugnant system of government" that murders, maims, and psychologically tortures its subjects.[69] "Armed struggle must be a movement intended to hit at the symbols of oppression," Mandela maintained in a 1993 interview, "and not to slaughter human beings."[70] For Mandela and so many other black South Africans, this was not so much a call to violence, but a call to life or self-preservation. This pro-self-defense mechanism, this interest in the preservation of physical and psychological health, paralleled concerns previously verbalized by Malcolm X in America.[71] David Garrow was therefore right in suggesting that Mandela, by combining a devotion to self-defense with a receptivity to peaceful negotiation and change, represented a blending of vital qualities found in Malcolm and King:

> Mandela in many ways can be viewed as an amalgam of the most impressive qualities in both Malcolm and King. Many African Americans for more than 20 years have sought to highlight the dissimilar though complementary strengths of those two men. In Nelson Mandela, South Africa— and the world—may well be witnessing the closest real-life parallel to that idealized joining of King and Malcolm that anyone is likely to see.[72]

This tendency to draw parallels between Mandela and African American leaders from the civil rights and black power movement was quite common in this period when people worldwide were still discussing the merits of nonviolence and violence as avenues to social change. The tendency also seemed quite natural and indeed understandable, coming as it did at a time when ethnic and racial tensions were developing across the globe, and when dramatic change was needed to avoid an uncontrollably violent situation in South Africa. While agreeing that Mandela displayed much that reminded the world of King, particularly in terms of the keenness of his intellect and the power of his courage and charisma, David Garrow concluded neverthe-less that differences in methods would have kept the two men from com-pletely finding common ground in the struggle:

> But for King, unlike Mandela, an absolutely total commitment to nonvio-lence, both spiritually and physically, was at the very center of his being, and would have limited his ability fully to support the struggle of the African National Congress.[73]

Although convinced of the problematics involved in "Comparing Mandela's unique status to other, almost mythical figures of recent times," Garrow went on to assert in 1990 that Mandela's manner and approach to the question of means made him more comparable to Malcolm X than to King:

> In bearing and demeanor, as in political tactics, the African American leader whom Mandela most closely parallels is not King but Malcolm X. Just as Malcolm in the last year of his life rejected the racial antipathies of his own earlier years and began moving toward positions that might have put him in tandem with King, Mandela, too, rejects the racial exclusiveness of South Africa's Pan Africanist Congress in favor of a multiracial democracy. . . . Neither man shies away from the need for black freedom by—in Malcolm's most famous words—"any means necessary," but both Mandela and Malcolm have articulated visions of racial justice and interracial cooperation that contradict racist notions. . . . No parallel should be overdrawn, how-ever, and Mandela is no more a duplicate of Malcolm than he is of King.[74]

Questions about whether or not nonviolence was more practical and moral than violence were not ones to be discussed between black and white South Africans in the early 1990s. Apartheid remained fundamen-tally a violent system, and those who supported or benefited from it were in no moral position to discuss with the oppressed the ethics of protest and the best means of attaining freedom. At that point, Mandela and black leaders in the PAC, the AZAPO, and other organizations felt that questions about the morality and practicality of nonviolent and violent means had to emerge exclusively out of the black South African experi-ence. Only after power was shared with black South Africans, they felt, would such questions become an issue of discussion between the races.[75] Malcolm X and black power advocates raised the same concern in their challenge to King in the 1960s.

Moreover, black South Africans knew that such questions could not be resolved on the basis of traditional Christian standards as defined by white people. Here again, they targeted an issue that King was compelled to consider in his discussions with African American nationalists on the moral failures of white churches. Indeed, it would have been self-defeating for blacks in South Africa to wrestle with questions about nonviolence and violence in light of Calvinism, the dominant ethical and theological tradition used by whites to preserve the status quo. Having sanctioned the institutionalized and organized violence of the apartheid government, while denouncing all forms of armed resistance on the part of blacks, white South Africans had denied the very essence of God as liberator of the oppressed.[76]

The tremendous philosophical differences between blacks and whites concerning nonviolence and violence became glaringly evident in the debates over the whole issue of amnesty in South Africa. The amnesty question had come to a head by 1993. The races generally disagreed as to whether or not there should be "Nuremberg-type trials" for white racists who had murdered blacks. The ANC categorically rejected a blanket amnesty for government security forces "because it would absolve killers and torturers." The apartheid government sought to convince blacks that whites who killed blacks were political prisoners like Nelson Mandela. But those who had used violence to preserve an evil system, blacks argued, could never be logically equated with those who engaged in armed rebellion against such a system. In this context, "violence was not just violence" for black South Africans.[77] Such a distinction would have been uncharacteristic of King in view of his belief that violence in all forms is immoral, impractical, and unacceptable. However, he would easily have seen the moral dilemmas implicit in equating the violence of the apartheid regime with that of anti-apartheid activists.

The problem of sexism presented still another barrier to genuine peace and community in South Africa in the early nineties. The oppression of women occurred at all levels of society, and it proved to be a very painful reality in the black South African struggle. "Black South African women," said Winnie Mandela in a 1990 speech, "suffer a disproportionately heavy burden of oppression."[78] Up to that point, black women in South Africa had refused to address their unique experience of oppression consistently, primarily because they preferred not to diminish the importance of the struggle of black South Africans as a whole against white racism. Such a strategy was understandable given the frequency with which whites sought to divide blacks. The subordination of women in the South African freedom struggle in the early nineties was not unlike Martin Luther King Jr.'s experiences with sexism in the civil rights movement.[79]

Many South African Christians had come to a vivid sense of their role in striking down barriers to peace and community in their country by the early 1990s. Having decided on the need for a *revolutionary ecclesiology*, such as that advocated by King and by the theologians who formulated *The Kairos Document* in 1985, black Christians took the lead in denouncing apartheid as a theological heresy and a pseudo-religion practiced only by those with a penchant for indulging in idolatry.[80] Building on steps taken in the 1980s with the SACC's "Standing for Truth" campaigns and its calls for "responsible resistance," they also challenged South Africans to promote tranquility and to actualize the communitarian ideal in all arenas of life, an ideal King so eloquently proclaimed and embodied in his own life. The message that emerged out of the SACC's "Emergency Summit" on political violence, held in Johannesburg in May 1992, was that the time for pious words and meaningless proclamations had ended.[81] Even the *amnesty question*, which remained a source of tension between the races, was addressed forthrightly by both black and white Christians who understood that community-building provided the key to a transformed and prosperous South Africa.[82]

The practical ways in which black South African church leaders sought to keep alive that Christian hope, that sense that the liberating power of God will triumph over human suffering and fragmentation, triggered thoughts of the black church in America during the King years. Leaders such as Allan Boesak, Frank Chikane, and Desmond Tutu continued to represent a voice of restraint and moderation as young black radicals clamored for retaliatory violence, particularly in the wake of the Chris Hani assassination. In June 1993, the Anglican archbishop Tutu and the Methodist bishop Stanley Mogoba brought together Nelson Mandela and Gatsha Buthelezi to explore ways of halting the frightening cycle of violence between the ANC and Inkatha.[83] During the same time, H. Mvume Dandala, a Methodist pastor and a facilitator of the Hostel Residents' Peace Initiative in Johannesburg, engaged in "a nonpartisan, inter-tribal initiative to keep peace" in anticipation of South Africa's first all-race elections.[84] Such activities were very much in harmony with King's powerful testimony concerning the church's responsibility as a symbol of peace and of the beloved community.

This sense of a need for a revolutionary ecclesiology brought black South African and black American Christians together in a manner that recalled King and Albert J. Luthuli, both of whom were Christian ministers. Early in 1993, L. Charles Stovall, a national board member of the Southern Christian Leadership Conference (SCLC) and a United Methodist pastor in Dallas, Texas, traveled to South Africa to observe and participate in peace initiatives at the invitation of the ANC and the SACC.[85] Also in 1993, Bernard Lafayette and James Orange, black clergymen who worked with King in the SCLC, united with churchmen in South Africa in training South Africans in the area of conflict resolution. In their work as agents of peace and reconciliation, African American and black South African churchpersons built on a tradition that has roots in King's and Luthuli's joint efforts to promote nonviolent change in South Africa.[86]

As black South Africans and their white allies worked for a society that lifts neighborly concern beyond race and ethnicity, they found less than adequate support from world leaders who struggled with their own divisions within the human family. As late as 1993, many political leaders had not faced the urgency of the South African situation as defined by King and anti-apartheid activists who followed him. By prematurely ending their sanctions against South Africa, the United States and the European community showed that the complete unraveling of the apartheid system was not one of their highest priorities.[87] Zambia, Zimbabwe, and other frontline states still represented "a force for pressure against the South African regime," but their primary concern rested with their own security and well-being. Nigeria remained one of several major African countries with business ties to South Africa.[88] The disposition of the global community toward South Africa suggested that it was still morally lax to the point of allowing a human tragedy comparable to the massive slaughter suffered by the American Indians, African slaves, and European Jews.

Nelson Mandela's trips abroad in the period from 1990 to 1993 were designed to keep the international pressure on South Africa. Of particular importance were his travels in the United States, where he associated with African Americans who reflected the values and example of Martin Luther King Jr. in their commitment to the anti-apartheid cause. Mandela first visited the United States in June 1990, spending eleven days in New York, Washington, D.C., Detroit, Los Angeles, Atlanta, and three other cities.[89] Weeks prior to the trip, African American newspapers and other media sources featured long and interesting stories of his life, giving considerable attention to how the freedom movement in South Africa related to the African American struggle and particularly to figures like King. In an interview with *Ebony,* Mandela spoke of the special ties between black South Africans and African Americans:

> [T]here are many similarities between us. We have learned a great deal from each other. . . . We have received tremendous support and encouragement from our brothers and sisters in America for our struggle. . . . This bond must continue and grow stronger as we continue in our fight for democracy and equality.[90]

Mandela referred in lofty terms to those African American leaders who had shifted the Free South Africa movement from the street demonstrations to the push for sanctions in the U.S. Congress in the 1980s, noting especially their willingness to go to jail for the cause:

> It was an impressive role for Black Americans to choose arrest. This was of tremendous importance to us. We not only regard Congressmen Bill Gray, Ron Dellums, and (TransAfrica's) Randall Robinson as friends, but as brothers who have done everything expected of them to help us sustain our struggle against South Africa. They and so many others deserve so much credit and praise.[91]

In his most widely televised speech during the 1990 trip, delivered to the U.S. Congress on June 26, Mandela alluded to the impact of America's noble traditions and symbols of freedom and participatory democracy on his people. "The day may not be far," he proclaimed, "when we will borrow the words of Thomas Jefferson and speak of the will of the South African nation." He further remarked:

> We could not have heard of and admired John Brown, Sojourner Truth, Frederick Douglass, W. E. B. Du Bois, Marcus Garvey, Martin Luther King Jr., and others, and not be moved to act as they were moved to act. We could not have known of your *Declaration of Independence* and not elected to join in the struggle to guarantee the people life, liberty, and the pursuit of happiness.[92]

Mandela's stay in Atlanta, Georgia, was highly symbolic, beginning as it did with him placing a wreath at King's gravesite at the Martin Luther King Jr. Center for Nonviolent Social Change.[93] Local newspapers stressed in bold headlines "the inevitable comparison" between Mandela and King.[94]

With the elegance of style so typical of great leaders, Mandela told the hundreds of blacks gathered at the Martin Luther King Jr. Chapel at Morehouse College that "it was your active engagement in the struggle against apartheid that has brought us to this moment." After mentioning the names of King, Paul Robeson, Harriet Tubman, Rosa Parks, and other black freedom fighters "who lit up our lives with pride," Mandela and his wife Winnie called upon all Americans to "help us build a united, non-racist, non-sexist, and democratic South Africa."[95] The atmosphere, charged with the singing of the African national anthem, rekindled thoughts of the spirit and struggles that had long united people of African descent across geographical boundaries.

This spirit of oneness was heightened by the honorary degrees and book of tributes presented to Mandela at the King Chapel. Johnnetta B. Cole, the president of Atlanta's Spelman College, praised Mandela for teaching "us enduringly about dignity in struggle." "At the feet of your elders, you learned of ancestral valor earned in epic struggles in defense of the fatherland," she continued. "You took up that struggle and carried it forward through bannings and bombs, through oratory and valedictory, through imprisonment, trial and isolation."[96] James T. Laney of Emory University told Mandela: "Here in Atlanta, where, more than a hundred and twenty-five years ago, an old way of life burned to the ground and a new way rose from the ashes, and where Martin Luther King Jr. first began to dream, you walk among us as a reminder of the best that we have sought, and of the good we still hope to achieve."[97]

Tributes equally significant and powerful were offered by top administrators from universities located in other parts of the United States. Jimmy R. Jenkins, the chancellor at Elizabeth City State University in North Carolina, declared that "the triad of Nelson Rolihlahla Mandela, Martin Luther King Jr., and Morehouse College, symbolize, in a very special way, the fight for freedom and the right to pursue a good and productive life by all people."[98] Robert E. Glennen, of Emporia State University in Kansas, praised Mandela as an example of the indomitability of the human spirit, noting that "the courage and leadership you have shown in the tradition of such charismatic leaders as Gandhi, Martin Luther King, and John Kennedy make it indeed an honor to greet you during your United States Freedom Tour."[99] In yet another expression of admiration and respect, Edmond L. Volpe, president of the College of Staten Island, highlighted Mandela's importance for all oppressed people. "Sustained by your profound commitment to Third World liberation by your wife, your friends, and your comrades," Volpe asserted, "you have followed the path of Moses and join Martin Luther King, Andrei Sakharov, and Lech Walesa, all leaders in the global walk to freedom that may prove to be the glory of this age."[100] John W. Shumaker, of Central Connecticut State University, ended the tributes on a dynamic note, likening Mandela's importance to oppressed South Africans to what a long line of black leaders mean to the struggle in America:

> You personify in your native southern Africa what a great many African Americans from Benjamin Banneker, Richard Allen, and Paul Cuffee in the eighteenth century, through Frederick Douglass, Sojourner Truth, and Harriet Tubman in the nineteenth, and Booker T. Washington, Mary McLeod Bethune, and the ever present W. E. B. Du Bois in the early twentieth century, to such leaders of our own generation as Martin Luther King Jr., Malcolm X, and Jesse Jackson have epitomized in the United States: struggle, principle, candor, insistence upon freedom now, and valiant heroism.[101]

Nelson Mandela's 1990 Freedom Tour led blacks and whites throughout the United States to think more seriously about the continuing relevance of King and the civil rights movement for the South African freedom struggle. Black preachers and politicians became more conscious of the need to promote King's dream for South Africa through education and various means of protest. In March 1992, Wyatt Tee Walker, a former King associate and leader of the Religious Action Network (RAN), joined numerous RAN congregations in a new anti-apartheid crusade. Convinced that African American churches had a special role to play in the crusade, they collected keys and presented them to the South African embassy and consulates all over the United States, "demanding that the South African government unlock apartheid jails and stop the violence." On April 4, 1992, the twenty-fourth anniversary of the King assassination, the Seattle Council of Churches in Seattle, Washington, launched a "Stop Apartheid Violence" campaign with a candlelight vigil at the Martin Luther King Jr. memorial monument in that city. On that same day, other events occurred that evoked King's memory in relation to South Africa. In Kansas, the Dr. Martin Luther King Jr. Memorial Committee, comprised of local churches and political organizations, staged a "Stop Apartheid Violence" campaign. In Tennessee, the Mid-South Center for Peace and Justice expressed its opposition to apartheid with a candlelight vigil at the newly opened Martin

Luther King Jr. memorial monument, located at the former Lorraine Motel in Memphis, the site of the King assassination.[102] For those involved in such events, King and the African American freedom struggle afforded a direct model for black liberation from apartheid.

Mandela's return to America in the summer of 1993 sparked events of a similar nature. At the National Association for the Advancement of Colored People's (NAACP) annual convention in Indianapolis, Mandela spoke once again of the ties between blacks in South Africa and the United States. "We stand here not as people from another land, but as part of you," he shouted, "part of the great family of Black people that is to be found in many parts of the world."[103] Memories of King pervaded the convention hall as the cries and songs of freedom burst forth like the mighty waves of an ocean. Upon receiving the W. E. B. Du Bois International Award from Benjamin F. Chavis, the NAACP's executive director, Mandela spoke in glowing terms of "our common struggle for emancipation."[104] Chavis responded with references to the symbolic importance of an ANC president joining the NAACP convention. His comments on the challenges confronting both black Americans and black South Africans reminded many of remarks made at the 1992 convention by Benjamin L. Hooks, his predecessor, who described "Martin Luther King Jr. and Nelson Mandela" as "genuine heroes of the long, long struggle for freedom."[105]

Promises of closer working relationships between blacks in America and South Africa resulted from Mandela's conversations with Chavis and other African American leaders in the early nineties. Leon Sullivan called for new business commitments to South Africa, noting especially the opportunities for black investment.[106] In late 1993, U.S. Secretary of Commerce Ron Brown, Representative Charles Rangel, and five black businessmen went to South Africa to explore business and investment opportunities for African Americans.[107] Missions of this kind continued into early 1994, as African American leaders combined their exploratory ventures with fund-raising efforts and other campaigns designed to prepare South Africa for her first all-races elections.[108] Especially notable was the South African tour of Representative John Lewis, who had marched with King in the American South. Like King, Lewis compared the struggle in South Africa to the civil rights movement, declaring that the day would soon come when apartheid would surrender to true democracy.[109]

The developing alliances between black Americans and black South Africans moved from the premise that the fundamental differences in their two situations were not as significant as the common experiences that so-lidified them. Black South Africans who visited the United States in the early nineties knew that African Americans were still victims of the same white supremacy that afflicted peoples of color in their own country. Joseph Leshaba, who spent a summer as an intern to Richmond, Virginia, city manager Robert Bobb, insisted in 1992 that the racial situation in the United States was essentially no different from that in his native South Africa, a point difficult to contest in light of the tensions surrounding the Rodney King beating and the plans of white supremacists to bomb black churches and kill black leaders. "There is still apartheid here, as far as I'm concerned," Leshaba observed. "Maybe they're just calling it by another name."[110]

While in Philadelphia in 1993, Nelson Mandela spoke in a similar vein, maintaining that "even in America, Black people are not yet treated as equals." With this understanding, Mandela sensed that black majority rule in South Africa, once established, would have important implications for the course of black freedom in the United States.[111] African American leaders such as Benjamin Chavis and Charles Rangel fully agreed, a position that explains Rangel's insistence on "the expansion of strong cultural ties" between blacks in the United States and South Africa.[112] In 1993, both Chavis and Rangel spoke of the relationship between African Americans and black South Africans in ways strikingly suggestive of King, who speculated in the 1960s, when the end of the apartheid regime appeared only a distant dream, that black liberation and empowerment in South Africa could become one of the greatest single international influences on his people in America.

King and the First Black Majority Government in South Africa

With its first free all-races elections, held in April 1994, South Africa moved a step closer to what Martin Luther King Jr. termed the beloved community. Nelson Mandela became the country's first black president, with approximately 62.6 percent of the vote, and his ANC won 252 of the 400 seats in parliament.[113] Major newspapers worldwide carried the story in bold headlines, with one stating, with some exaggeration, that "Mandela Is Named President, Closing the Era of Apartheid."[114] A central figure in the elections, Mandela was characterized as "an almost godlike Moses-figure leading his people from prison to the non-racial democratic promised land."[115] According to one observer, "A banner of Martin Luther

King Jr. bobbed amid the sea of Mandela posters and Mandela Umbrellas and Afro-picks and badges that the crowd carried in screaming, 'Nelson! Nelson!'" "We are free today! We are free today!" cried Desmond Tutu, the long-time anti-apartheid activist whom many still compared to King.[116]

The dramatic reports of victory, the shouts of joy, and the expressions of hope were punctuated by singing and dancing, with one art form propelling the other in a fashion markedly *African*. Chanted resistance and liberation songs "swelled spontaneously" in homes, public buildings, and on trains, and some black South Africans were seen "leaping, scuttling and backsliding into a pounding version of 'Hold On, Boys,' a work-song for barracks laborers near the breaking point, a song intended to snatch courage from intimidation."[117] With African Americans present for the announcement of the historic triumph, some sang "We Have Overcome," reviving thoughts of the spiritual energy that undergirded King and his people's struggle in America. Foot-stomping dances known as toyi-toyi occurred for hours, dances that black South Africans had "turned into a swarming political art form in defeating racist oppression."[118] Nelson Mandela and Coretta Scott King, in the words of one reporter, "danced the night away."[119] The whole scene, wrote James M. Wall, testified to Martin Luther King Jr.'s claim that "no lie can live forever":

> Let the election of Nelson Mandela as prime minister of South Africa stand as dramatic testimony that, in the phrase often used by Martin Luther King Jr., "truth crushed to earth shall rise again." Suffering and falsehood prevail in Bosnia, Israel/Palestine, Haiti and elsewhere, but South Africa demonstrates that, while it may take a while, truth shall rise again.[120]

The triumph of Mandela and the ANC came only after they had encountered stern opposition from anti-election militants, a development quite in line with King's view that growth and change come through struggle.[121] As late as March 1994, Mangosuthu Gatsha Buthelezi's Inkatha Freedom Party, a coalition of Afrikaner nationalist groups, and the government of the Bophuthatswana homeland threatened to boycott and challenge the elections. These three elements' insistence on a great degree of regional autonomy conflicted in important ways with Mandela's and the ANC's vision of a united and democratic South Africa. By early April 1994, Inkatha and Bophuthatswana, due to negotiations and a desire not to be completely isolated from the new South African government, had ended their opposition to the elections.[122] Many Afrikaner nationalists united under General Constand Viljoen, agreed to participate in the process, and vowed to become the third largest party in the new parliament, a position from which they hoped to advance their ideal of a separate Afrikaner state.[123] A few Afrikaners grew increasingly alienated from and opposed to the process, responding to Mandela's call for peaceful, nonracial elections with threats of violence. These Afrikaner extremists carried out a wave of bombings that killed twenty-one on the eve of the elections.[124] The ANC's struggle to circumvent the tactics of anti-election militants afforded a classic example of how, in the words of King, "the emergence of the new" always confronts "the recalcitrance of the old."[125]

Efforts to sabotage South Africa's 1994 elections ultimately surrendered to a spirit of negotiation and coalition building. Delegations from numerous political parties met at various times to hammer out a process of nonracial elections. Voter education offices were set up throughout South Africa, and grass-roots, door-to-door campaigns to encourage voter participation were launched.[126] The ANC's efforts along these lines received considerable moral and financial support from the NAACP, the Southern Christian Leadership Conference (SCLC), and the Martin Luther King Jr. Center, thus bringing to mind a tradition of association and working relationships that became well established in the joint anti-apartheid campaigns of King and Albert Luthuli. Beginning in September 1993, representatives of the NAACP made six trips to South Africa to assist the ANC in the transition to full democratic rule.[127] The leaders of the NAACP and other civil rights organizations felt a moral as well as a practical responsibility to keep African Americans involved in developments in South Africa, a feeling expressed by W. E. B. Du Bois and Paul Robeson before King articulated it in the most sophisticated terms.

Nelson Mandela's victory speech, delivered May 9, 1994, pictured a South Africa in search of a new identity. After declaring "in the spirit of Dr. Martin Luther King Jr. that South Africa was 'free at last,'" he raised the image of a South Africa built around the values and resources of the masses.[128] "We are beginning a new era," Mandela proclaimed. "We are moving from an era of pessimism and division to an era of hope and unity."[129] In his inaugural speech, given on May 10, 1994, Mandela reaffirmed this vision as he presented a part of his blueprint for a new multiracial South Africa before a crowd that included over forty heads of state, some of whom, like Vice President Albert Gore, spoke proudly of the relationship between the African American and black South African struggles.

"The time for the healing of the wounds has come," Mandela said. "The moment to bridge the chasms that divide us has come." These words struck a responsive chord in the hearts of Coretta Scott King, Bernice King, and Martin Luther King III, family members of the slain civil rights leader, who "were on hand to see King's dream come true in South Africa." As the enthusiasm of the 140,000 spectators reached fever pitch, with African American and black South African freedom songs rising and falling in perfect harmony, Mandela went on to describe the ideal society for which all South Africans of goodwill would strive, a society embodying all the dimensions of what King would call the beloved community:

> We pledge ourselves to liberate all our people from the continuing bondage of poverty, deprivation, suffering, gender and other discrimination. We succeeded to take our last steps to freedom in conditions of relative peace. We commit ourselves to the construction of a complete, just and lasting peace.[130]

It is generally accepted that the April 1994 elections "strengthened the culture of negotiation and reconciliation" in South Africa.[131] This became most evident in Mandela's shaping of a "power sharing Government of National Unity." Consolidated a day after Mandela's inauguration, this government included even former rivals like F. W. de Klerk (second deputy president) and Gatsha Buthelezi (deputy minister of home affairs), and women activists such as Winnie Mandela (Deputy Minister of Arts, Culture, Science & Technology).[132] Mandela's 27-member cabinet—in which the ANC holds eighteen seats, the National Party six, and Inkatha three—has been called "a loveless marriage of convenience" since "there is no democratic alternative."[133] The new South African government most certainly reflects what Martin Luther King Jr. and Albert Luthuli had in mind when they, and numerous anti-apartheid activists before and after them, spoke of nonracial democratic rule. However much this Government of National Unity resembles King's idea of the beloved community, it is believed, at the same time, that its "eclectic, even explosive mix of personalities, backgrounds and styles" will "challenge Mr. Mandela's promise to govern by consensus."[134]

But Mandela's determination to maintain a unified government that inspires "a businesslike vision of common national purpose" is as strong as that King displayed in his push for genuine participatory democracy in America. In his first "State of the Nation" speech, delivered May 24, 1994,

Mandela called for "a people-centered society," declaring that "the burden of the past lies heavily on all of us, including those responsible for inflicting injury and those who suffered." Mandela insisted on the advancement of a "new tolerance" that would end even the use of racial epithets, which means that blacks should no longer be referred to as "kaffir" and whites as "baas."[135]

The new black majority government will undoubtedly increase the possibility for the kind of working relationships between Americans and South Africans that King hoped for and promoted. This should happen particularly in the case of African Americans and black South Africans, who consciously share a kinship that goes beyond their African ancestry. Even before the new government was elected, African Americans began to move to South Africa. Responding to "an open-door invitation to be a part of the new South Africa," African Americans—such as the businessman Leyland Hazelwood and Phyllis Crockett, a former White House reporter for National Public Radio—have already set up residence in South Africa. Mandela challenged African Americans early in 1994 "to come home," to "help us rebuild," and to "come to your country and reclaim it." Acknowledging that "American blacks have given much to the liberation of South Africa," Walter Sisulu, the 82-year-old deputy president of the ANC, echoed Mandela's invitation, noting that "I should be the first to welcome" them.[136] A new South Africa, drawing on the resources and talents of African Americans and black South Africans, will add much to the fulfillment of King's dream for humanity. However, if the continuous flow of African Americans into South Africa causes tensions between them and peoples of color in that land, who are still pushing for equality of opportunity, King's dream will encounter frustrations and challenges heretofore unimagined.

CHAPTER 6

SOARING ON THE WINGS OF PRIDE
King and the Future of South Africa

I look at a bird and I see myself; a native South African soaring above the injustices of apartheid on wings of pride, the pride of a beautiful people.

Miriam Makeba, 1994[1]

Ensuring equality of genders in the new South Africa will be a tough battle.

Felicia Mabuza-Suttle, 1994[2]

I believe we are well-set on the road to sustainable development of all our people and communities.

Jay Naidoo, 1995[3]

South Africa is widely viewed today as the most important example of how a society might move beyond racial and tribal factionalism to assume a nonracial, relatively egalitarian posture. Terms like "individual freedom," "group rights," "participatory democracy," "power sharing," and "human community" are assuming new meanings among South Africans, and the world community is no longer flooded with daily news reports about the brutal and hegemonic nature of apartheid and white supremacist rule. In short, it appears that Martin Luther King Jr.'s concept of a thoroughly integrated society—a society characterized by mutual acceptance, true intergroup and interpersonal living, and shared power—is no longer an impossible and unrealizable dream for South Africa.[4]

But South Africa is also in a time of crisis. The rumblings of discontent in the Government of National Unity (GNU), ethnic group competition, wide economic disparities, and unresolved gender issues are making the transition to genuine participatory democracy extremely difficult.[5] South Africa is still what one writer once termed "a conflict-torn nation" struggling "to come to terms with itself," and what another has labeled ambivalently "that troubled, promising land."[6] In his recent autobiography, Nelson Mandela, whose policy-making role is quickly overwhelming his image as "the great unifier," spoke of a South Africa still in search of freedom for the oppressor and the oppressed:

> Some say that has now been achieved. But I know that is not the case. The truth is that we are not yet free; we have merely achieved the freedom to be free, the right not to be oppressed. We have not taken the final step of our journey, but the first step on a longer and even more difficult road. For to be free is not merely to cast off one's chains but to live in a way that respects and enhances the freedom of others. The true test of our devotion to freedom is just beginning.[7]

This chapter treats the meaning and significance of Martin Luther King's life and message for South Africans today and in the future. Attempts are made to relate King to questions confronting South Africa's new Government of National Unity, to underscore his significance for the mounting crusade for gender equality in South Africa, and to explain how his ideas can influence South Africa's continuing transformation in the twenty-first century.

King and Questions Confronting the Government of National Unity

South Africa's struggle to become what Nelson Mandela called "a rainbow nation" in search of a new and more genuine communitarian ideal began with its power-sharing Government of National Unity in 1994. The spirits of South Africans ran high as they evoked the names of great African American and black South African freedom fighters, and as they danced to the melodic sounds of songs from the anti-apartheid crusade and the civil rights movement in America.[8] But something has happened in South Africa since that time—something quite profound, but not beyond the limits of human understanding. Celebration has given way to sober reflection, and shouts of optimism have surrendered to the often painful recognition that evil systems do not disappear overnight. "Mandelamania," as it was called in 1994, has waned amidst the growing realization that one man alone cannot perform political and economic miracles in a society long beset by problems too complex for any logical human being to comprehend in simple terms. Because of this state of affairs, South Africans find themselves confronted with serious questions that will require clear and careful answers if their nation is to become, in the words of Martin Luther King Jr., "a society at peace with itself."[9]

The question of how to best maintain a strong Government of National Unity confronts South Africans with great force and urgency. Since its inception, the power-sharing government, which reflects South Africa's racial and ethnic diversity, has been projected as the model for what that nation as a whole should be.[10] But the Government of National Unity remains a "fragile cohesion" with an uncertain future. First, there are black nationalists in South Africa, most notably the Pan-Africanists, who feel that Mandela is pandering to whites, and who believe that the government should function on a straight foundation of black majority rule rather than compromise to include non-black elements.[11] Such sentiments are not likely to vanish. Mandela's only recourse in this situation, given his goals for South Africa, is to keep emphasizing a point that Martin Luther King Jr. consistently made—namely, that black supremacist rule can be as immoral as white supremacist rule.

A second problem involves the Government of National Unity's struggle to adjust to its new role. The African National Congress (ANC) has experienced great difficulty in moving from essentially "a social movement/liberation organization" to "an efficient, electorally geared political party." Some ANC activists prefer to remain a liberation organization to ensure that the government's Reconstruction and Development Programme (RDP) reflects the spirit and concerns of grass-roots supporters.[12] Only in this way, they argue, can the government succeed in promoting affirmative action, collective bargaining, social security, a fair wage scale, and other benefits for those at the bottom of the economic ladder. There is also the view that the ANC, when operating as a liberation organization, can best empower people to exercise their rights and responsibilities in their own localities.[13] The idea of a political party that embraces a strong liberation ethic is consistent with sentiments advanced by King, Mohandas K. Gandhi, and Albert J. Luthuli.

The slow pace of South Africa's transformation is yet another problem facing the Government of National Unity. The quality of life is not shifting in dramatic and positive ways for most black South Africans at the grass-roots level. Grass-roots supporters of the Mandela government "want to see both material benefits" and "some meaningful white atonement for apartheid crimes," and the government's failure to meet their great expectations is causing many to become frustrated and hopeless.[14] The problem is exacerbated by the fact that South Africa's black middle class is growing and benefiting immensely from the recovery. Caught up in the euphoria of having "made it," they no longer share common goals with poor blacks.[15] King was beginning to see the same disturbing trend in America when he was assassinated. Of equal concern is the perception, found increasingly among poor black South Africans, that the Mandela government is protecting the economic interests of whites at the expense of blacks.[16]

The Government of National Unity is discovering daily that it must go beyond what one commentator calls "traditional anti-apartheid approaches" in order to purge South Africa of the racism, economic injustice, sexism, and violence that continue to threaten the well-being and survival of its peoples. The mere existence of a black majority government has not eliminated racist sentiments from the minds of white South Africans, for many of them are now engaging in the politics of denial "to foster a kind of self-assurance that their oppression of blacks has not been all that bad."[17] Ameliorating the economic legacy of apartheid is proving to be equally complicated, thus substantiating Martin Luther King Jr.'s claim that achieving economic justice is always a more complex and costlier undertaking than attaining basic constitutional rights.[18] Economic issues become all the more complicated and difficult to address when related to the problem of gender discrimination, a point that is becoming increasingly clear to South Africa's Government of National Unity.[19] When the problem of violence in South Africa enters the equation, it becomes obvious that the country's problems are too enormous for any government, however powerful and efficient it might be, to correct in a short time frame.

The question of what should be the precise nature of the new South Africa's relationship to the outside world is one of mounting significance. The Government of National Unity's approach to this question will determine in large measure its success in combating the evils of racism, economic injustice, classism, sexism, and violence. King often said that South Africa's quest for internal community and peace would depend largely on the quality of her links with the external world. While recognizing that South Africa needs the economic and moral support of the global community to ultimately become a truly nonracial, economically just, nonsexist, and peaceful society, Nelson Mandela, on the other hand, insists that his country will one day teach the world how true democracy should function. Quoting the late Albert Luthuli, Mandela declared:

> I personally believe that here in South Africa, with all our diversities of color and race, we will show the world a new pattern for democracy. . . . I think that there is a challenge to us in South Africa to set a new example for the world.[20]

In making this statement, Mandela is not oblivious to the political and cultural impact that South African artists and writers have had, and continue to have, on the international community. Following the example of African American artists/ activists like Paul Robeson, Harry Belafonte, Stevie Wonder, and Gil Scott-Heron, black South African "artists such as jazz trumpeter Hugh Masekela, singer Miriam Makeba, pianist Abdullah Ibrahim (also known as Dollar Brand), actor Zakes Mokae, and producer-playwright Mbongeni Ngema" have long "used their time on the stages of the world to keep the plight of black South Africans in the international spotlight."[21] Their "songs and stories of hope and joy," of "pain and struggle," have "expanded the cultural vocabulary" of the world, and have taught people everywhere something profound about the indomitability of the human spirit.[22] The same can be said of South African writers such as Gcina Mhlophe, Mark Mathabane, and Don Mattera, who have been influenced over time by the words and ideas of Gwendolyn Brooks, James Baldwin, Maya Angelou, Claude McKay, Countee Cullen, and a host of other African Americans.[23] This sense of black South Africa's enduring cultural and political impact on the world community, through the performed and literary arts, was entertained by Martin Luther King Jr. as he pondered, on an intellectual plane, those values and virtues that both black South Africans and African Americans could bring to the shaping of a new humanity.[24]

The extent to which the Government of National Unity will be successful in meeting the many challenges it faces is open to debate. Uncertainties abound, as do questions of just how long this power-sharing government will survive. Signs of the unraveling of Mandela's government are already evident, raising new doubts about the Government of National Unity as a microcosm of the kind of ideal society King, Gandhi, and Luthuli envisioned for South Africa. Joe Slovo, the Minister of Housing and Welfare, died in January 1995, leaving a position that will be difficult to fill with someone of his enormous gifts and popularity.[25] In March 1995, Winnie

Mandela, the Deputy Minister of the Arts, Culture, and Science, was fired for insubordination and for sowing discord in the government, a development that is generating new questions among Pan-Africanists, Unionists, and the poor about Mandela's leadership and tolerance of dissent.[26] Mangosuthu Gatsha Buthelezi, the Minister of Home Affairs and head of the Inkatha Freedom Party, is constantly threatening to withdraw from the Government of National Unity, a move that would undoubtedly trigger a resurgence of the conflict and violence that clouded relations between the ANC and Inkatha in the late 1980s and early 1990s.[27]

Such tensions and evidences of instability are typical of what confronts new governments, a point King perceptively advanced in his last book.[28] Nelson Mandela has quickly discovered that the life of the freedom fighter is quite different from that of the government leader. To be sure, he now knows from experience that it is much easier for an outsider to criticize government policies than for an insider to do so. Nothing substantiates this more than Mandela's recent warning against dissenters in his society. "Hit with demands from public workers for better pay, agitation by black police over lingering discrimination, and white protests about black children in their schools," says one political analyst, Mandela recently "leveled his fiercest fusillades at radical politicians, Unionists, and civic leaders who want to squeeze money out of the government with strikes, boycotts, and holding public officials hostage in their offices."[29] Mandela went on to criticize South Africans for "expecting free housing, electricity, and other services," and noted that "a minority who sought disruptions to further their own ends had 'misread freedom to mean license.'"[30] Challenges of this nature, encountered on a daily basis by Mandela, support King's oft-repeated claim that it is always difficult for oppressed people to maintain a proper relationship between freedom and responsibility.

King and the Mounting Crusade for Gender Equality

In a speech delivered after his release from prison in February 1990, Nelson Mandela paid tribute "to the mothers and wives and sisters of our nation," asserting that "you are the rock-hard foundation of our struggle." "Apartheid has inflicted more pain on you than anyone else," he added.[31] In a recent essay, Laura B. Randolph expressed similar sentiments, declaring that she wishes South Africans could tell their daughters that "Mandela's election was the death rattle for sexism as well as racism." "I wish they could tell them," continues Randolph, "that in the South Africa of the twenty-first century, the oppression of women, like the oppression of blacks, will vanish like the hopes of white extremists for three more centuries of white rule."[32] But the election of Mandela and the establishment of the Government of National Unity have not brought an end to gender discrimination, despite the fact that women comprise roughly one fourth of the four hundred–seat National Assembly and a third of the seats in the nine provincial legislatures.[33] Women constitute about 53 percent of South Africa's population, but men clearly control the structures and institutions of the society.[34] In a word, sexism is institutionalized in the laws, customs, and practices of South Africa.[35] The same remains true in the United States as well, some thirty years after Martin Luther King Jr. included women in his vision of the beloved community.

The problem of gender discrimination in the South African context finds expression in various ways. Until recently, laws required South African women to obtain the signature of a man in order to "secure loans, apartments, even telephones."[36] Black South African women represent the poorest segment of society, and they constantly live in fear of being beaten, raped, or violated in other ways. Women who have more children than they can possibly support do not have legal access to abortion when faced with unwanted pregnancies.[37] In the workplace, women are treated like second-class citizens, earning far less than men in almost all occupations that include both sexes. In the home, women are expected to handle the cooking, cleaning, child rearing, and other traditionally female responsibilities.[38] Bridgette Mabandla, a widely known activist now serving in parliament, related the plight of South African women in these terms:

> Most South African women are quite literally barefoot, pregnant, and in the kitchen. We do not control our bodies. We are scarce in leadership positions. We are absent from history books. We are even disallowed from many priesthoods.[39]

Before the 1994 elections, black South African women refused to devote themselves fully to the fight against gender discrimination for essentially two reasons: first, because of the perception that the struggle against racism and white supremacist structures was more important or urgent; second, because of the widespread recognition that the white supremacist system would use issues of gender to further divide and ultimately conquer the black South African community, thereby preserving the structures of apartheid. The same patterns of logic were employed by African

American women in the 1960s, when Martin Luther King Jr. and other male figures dominated the leadership and agenda of the civil rights movement. But the election of Nelson Mandela and the establishment of black majority rule provided the avenue for the forces against sexism to press their claims on an unprecedented level. By the fall of 1994, South African women had presented to the new government "The Women's Charter," a list of demands that they hope will be addressed in the nation's permanent constitution.[40] This matter is still evoking much concern, debate, and discussion in various circles of the Government of National Unity. The election of seventy women among the four hundred lawmakers of South Africa's parliament in 1994 is a hopeful sign, but the full liberation of women will undoubtedly take time. It will be the dominant issue confronting South Africans in the twenty-first century.[41]

There are some differences of opinion about the form that the South African women's movement will take in the future. Felicia Mabuza-Suttle, a television talk-show hostess often called "the Oprah Winfrey of South Africa," believes that only women can launch the struggle. This approach undermines King's, Luthuli's, and Mandela's idea of a collective role, embracing men and women, for the liberation of all. "The struggle for national liberation has long been fought by both men and women," Mabuza-Suttle recently explained. "However, the struggle for the liberation of women will be fought by women—black and white—alone."[42] This view stems from the sense that the Government of National Unity, like the previous apartheid government, still places women in an inferior position.[43] However perceptive this idea of a struggle spearheaded only by black and white women may seem, it does not address the continuing problem of racism that warps the thinking of white women—a problem that could make a unified women's movement to overcome gender discrimination impossible.

Another view, represented by Winnie Mandela, holds that the black South African women's movement must be kept separate from that of white South African women. "Reviled by whites, Asians, and mixed-race-voters" because of "her penchant for race-baiting, she constantly criticizes the Government of National Unity for pandering to whites."[44] Winnie Mandela's notion of a separatist movement for the liberation of black South African women also contradicts views held by King and Luthuli, and more recently by Nelson Mandela, all of whom emphasize a collective role for the "whole people" in the drive for genuine South African freedom. The extent to which Winnie Mandela's ideas regarding women's liberation will materialize is not clear, especially since she is now alienating female supporters in the ANC Women's League, an organization she serves as president, and one that constitutes "a key component of her political base."[45]

Most black South African women feel that the struggle for their liberation should remain a vital part of the total effort to destroy the last vestiges of apartheid. The view here is that any attempt to develop a movement strictly along the lines of gender could undermine continuing efforts to completely eliminate racism, and will inevitably result in even more tensions and divisions between men and women. King's conception of the beloved community suggests that he would wholeheartedly agree with such a perspective.

As the women's movement gains more momentum in South Africa, black women will most likely emerge as its most important leaders. Undoubtedly, most of the movement's vitality will come from black women, who have much to contribute to a viable liberation ethic for all South Africans. South Africans have much to gain, in terms of cultural enrichment and political liberation, from the songs of Miriam Makeba, from the political leadership and insights of Winnie Mandela, Albertina Sisulu, and Lindiwe Mabuza, and from the efforts of Felicia Mabuza-Suttle to encourage meaningful dialogue between the races.[46] However, a movement for further liberation in South Africa, drawing on the experiences and resources of not just black women, but women in general, would reflect more adequately the beloved community ideal as articulated by King.

As was the case in the past, black South African women will continue to find rich resources of thought and feeling in African American women as they shape their dream and struggle. Motlalepula Chabaku, the black South African clergywoman, has consistently spoken to the meaning of persons like Harriet Tubman and Rosa Parks for the struggle of women in her country.[47] Others have referred to the importance of Gwendolyn Brooks and Maya Angelou. Of course, African American women have been deeply influenced and inspired by the struggle of black South African women against apartheid as well.[48] Black women in both countries will undoubtedly continue to influence each other as they attack, in a more consistent and organized fashion, the evils of sexism. Such mutual sharings and exchanges are in line with King's notion of a necessary and positive working relationship between African Americans and South Africans.

The ways in which black womanist theologians and ethicists in America have incorporated King into their analyses of their unique experience and struggle could prove instructive for black South African women. Katie G. Cannon contends that King's moral and conceptual resources are relevant for an ethic of liberation for black women, especially when one considers the implications of his notion of *imago Dei* (divine image), his idea of love as grounded in justice and social change, and his communitarian vision for addressing gender inequities.[49] Jacquelyn Grant and Delores S. Williams have noted the value of King's idea of redemptive suffering as part of the survival ethic of black women, but they feel on the other hand that this idea alone does not provide adequate substance for their liberation.[50] Kelly Brown Douglas suggests that King interpreted the message of Jesus Christ in ways that are liberating and uplifting for black men and women.[51] Cheryl Townsend Gilkes views King as an important intellectual source of the Afrocentric vision of black women like Alice Walker, who has made communal self-love, the vitality of African American culture and history, and unified black struggle central themes in her writing.[52] All of these African American womanists afford insights, based on their reading of King, that can enhance the liberation and wholeness of black South African women.

However, black South African women must read these sources critically, because their experiences and struggles have been in some ways different from those of their African American counterparts.[53] Even as they continue to look to African American women for intellectual, moral, and spiritual support, they will undoubtedly discover their greatest resources in their own historical and cultural experiences. The same applies in instances where African American women are seeking support and inspiration from black South African women. Also, black South African women would do well to approach King's message and moral activism in the same critical and analytical manner as that taken by black South African men such as Desmond Tutu and Allan Boesak. That is to say, they must learn from King while rejecting those parts of his legacy that are inapplicable to the South African context.

No one can predict what the Government of National Unity will do in the future to eliminate the problem of gender discrimination in South Africa. Some South Africans feel that Nelson Mandela's recent firing of Winnie Mandela, "for having been seen as insubordinate to her husband, boss, and president," is an indication that the government will not break cleanly with tradition in its treatment of women.[54] If this is the case, then one of the most tragic aspects of the old apartheid system will continue to diminish the image of South Africa in the eyes of the world. If, on the other hand, Mandela symbolizes what one scholar terms a "nonsexist South Africa," that country will emerge as a beacon of hope.[55] And King *redivivus* would rejoice.

King and South Africa: Today and the Years Ahead

Given the changing state of affairs in South Africa, and the purpose of this study, it is quite proper to discuss those aspects of Martin Luther King Jr.'s life and thought that can be related to the South African context today and in the future. Thus, we ask: Are King's theological and ethical reflections on the meaning, significance, and actualization of human community still relevant for South Africans, especially since apartheid as a legal system no longer exists? Is nonviolence, as understood and practiced by King, the only moral and practical method available to South Africans in their continuing quest for a more just, peaceful, and integrated society? Are King's ideas concerning the moral obligation of the international community toward South Africa still applicable? No serious analysis of King's meaning for South Africa can avoid these questions.

King really believed that the beloved community, "an inclusive and interracial society characterized by 'freedom and justice for all,'" could find fulfillment in South Africa.[56] By all measurable standards, that belief found some vindication in the early 1990s with the dismantling of *de jure* apartheid and the establishment of black majority rule. Many of the barriers to human community have crumbled, and South Africans of all racial and ethnic backgrounds are integrating their talents and resources for the uplift of the total society. While standing on the threshold of a rebirth, South Africa is also facing an unprecedented identity crisis, owing in part to the chasms that still divide its people.[57] That is why King's vision of a community that transcends all artificial human barriers, and yet one in which "the individual soul" is not "shackled by the chains of conformity," will remain pertinent for the South African context in the years ahead.[58]

Nelson Mandela is currently the most important symbol of community in South Africa. His Government of National Unity and Reconciliation is a metaphor for what he envisions for his country as a whole. However, many agree that "a culture of political tolerance will have to be created" before Mandela's brand of power sharing can be effective.[59] Tensions have already surfaced over the firing of Winnie Mandela. Reports suggest that Nelson Mandela and Frederik de Klerk, Second Executive Deputy President, are enemies, and many ANC members remain uncomfortable with the appointment of Gatsha Buthelezi in Home Affairs. Buthelezi, it is believed, could continue to "act as a spoiler" by "pressing for major revisions in the interim constitution, which he regards as 'fundamentally flawed.'" The Inkatha leader has already referred to the "so-called Government of National Unity," leaving "the impression that he is both in the government and yet keeping it at arm's length."[60] Equally disturbing is the fact that General Constand Viljoen, the former chief of the South African Defence Force (SADF) and now leader of the extremist, right-wing Freedom Front, has refused to serve in Mandela's cabinet, a move designed perhaps to appease Afrikaner separatists.[61] If Mandela dies, resigns, or is forced out in the near future, or if he fails to control elements on the right and the left, South Africa's search for reconciliation and community will suffer a severe setback. Martin Luther King Jr.'s image of an organization in which people differ while still uniting around common goals is instructive when approaching problems of this kind.[62]

Despite Mandela's expressed intention to be the president of all South Africans, and to lead in the creation of "a rainbow nation at peace with itself and the world," South Africa remains a highly fragmented society.[63] One of the greatest misconceptions promoted in recent times is that apartheid, in all of its crude dimensions, came to an end with the election of Mandela and the establishment of a black majority government. Such a conclusion erroneously implies that apartheid is merely a legal or governmental system. To the contrary, apartheid is a way of life, a state of mind, and it reflects something very deep in the South African character that has to do with violence, machismo, and color consciousness. King consistently made this point decades ago. There is more than ample proof that the transition from a segregated society to what King called an "integrated society" has not yet occurred.[64] Many Afrikaners, suffering from the same moral and spiritual malady that afflicted white America during and after the King years, still cannot look on a black African as an equal. Moreover, as one observer recently stated, "Whites are scared of black revenge, expropriations of land, heavy taxation, and a declining currency and standard of living," and the racist rhetoric and growing anger of Afrikaner nationalist extremists and separatists could still invite race war.[65]

The complete obliteration of apartheid seems all the more uncertain when one considers the immense degree to which white racism continues to intrude on the psyche of other racial groups in South Africa. Bombarded with positive images of whiteness and extremely negative depictions of blackness over time, many blacks unconsciously resent themselves and others who share their skin color. Many Coloreds still view light skin as a status symbol and dark skin as a stigma, and "they look down on blacks" and are threatened by black numerical superiority.[66] The fact that Coloreds and Asians received more privileges than blacks under the old system of *de jure* apartheid is not likely to be soon forgotten in the African community.

Because color discrimination among the oppressed was not foreign to King's struggle in America, his theory of human dignity is relevant for South Africans who are determined to eliminate every vestige of racism. King held that all humans are made in the divine image, are subject to Christ's universal love, and are therefore creatures with dignity and worth.[67] Consequently, racism or color discrimination in any form is tainted with sin and can only diminish humanity in general. By combining a selective use of King's thought with the most enlightened conceptions of personhood from their own traditions, South Africans, as has been the case with Allan Boesak and Desmond Tutu, might formulate the kind of personalistic philosophy necessary for active and unconditional participation in the building of community. As they pursue this task, they will inevitably confront the same question King faced in promoting interracial harmony and coalitions in the United States; namely, how racial and ethnic pluralism can be preserved and respected even as people engage in the shaping of the beloved community.

King's thought also has something to offer in the struggle to overcome the most divisive aspects of tribalism. Tribalism continues as one of the cornerstones of the apartheid system. "However artificial in their origins," writes George M. Fredrickson, "tribal loyalties are nevertheless important for many Africans," and the ANC's failure "to plan for their containment" will only ensure lasting instability.[68] King maintained that the individual spirit should never be so "bound by the manacles of party allegiance" that one finds it impossible to live on terms of harmony and peace with those of other party affiliations. He saw humans as social beings created to live in community, as persons who are by nature related to and dependent on one another. Put another way, humans are not completely self-sufficient, but, rather, social beings who find authentic existence and fulfillment through social contact and social relations under the guidance of a personal God who works for universal wholeness.[69] The future of *de facto* apartheid hinges to a considerable degree on how well this lesson is learned by the Zulus, the Xhosas, and other tribal groups in South Africa.

The same applies in reference to the problem of sexism. Doing theology and ethics in dialogue with King, around the beloved community concept, can be helpful in clarifying and resolving the issue of female subordination, despite the fact that the civil rights leader failed to adequately emphasize the unique experiences of women under oppression and the need for their liberation. In this regard, and in the case of racism and tribalism as well, King's principle of the social nature of human existence also provides a basis for reflection. Moving from the premise that "all life is interrelated," King knew that men can never be what they ought to be until women are what they should be. His insights into the essential oneness of humanity under a loving and rational God are useful for a healthy and constructive critique of sexism in the South African context.[70]

Economic inequality and poverty remain as perhaps the most visible manifestation of the apartheid legacy. Millions of people of color in South Africa are still impoverished and landless, wasting away in the townships, squatter camps, and informal settlements. "Their living conditions," according to one estimate in early 1994, "are the worst in the world."[71] Millions live in tin and cardboard shacks without clean drinking water, electricity, and adequate sanitation. Forty-five percent of South Africa's blacks are jobless, and the unemployment rate exceeds 50 percent for young township dwellers. Many with jobs endure extremely poor working conditions and low salaries, calling to mind the situation King encountered in the context of southern Jim Crowism. The per capita income for whites is currently 9.5 times that of blacks. About 60,000 white farmers control 87 percent of the land. Moreover, the state of black education is worse than anything imaginable in the modern world. A black South African child has a better chance of dying before age five than of completing high school, and some 50 percent of the country's 30 million blacks are illiterate.[72] "Alleviating the stark disparities between South Africa's 30.8 million Black, Asian and mixed-race people and the country's 7 million Whites," a commentator wrote in the summer of 1994, "is both a moral and political imperative for the ANC."[73] Dealing with such disparities will not be impossible if Mandela's government truly understands, as King did

Albert J. Luthuli, the last nonviolent leader of the ANC, communicated with Martin Luther King Jr. in the 1950s. Photo courtesy of George M. Houser.

Walter Sisulu, Secretary-General of the ANC, at his home in 1954. Photo courtesy of George M. Houser.

E. S. Reddy, the Principal Secretary of the U.N. Special Committee on the Policies of Apartheid of the Government of the Republic of South Africa, sought King's testimony against apartheid in 1963. Photo courtesy of E. S. Reddy.

Donald Harrington, one of t organizers of AFSAR, which 1953 became the ACOA. Ph courtesy of Donald Harringt

Kenneth Kaunda, a future leader of southern Africa, on a speaking tour in the United States, April 1960. Photo courtesy of George M. Houser.

Dorothy I. Height, president of the NCNW, and the only African American woman who associated with King and other major civil rights leaders at the highest level of the ANLCA in the 1960s. Photo courtesy of the National Council of Negro Women.

Dennis Brutus, the South African leader and exile, solicited King's support for South African political prisoners in 1967. Photo courtesy of Dennis Brutus.

Peter Mansfield, a president of the NUSAS, sought King's services as a lecturer on behalf of the NUSAS in the 1960s. Photo courtesy of Peter Mansfield.

Ian Robertson, another NUSAS president who also exchanged letters with King in the 1960s. Photo courtesy of Ian Robertson.

Desmond Tutu, the Anglican bishop and Nobel Peace Prize recipient, reflected King's influence in South Africa in the 1970s. Photo courtesy of Jann Cather Weaver/UCC Office of Communication.

Soweto priest Buti Tlhagale, who wrote that King's "peace at all costs doctrine" was not borne out by the black South African experience. Photo used by permission of Mzi Oliphant.

Allan Boesak, the Reformed minister and South African leader, whom some regarded as "a disciple of King" in the 1970s. Photo courtesy of Maryknoll Missioners.

Nelson Mandela in South Africa in June 1990, four months after his release from prison. Pictured with Michael Geffrard, member of Mayor David Dinkins's trade mission to prepare New York businesses for post-apartheid relations. Photo courtesy of Eddie Mae Jones.

a generation ago, that economic injustice, like racism, tribalism, and sexism, is as much a theological problem as it is a moral and political issue. South Africa cannot afford to enter the twenty-first century with glaring economic disparities among its people. The message echoing through the life of King is that a few South Africans cannot remain rich and profitable while most languish in grinding poverty, especially if the beloved community is to become real.

Rebuilding South Africa's infrastructure is now the challenge. Economists estimate that the cost of such an endeavor will exceed $20 billion over the next five years, $9 billion more than the amount already targeted by the ANC's Reconstruction and Development Programme for that same period.[74] But the challenge goes beyond the possible cost of nation building. An equally formidable challenge rests in meeting the high expectations of black South Africans, who, after decades of social and economic oppression, are most impatient for improvements in their quality of life, despite the significant constraints on what can actually be achieved in the near future. This is not likely to change, even as Mandela, faced with the realities of government, calls for patience and understanding.[75] As King always said, the word "wait" rings in the ears of the destitute with piercing familiarity, and those who fail to make equality a reality risk the inevitability of revolution.

Yet another challenge exists in the fear and reservations of whites, who have been assured by Mandela that black power will not mean radical changes in their standard of living. The likelihood of Mandela keeping such a promise is minimal, because land reform and redistribution and other meaningful programs of reform for blacks, Coloreds, and Asians cannot be implemented apart from a decline in the social and economic status of whites. Despite his claim that "There is no need whatsoever for us not to be able to raise the position of Africans, Coloureds, and Indians to the same level as Whites," Mandela faces a dilemma not entirely unlike that experienced by Martin Luther King Jr. and other civil rights proponents in America; namely, how to address the distinctive needs of people of color while meeting demands for peaceful coexistence between all racial and ethnic groups.[76] Such dual allegiances, as King's own life testifies, are at the same time inevitable and difficult to maintain, especially given the potential for racial misunderstanding and fragmentation.

Questions linger in the minds of many about the wisdom of Nelson Mandela's approach to social and economic change. He has already vowed to avoid "permanent" new taxes, to control inflation, to lower the government deficit and interest rates, to maintain a stable currency, to court investment, and to promote growth.[77] He supports free health care, nutritional programs, and education for needy children, and is now developing electrification and public works projects to create jobs and to clean up black townships. Where once Mandela sounded like King in calling for basic structural changes in South Africa's capitalistic system, he has not engaged in a radical redistribution of the country's wealth through high taxes and the confiscation of white-owned properties, feeling that such programs will result in the flight of white capital, the exodus of skilled whites, and the discouragement of foreign investment.[78] Political realities have convinced Mandela of the need "to make compromises with capitalism as much as with democratic socialism."[79] Mandela and the ANC have been forced "to undergo an intellectually wrenching and politically precarious evolution away from" their "socialist roots and toward a more market approach to economic development," according to one report, much to the disgust of the "rank-and-file South African."[80]

Although Mandela promised that he would not operate entirely within the structures already in place, some black South Africans feel that he is being co-opted by establishment politics. Many grass-roots blacks are discovering that they no longer have access to him. Still others raise questions about his plans for land redistribution. If the Mandela government fails to create a new South Africa, it will lose political support to the more militant elements in society, who feel that a radical restructuring of the system, not cosmetic reform, is needed. Be that as it may, Mandela feels that well-developed and carefully calculated programs of reform are the best route to a South Africa free of political turmoil, economic calamity, and ethnic strife.[81] At the same time, he has shown an openness to compromise and some tolerance for the right of citizens to criticize any reforms that they deem unjust. Mandela's choice of a democratic government that gives priority to the needs and security of all citizens, and that allows the people the *right* to protest for *right* within reasonable limits, easily squares with the type of political system advocated by Martin Luther King Jr. for both South Africa and the United States.

As South Africa strives for the kind of broad racial cooperation that can lead to the economic well-being of all her citizens, she will need the assistance of the world community in terms of investment and trade. Mandela has already appealed to "important players in the world economy," encouraging them to consider South Africa as "an attractive destination for the enormous capital resources held by the institutions you represent."[82] Some firms that previously severed ties with South Africa are now returning, but chronic violence, labor unrest, political uncertainties, and feelings of uneasiness about Mandela's economic policies are making "many companies reluctant to invest." Nothing is more consistent with King's dream than America's pledge to help restore South Africa's economic stability in a multiracial environment. Vice President Albert Gore, imbued with the spirit of multiparty democracy he witnessed at Mandela's inauguration, responded well to calls for a "Marshall Plan" for Africa. Now that sanctions have been lifted, a United States aid package of approximately $160 million is available to South Africa.[83] If U.S. aid is administered as a surreptitious means to control South Africa, rather than out of a spirit of genuine reconciliation and hope, it will violate the kind of wholesome and mutually beneficial relationship that King envisioned for the two countries. U.S. assistance to South Africa must ultimately be oriented toward building what President Bill Clinton defines as "a broader and deeper relationship between our country and all of Africa."[84] Nothing short of this will suffice, considering the realities of the post–cold war world. As King believed in his time, and as leaders like Jesse Jackson feel today, African Americans will become key players in establishing and maintaining the integrity of any economic relationship between the United States and South Africa.[85]

There is considerable discussion in ecclesial circles about what should be "the role of the church and the nature of Christian witness" in South Africa's future. As John W. de Gruchy recently observed, "newly emerging realities" in South Africa "have begun to reshape the character of the church struggle in terms of the responsibility of the church in the process of the transition to democracy."[86] The dominant task now confronting the church and religion is overcoming *de facto* apartheid and the bitter legacy of *de jure* apartheid. This is why Martin Luther King Jr.'s idea of a socially and politically involved church, and yet one that is sustained by its vital liturgical life and experiences of personal piety, remains so relevant for South Africans. King believed that Christianity, and any religion for that matter, should change the hearts of people, thus ridding them of fear, deception, hatred, greed, and other negative internal attitudes that prevent genuine community. Here lies a special challenge for black Christians, who constitute the majority in South Africa's churches, and who have led in keeping alive that *Christian hope*—that sense that the liberating plans of God will find fulfillment. On another level, Linda E. Thomas explains how African indigenous churches might continue to serve as "a cultural system of political resistance" by keeping alive the relationship between spirituality and social transformation, and by criticizing, reshaping, and redefining the rituals and symbols long imposed upon them by an oppressive white Western missionary Christianity.[87] If King's thought is to be taken as a guide, then all Christians, Muslims, Jews, African traditionalists, and those of other religious persuasions have an obligation to empower South Africans spiritually and morally for the kind of transformation that results in reconciliation, patriotic cooperation, and genuine interpersonal and intergroup living.

What King wrote and said about education can also be related to South Africa's future development. King believed that education, like religion, is needed to change bad attitudes that keep people from living a communal and prosperous existence. He referred to education as "a most vital and indispensable element," and noted that revolution must be brought into the educational system before it can be successful in the social, political, and economic arenas of a society.[88] Having essentially the same view of education, President Nelson Mandela said in June 1994, on the eighteenth anniversary of the Soweto uprising, that "the government is convinced that among the first challenges that we need to address is to inculcate the culture of learning and teaching in all schools."[89] Black South Africans who previously knew overcrowded classrooms, undertrained teachers, and a shortage of textbooks and other resources are now flocking to classrooms to attain the skills needed to assume leadership roles in a new and more inclusive South Africa.[90] Educators report that "a culture of learning" is "starting to displace the culture of resistance."[91]

The ANC's idea of an educational process that prepares people "not only for work but to take part in a democratic system" clearly coincides with ideas expressed by King as he considered the tragic effects of ignorance in both the American South and South Africa.[92] King felt that through proper educational methods, individuals could come to a healthy sense of their own essence as social beings who find authentic existence through relations with others. His insistence on the brand of education that makes people think critically and creatively, and that forces them to keep an open and analytical mind in the search for truth, has meaning and significance for all South Africans as they seek to overcome that maze of myths and stereotypes that have long separated them along the lines of race, tribe, class, and gender.[93] Like whites and African Americans under southern Jim Crow, generations of South Africans have been victimized by a blatant and vicious system of miseducation. Only through a powerful system of re-education can they, in the words of King, recognize the "basic fact of the interrelated structure of all reality."[94] This process of re-education has already developed to some extent under the Mandela government. Today, more black children have an opportunity to learn in an atmosphere that fosters acceptance, understanding, self-worth, and tolerance for human differences.

"Democratic access to education" is presenting a special challenge for black South Africans, who are developing a new sense of themselves, their place in society, and their destiny. Much of this challenge involves studying, coming to terms with, and preserving their history and culture, one that King put before his people in the American South.[95] Unfortunately, history "is fast disappearing as the rush to embrace a new order threatens to erase the last physical evidence of South Africa's apartheid past." Humiliating public signs that once designated separate entrances for whites and people of color have been taken down or painted over, passes carried by blacks as a badge of identity have been burned, "hovels in camps once occupied by black laborers have been razed or refurbished," and "historians worry that documents and other artifacts of oppression will be lost or destroyed, along with the country's collective memory."[96]

From the standpoint of culture, witchcraft, the presence of witch doctors, the practice of tribal justice, and other traditions are being threatened as Western influences impinge on the educational process.[97] The threats to history and culture are compounded by young blacks' "disdain for the stories of their elders."[98] If education leads black South Africans to look only to the white West for cues on how to think, communicate, and behave, instead of taking on roles that truly reflect their African heritage, they will destroy themselves. King suggested the same to his people in America, and his concept of freedom and dignity, gained through an appreciation of one's past, is applicable for black South Africans who wish to make the fullest possible use of new educational opportunities.[99] To a much greater extent than was the case with African Americans during the King years, black South Africans are compelled, through the mediums of education and government, "to combine traditional African culture and modern democracy."[100]

King's emphasis on the importance of legislation and court action in regulating the behavior of those who stand against peace and community is as relevant for South Africans as his views on religion and education. King consistently argued that a vital part of any people's struggle for freedom and wholeness, indeed for the beloved community, must necessarily come "through legalism and legislation." "The law may not change the heart," he once wrote, "but it can restrain the heartless."[101] In the past, the law was used in South Africa to oppress blacks and to erect physical barriers to interracial community. Now that a black majority government is in place, legislation and court action can be employed to ensure the greatest possible measure of justice, peace, and harmony. The question of legal means must be considered in any analysis of the relationship of King's moral vision and ethical perspective to issues facing South Africans in the years ahead.

The same can be said in reference to South Africa's current and future efforts to deal with its "explosive history of racial, ethnic, and tribal violence." The question remains: "Can an infant democracy heal the searing wounds 'of a violent past' and 'bind up all the diverse people of South Africa?'"[102] To be sure, tribal violence and racial murders have declined significantly, but will this pattern continue? As late as July 1994, ANC and Inkatha backers were killing each other in the troubled township of Tokoza.[103] Right-wing extremists, uncertain about the future of the Afrikaner, still pose a violent threat for the new government. In a culture stained by a history of both political and criminal violence, such concerns remain paramount. They are exacerbated by South Africa's recent move to design sophisticated nuclear weapons.[104] The church leader Allan Boesak recently commented, in terms that recall Martin Luther King Jr., that "my immediate concern about the future lies in the question of violence."[105]

But there are hopeful signs. Since the transition began in 1990, courses on peace making have been taught in South African schools. Students are developing a fundamental belief in the sacredness of life, even when that life is cloaked in blackness.[106] On another level, steps are being taken by the Mandela government to convert what was once the most brutal police force in the world into one that respects, serves, and protects all South African citizens. Such efforts should reap positive benefits as more blacks and women join the South African Police Service. The issue of reparations for those most victimized by Gestapo-type police tactics, and by apartheid in general, is also a topic of discussion and reflection in academic circles. The ideas of King, Gandhi, and Luthuli are still central in this process. Equally important is the fact that amnesty legislation has been enacted, pardoning thousands of former political prisoners and members of the ANC's military wing. Amnesty is also being considered in the case of those "who committed offenses in defense of apartheid," a move that will long be controversial.[107] Even so, South Africa's attempts to transform its violent culture points to a brighter future for the region, not only for South Africans themselves, but for neighboring states that were for so long victims of "an unholy alliance between apartheid and the Western democracies."[108]

The beloved community as defined by King will not easily be achieved in South Africa. But the potential is still there, especially given the propensity of Africans for community-based societies. The *land* question and the redistribution of the nation's wealth across racial, ethnic, and tribal boundaries remain an obstacle to the full realization of the beloved community ideal. If blacks continue to hold political power without sufficient land and economic power, South Africa will become a *microcosm of Americanism*. If some Afrikaner extremists and black tribal groups press for voluntary geographic separation in the future, *de facto* apartheid will merely continue while assuming yet another form. If strong, consistent efforts are not devoted to ending bigotry, South African racism could become as sophisticated and insidious as American racism, thus reviving the potential for intense civil conflict. On the other hand, if South Africans build upon common denominators, and succeed in wresting peace and community out of the throes of violence and fragmentation, they will become a beacon of economic and political prosperity for all of southern Africa. Indeed, South Africa will become a model for the world, and especially for the United States, a nation still haunted by racial strife and economic injustice despite the sacrifices made by Martin Luther King Jr. and others.

The future of South Africa will be shaped by the values and talents of all her citizens. It will be shaped by white extremists who remain victims of their own lethal folly, by well-meaning white liberals and moderates, by Asians and Coloreds who have not lost touch with their own best instincts, by black men and women who know the deepest pain of apartheid, and by black youths who are imbued with what Nelson Mandela once called "the spirit of no surrender."[109] But the task of achieving a new and more genuine human ideal in the South African context rests more with those who know the true meaning of oppression. Only they can, in the spirit of Martin Luther King Jr. and in the words of an old South African freedom song, "show us the way to freedom."

NOTES

Introduction

1. "Martin Luther King Jr. and Mahatma Gandhi," *Negro History Bulletin,* vol. XXI (May 1968): 4–5; "Martyrdom Comes to America's Moral Leader," *Christian Century,* vol. LXXXV (17 April 1968): 475; Adam Fairclough, *To Redeem the Soul of America: The Southern Christian Leadership Conference and Martin Luther King Jr.* (Athens: University of Georgia Press, 1987): 1–405; and Richard Lentz, *Symbols, the News Magazines, and Martin Luther King Jr.* (Baton Rouge: Louisiana State University Press, 1990), 1–342. King's importance as a world leader and symbol was clearly reflected in his approach to world problems as both a writer and activist. See Martin Luther King Jr., *Where Do We Go from Here?: Chaos or Community* (Boston: Beacon Press, 1968), 167–91; King, *The Trumpet of Conscience* (San Francisco: Harper and Row, 1967), 21–78; and William R. Miller, "The Broadening Horizons: Montgomery, America, the World," in C. Eric Lincoln, ed., *Martin Luther King Jr.: A Profile* (New York: Hill and Wang, 1970), 40–71. For the most extensive treatment of King in relation to the global context, see Lewis V. Baldwin, *To Make the Wounded Whole: The Cultural Legacy of Martin Luther King Jr.* (Minneapolis: Fortress Press, 1992), 163–313.

2. This subject is largely neglected even in important articles such as Milfred C. Fierce, "Selected Black American Leaders and Organizations and South Africa, 1900–1977: Some Notes," *Journal of Black Studies* 17, no. 3 (March 1987): 305–25. Surprisingly, even highly regarded King scholars have suggested that King's anti-apartheid activities and views on South Africa are too limited to merit treatment in a book-length manuscript, or have implied that the subject has not been ignored, despite evidence to the contrary. James H. Cone declares that even in relation to King's "strong opposition to South Africa, he seems to have limited that opposition primarily to a few speeches about it, and only brief references to it in most of his other speeches." David J. Garrow insists that my claim that King's anti-apartheid activities and attitude toward South Africa have been "virtually ignored" is "too strong a declaration unless one appends a footnote identifying some number of specific King books that don't make any . . . references to Africa." Such comments are a barometer of the extent to which Americans lack fa-

miliarity with King's contributions to liberation movements outside the United States. From James H. Cone to Lewis V. Baldwin (18 February 1987); and From David J. Garrow to Lewis V. Baldwin (5 December 1988). Among King scholars, there is still the belief that any serious attention to King in relation to "black" or "African" issues undermines the depth of his beloved community vision. I submit that King's concern for Africa and African struggles was not antithetical to, but consistent with, his ideal of the beloved community.

3. For the first extensive treatments of King in relation to South Africa in published form, see the following by Lewis V. Baldwin: "Martin Luther King Jr.'s 'Beloved Community' Ideal and the Apartheid System in South Africa," *Western Journal of Black Studies* 10, no. 4 (winter 1986): 211–22; "The Deferred Dream of Martin Luther King Jr.: The United States and South Africa," Part I, *National Baptist Union-Review* 91, no. 9 (August 1987): 4 and 6; "The Deferred Dream of Martin Luther King Jr.: The United States and South Africa," Part II, *National Baptist Union-Review* 91, no. 12 (October 1987): 6–7; "Toward the Dawn of Freedom: Martin Luther King Jr.'s Vision of an Independent Africa," *African Commentary* II, issue 3 (March 1990): 6–8; and "The Vision of Martin Luther King Jr. and the Apartheid System in South Africa," *Journal of Religious Studies* 16, nos. 1 and 2 (winter 1991): 22–45. For other recent important statements on King and South Africa, see George M. Houser, *No One Can Stop the Rain: Glimpses of Africa's Liberation Struggle* (New York: The Pilgrim Press, 1989), 108, 120, 124, 256, 266, 349; and Houser, "Freedom's Struggle Crosses Oceans and Mountains: Martin Luther King Jr. and the Liberation Struggles in Africa and America," in Peter J. Albert and Ronald Hoffman, eds., *We Shall Overcome: Martin Luther King Jr. and the Black Freedom Struggle* (New York: Pantheon Books, 1990), 189–92.

4. Lewis V. Baldwin, "Martin Luther King Jr.'s 'Beloved Community' Ideal and the Apartheid System," 211.

5. The basic principles embodied in King's communitarian ideal are brilliantly discussed in Kenneth L. Smith and Ira G. Zepp Jr., *Search for the Beloved Community: The Thinking of Martin Luther King Jr.* (Valley Forge, Pa.: Judson Press, 1974), 119–40; and Walter E. Fluker, *They Looked for a City: A Comparative Analysis of the Ideal of Community in the Thought of Howard Thurman and Martin Luther King Jr.* (Lanham, Md.: University Press of America, 1989), 81–172. Also see Baldwin, *To Make the Wounded Whole*, 163–313.

6. King, *Where Do We Go from Here?*, 167–68.

7. Smith and Zepp, *Search for the Beloved Community*, 119; Fluker, *They Looked for a City*, 110–28; Walter E. Fluker, "They Looked for a City: A Comparison of the Ideal of Community in Howard Thurman and Martin Luther King Jr.," *Journal of Religious Ethics* 18, no. 2 (fall 1990): 33–50; and Baldwin, *To Make the Wounded Whole*, 245–313.

8. Fluker, *They Looked for a City,* 110–13.

9. Ibid., 82–88; Lewis V. Baldwin, *There Is a Balm in Gilead: The Cultural Roots of Martin Luther King Jr.* (Minneapolis: Fortress Press, 1991), 4–5, 104, 171–73; Baldwin, *To Make the Wounded Whole,* 163–313; Smith and Zepp, *Search for the Beloved Community,* 119–49; Kenneth L. Smith, "The Radicalization of Martin Luther King Jr.: The Last Three Years," *Journal of Ecumenical Studies* 26, no. 2 (spring 1989): 278; and John J. Ansbro, *Martin Luther King Jr.: The Making of a Mind* (Maryknoll, N.Y.: Orbis Books, 1982), 29–36 and 163–97.

10. Baldwin, *There Is a Balm in Gilead,* 172; and Fluker, *They Looked for a City,* 81–128.

11. Smith and Zepp, *Search for the Beloved Community,* 119.

12. King, *Where Do We Go from Here?,* 173–91; King, *The Trumpet of Conscience,* 67–78; and Fluker, *They Looked for a City,* 120–43.

13. King, *Where Do We Go from Here?,* 173–74.

14. Fluker, *They Looked for a City,* 110–52.

15. Baldwin, *There Is a Balm in Gilead,* 15–90; and Lewis V. Baldwin, ed., *Toward the Beloved Community: Martin Luther King Jr. and South African Apartheid,* unpublished manuscript (1994), 15–16, Archives of the Martin Luther King Jr. Center for Nonviolent Social Change, Inc., Atlanta, Georgia.

16. Baldwin, ed., *Toward the Beloved Community,* 17.

17. Ibid.

18. George M. Houser insists that "Martin Luther King Jr. was not essentially a Pan-Africanist, although his and Du Bois's positions had a great deal in common." Houser's point is questionable to the extent that King did accept aspects of the central view of Pan-Africanists; namely, that "people of African descent throughout the world have common cultural characteristics and share common problems as a result of their African origins, the similarity of their political oppression and economic exploitation by Western civilization, and the persistence and virulence of racist theories, attitudes, and behavior characterizing Western contact with people of African descent." However, King was too much of an integrationist and a believer in a common culture shared by blacks and whites in America to fit neatly into the tradition of Pan-Africanism. See Albert and Hoffman, eds., *We Shall Overcome,* 183; John H. Bracey Jr. et al., eds., *Black Nationalism in America* (New York: Bobbs-Merrill, 1970), xxix (introduction); and Baldwin, *To Make the Wounded Whole,* 163–244.

19. Baldwin, *To Make the Wounded Whole,* 245–313.

20. At various times during his career as a civil rights leader, King used the metaphors "New South," "American Dream," and "World House" to articulate his vision of community in intellectual terms. Interestingly enough, King embodied this progression in his own person because he moved from being a little-

known southern black preacher to a national leader and ultimately to a world figure. See James M. Washington, ed., *A Testament of Hope: The Essential Writings of Martin Luther King Jr.* (New York: HarperCollins, 1986), 112–16; Martin Luther King Jr., "Bold Design for a New South," *Nation,* 30 March 1963, 259–62; King, "The American Dream," unpublished speech delivered at Plymouth Church of the Pilgrims, Brooklyn, New York (10 February 1963): 1–3; and King, *Where Do We Go from Here?,* 167–91.

1. The Politics of Race

1. Philip S. Foner, ed., *Paul Robeson Speaks: Writings, Speeches, Interviews, 1918–1974* (Secaucus, N.J.: Citadel Press, 1978), 288.

2. Quoted in Alex La Guma, ed., *Apartheid: A Collection of Writings on South African Racism by South Africans* (New York: International Publishers, 1978), 25–26.

3. From James A. Pike and Martin Luther King Jr. to Members and Supporters of the ACOA (25 February 1958), The ACOA Collection, Amistad Research Center, Tulane University, New Orleans, Louisiana.

4. Martin Luther King Jr., *Stride Toward Freedom: The Montgomery Story* (San Francisco: HarperCollins, 1958), 15–107; King, "Recommendations to the Dexter Avenue Baptist Church for the Fiscal Year 1954–55," unpublished document, 1–7, The Martin Luther King Jr. Papers, Special Collections, Mugar Memorial Library, Boston University, Boston, Mass.; From the Pulpit Committee of the Dexter Avenue Baptist Church to Martin Luther King Jr. (10 March 1954), King Papers, Boston University; From Martin Luther King Jr. to the Dexter Avenue Baptist Church (14 April 1954), King Papers, Boston University; "Report of the Montgomery Improvement Association, Inc." (14 March 1957), 1–4, King Papers, Boston University; "Report of the Montgomery Improvement Association, Inc." (18 April 1957), 1–4, King Papers, Boston University; From Martin Luther King Jr. to President Dwight Loder of Garrett Biblical Institute (5 August 1958), The Garrett Library, Evanston, Ill.; and "Report of the Southern Christian Leadership Conference: Plans of Action for a South-Wide, Year-Round Voter-Registration Program" (February 1959), 1–8, King Papers, Boston University.

5. The ANC activist Walter Sisulu reported that "I knew Daddy King because we had correspondence with him in the early 1950s." See Steve Harvey, "Struggle Recalls King's, but Strategies Differ," *Atlanta Journal and Constitution,* 17 June 1990, D-2; and Mark Sherman and Marcia Kunstel, "Activist Continues Push for Black South Africans' Political Freedom," *Atlanta Journal,* 27 June 1990, A-9.

6. Albert J. Luthuli, *Let My People Go* (New York: McGraw-Hill, 1962), 83–84. Given Martin Luther King Sr.'s active involvement with Atlanta's Negro Leadership Coalition in the 1940s, it would have been virtually impossible for

him not to know of Luthuli's visit and activities in the city. See Martin Luther King Sr., *Daddy King: An Autobiography*, with Clayton Riley (New York: William Morrow, 1980), 111.

7. Luthuli spoke at at least one black college in Atlanta. King was an assistant minister at his father's church in that city at this time. Considering the active involvement of the black church community in welcoming Luthuli to Atlanta, and bearing in mind Daddy King's role as a well-known leader in that city, it is highly unlikely that young Martin remained totally unmindful of Luthuli's presence in and possible impact on the black community there. See Luthuli, *Let My People Go*, 84.

8. Martin Luther King Sr. visited various parts of the world in the 1930s and 1940s, and was known to invite preachers from abroad to speak at Atlanta's Ebenezer Baptist Church, where he pastored. See Clayborne Carson et al., eds., *The Papers of Martin Luther King Jr.: Called to Serve, January 1929–June 1951* (Berkeley: University of California Press, 1992), 77, 80, 87; and Interview with Philip Lenud (7 April 1987).

9. Edward A. Jones, *A Candle in the Dark: A History of Morehouse College* (Valley Forge, Pa.: Judson Press, 1967), 35–36, 214–15, 276–82; and Benjamin E. Mays, *Born to Rebel: An Autobiography* (New York: Charles Scribner's Sons, 1971), 149–61, 233, 254–60. The impact of King's family background and education on his understanding of the world will become clearer as scholars devote more attention to his global significance. Some attention to the subject is given in Lewis V. Baldwin, *To Make the Wounded Whole: The Cultural Legacy of Martin Luther King Jr.* (Minneapolis: Fortress Press, 1992), 245–313.

10. Mays, *Born to Rebel*, 152; and Interview with Lenud (7 April 1987).

11. Jones, *A Candle in the Dark*, 35–36, 214–15, 276–82; Mays, *Born to Rebel*, 149–61, 233; and Interview with Lenud (7 April 1987).

12. King, *Stride Toward Freedom*, 96.

13. Constance De Jong and Philip Glass, *Satyagraha: M. K. Gandhi in South Africa, 1893–1914* (New York: Tanam Press, 1983), 9; and Louis Fischer, *Gandhi: His Life and Message for the World* (New York: New American Library, 1954), 21–49.

14. This contention finds some support in John J. Ansboro, *Martin Luther King Jr.: The Making of a Mind* (Maryknoll, N.Y.: Orbis Books, 1982), 1–3; and Interview with Lenud (7 April 1987). King occasionally made fleeting references to Africa in some of his student papers at Crozer. See Carson et al., eds., *The Papers of Martin Luther King Jr.*, 215, 410.

15. Coretta Scott King, *My Life with Martin Luther King Jr.* (New York: Avon Books, 1969), 164.

16. King and Scott discussed extensively possible ways of eliminating South African apartheid. See "Conversation in Ghana," *The Christian Century* LXXIV,

no. 15 (10 April 1957): 446–48; and from Michael Scott to Martin Luther King Jr. (23 January 1958), King Papers, Boston University. King made an important reference to Scott in relation to South Africa in Martin Luther King Jr., "Introduction," in *Southwest Africa: The U.N.'s Stepchild* (New York: The American Committee on Africa, 1958–59), 1, King Papers, Boston University.

17. "Conversation in Ghana," 446–48. King apparently made available to Bishop Ambrose Reeves several copies of his *Stride Toward Freedom* (1958), an account of events surrounding the Montgomery bus boycott in 1955–56. From G. McLeod Bryan to Martin Luther King Jr. (10 October 1959), King Papers, Boston University; and From E. S. Reddy to Lewis V. Baldwin, (14 September 1993).

18. "Conversation in Ghana," 446–48; From Martin Luther King Jr. to Galal Kernahanof (29 April 1957), King Papers, Boston University; and William D. Watley, *Roots of Resistance: The Nonviolent Ethic of Martin Luther King Jr.* (Valley Forge, Pa.: Judson Press, 1985), 68. After returning to Montgomery from Africa, King spoke at length on liberation movements on the continent, referring at points to the Union of South Africa. See Martin Luther King Jr., "The Birth of a New Nation," transcript of a speech (14 April 1957): 1–22, King Papers, Boston University.

19. See "Conversation in Ghana," 446–48; and Martin Luther King Jr., "On South African Independence," a speech in London, England (7 December 1964): 1–2, Archives of the Martin Luther King Jr. Center for Nonviolent Social Change, Inc., Atlanta, Georgia. This 1964 speech can also be found in *Four Decades of Concern: Martin Luther King Jr.* (Atlanta: The Martin Luther King Jr. Center for Nonviolent Social Change, Inc., 1986), 18–19.

20. From Martin Luther King Jr. to Enoch Dumas (11 January 1960), King Papers, Boston University. King kept in his personal files numerous newspaper clippings on South Africa, reports of the ACOA on apartheid, and ANC publications such as *Mayibuye: Bulletin of the ANC* and *Spotlight on South Africa: News Digest*. Such sources can be found at Boston University and in the King Center Archives in Atlanta. For an important reference to King's knowledge of the Defiance Campaign, see From Martin Luther King Jr. to Albert J. Luthuli (8 December 1959), King Papers, Boston University; and George W. Shepherd, "Who Killed Martin Luther King's Dream?: An Afro-American Tragedy," *Africa Today* 15, no. 3 (April–May 1968): 2. In the 1950s, King also mentioned South Africa in his foreword to Richard B. Gregg, *The Power of Nonviolence* (Nyack, N.Y.: Fellowship Publications, 1959). In March 1952, the 58-year-old Manilal Gandhi, who resided in South Africa, began a 21-day fast in protest against apartheid laws. In the settlement at Phoenix, Natal, founded by his father, he declared that his fast "was to prepare him for the part he would take in a nationwide protest demonstration planned by an organization called the African National

Congress." For references to Manilal Gandhi's role in the Defiance Campaign, see "Gandhi's Son Begins Fast Against Race Segregation," *New York Times,* 7 March 1952, 2.

21. "Foe of Apartheid: Albert John Luthuli," *New York Times,* 24 October 1961, 1, 22; Liane Rozzell, "A Gesture of Honor," *Sojourners* (December 1984): 4; and King to Luthuli (8 December 1959).

22. King to Luthuli (8 December 1959); King to Dumas (11 January 1960); and George M. Houser, "Freedom's Struggle Crosses Oceans and Mountains: Martin Luther King Jr. and the Liberation Struggles in Africa and America," in Peter J. Albert and Ronald Hoffman, eds., *We Shall Overcome: Martin Luther King Jr. and the Black Freedom Struggle* (New York: Pantheon Books, 1990), 189.

23. Harvey, "Struggle Recalls King's," D-2; From James W. King to Martin Luther King Jr. (25 March 1964), The King Center Archives; "Roundup: Foreign Tributes to Dr. King," *Christian Century* 85, no. 19 (8 May 1968): 629–30; and Lewis V. Baldwin, ed., *Toward the Beloved Community: Martin Luther King Jr. and South African Apartheid,* unpublished manuscript (1994), 303, King Center Archives.

24. Bryan to King (10 October 1959); King to Luthuli (8 December 1959); and G. McLeod Bryan, "Statement on South Africa," unpublished document (October 1959): 5–6, King Papers, Boston University.

25. King to Luthuli (8 December 1959); Shepherd, "Who Killed Martin Luther King's Dream?," 2; Martin Luther King Jr., "My Trip to the Land of Gandhi" (1959), in James M. Washington, ed., *A Testament of Hope: The Essential Writings and Speeches of Martin Luther King Jr.* (San Francisco: HarperCollins, 1986), 23–30; and King, "Farewell Statement," Delhi, India (9 March 1959): 1, King Papers, Boston University.

26. See Mokgethi Motlhabi, *Challenge to Apartheid: Toward a Moral National Resistance* (Grand Rapids, Mich.: William B. Eerdmans, 1988), 144–46.

27. Baldwin, ed., *Toward the Beloved Community,* 15–16 and 301–2.

28. Martin Luther King Jr., "Statement Regarding the Legitimacy of the Struggle in Montgomery, Alabama" (4 May 1956): 1, King Papers, Boston University; and Baldwin, *To Make the Wounded Whole,* 247–50.

29. From Martin Luther King Jr. to J. Ellis (6 February 1960), King Papers, Boston University; and Lewis V. Baldwin, *There Is a Balm in Gilead: The Cultural Roots of Martin Luther King Jr.* (Minneapolis: Fortress Press, 1991), 192–93.

30. Sterling Stuckey, *Slave Culture: Nationalist Theory and the Foundations of Black America* (New York: Oxford University Press, 1987), 356.

31. Ibid.; Baldwin, *There Is a Balm in Gilead,* 75–76; and James H. Cone, *Martin and Malcolm and America: A Dream or a Nightmare* (Maryknoll, N.Y.: Orbis Books, 1991), 280–82. It appears that King became less concerned about being associated with the radical left during the last three years of his life

(1965–68), the period during which he became more "radical," a conclusion seemingly supported by his public stands on Vietnam and his acceptance of democratic socialism as an economic and political philosophy. See Martin Luther King Jr., "A Time to Break Silence" (1967), in Washington, ed., *A Testament of Hope*, 231–44; Kenneth L. Smith, "The Radicalization of Martin Luther King Jr.: The Last Three Years," *Journal of Ecumenical Studies* 26, no. 2 (spring 1989): 270–88; and Adam Fairclough, "Was Martin Luther King a Marxist?," *History Workshop*, vol. 15 (spring 1983): 117–25.

32. Stuckey, *Slave Culture*, 355–58; and Baldwin, *There Is a Balm in Gilead*, 75–76.

33. William Watley persuasively contends that after the Albany campaign (1961–62), in which the Kennedy administration's response was "lethargic," King viewed the federal government "more warily" and became increasingly critical of the FBI. See Watley, *Roots of Resistance*, 70.

34. George M. Houser, *No One Can Stop the Rain: Glimpses of Africa's Liberation Struggle* (New York: The Pilgrim Press, 1989), 12–20; From George M. Houser to Lewis V. Baldwin (9 October 1987); and Interview with George M. Houser (26 May 1993).

35. Houser, *No One Can Stop the Rain*, 20; and Interview with Houser (26 May 1993).

36. From Harold L. Oram to Donald Harrington (11 September 1957), ACOA Collection, Amistad Center, Tulane University.

37. For a brilliant discussion of King's beloved community ideal, see Kenneth L. Smith and Ira G. Zepp Jr., *Search for the Beloved Community: The Thinking of Martin Luther King Jr.* (Valley Forge, Pa.: Judson Press, 1974), ch. 6. George M. Houser reports that "The ACOA was interracial. Our board happened to be almost equally divided between black and white." Donald Harrington, Norman Thomas, Roger Baldwin, and George Houser were the whites involved, and the blacks included Charles Trigg, Conrad Lynn, Bayard Rustin, and A. Philip Randolph. See Houser, *No One Can Stop the Rain*, 265; and From George M. Houser to Lewis V. Baldwin (14 May 1994).

38. Houser, *No One Can Stop the Rain*, 12, 63; and interview with Houser (26 May 1993).

39. From George M. Houser to Walter Mildenberg (7 November 1957), ACOA Collection, Amistad Center, Tulane University; Houser, *No One Can Stop the Rain*, 12–61; and interview with Houser (26 May 1993).

40. From the Special Nominating Committee to the Members of the Executive Board of the ACOA (26 June 1957), ACOA Collection, Amistad Center, Tulane University; and Oram to Harrington (11 September 1957). Throughout the late 1950s, King's name appeared on ACOA stationery along with those of Reinhold Niebuhr, Harry Emerson Fosdick, and others who influenced his thought and outlook on the world.

41. Baldwin, ed., *Toward the Beloved Community*, 305; telephone interview with George M. Houser (23 July 1987); From George M. Houser to Lewis V. Baldwin (9 October 1987); interview with Houser (26 May 1993); and From George M. Houser to Martin Luther King Jr. (22 November 1957), ACOA Collection, Amistad Center, Tulane University.

42. Houser to Mildenberg (7 November 1957); Interview with Houser (26 May 1993); From George M. Houser to Martin Luther King Jr. (12 November 1959), King Papers, Boston University; and From Ann Morrissett to Martin Luther King Jr. (10 December 1959), ACOA Collection, Amistad Center, Tulane University.

43. From Eleanor Roosevelt, James A. Pike, and Martin Luther King Jr. to Friends and Supporters of the ACOA (July 1957), King Papers, Boston University; From George M. Houser to Irwin Kern (13 August 1957), ACOA Collection, Amistad Center, Tulane University; and Houser, *No One Can Stop the Rain*, 123–24.

44. From Houser to Kern (13 August 1957); and From George M. Houser to Diarmuid O'Scannlian (22 August 1957), ACOA Collection, Amistad Center, Tulane University.

45. *Declaration of Conscience: An Appeal to South Africa*, drafted by the American Committee on Africa (10 December 1957): 1–2, King Papers, Boston University; and From George M. Houser to Paul Moore (13 September 1957), ACOA Collection, Amistad Center, Tulane University.

46. *Declaration of Conscience*, 1–5. A partial listing of the signatories appears at the end of this document.

47. Ibid.

48. Martin Luther King Jr., "Apartheid in South Africa," an unpublished speech (12 July 1963): 1–3, King Center Archives. This speech was ghostwritten for King by Collin Gonze, a staff member of the ACOA who had lived in South Africa for several years. However, in preparing the speech, Gonze took words out of King's mouth instead of putting them into his mouth. King was scheduled to deliver the speech before the United Nations Committee on Apartheid on 16 July 1963, but did not because of other commitments.

49. From George M. Houser to Julius Mueller (18 September 1957), ACOA Collection, Amistad Center, Tulane University; and Houser, *No One Can Stop the Rain*, 124.

50. See especially "Bias Appeal Scored by South Africans," *New York Times,* 13 December 1957, 17; and John Hughes, "South Africa Retorts to Racial Critics," *Christian Science Monitor,* 13 December 1957, 16.

51. See *The A.C.O.A. Reports on the Declaration of Conscience* (9 January 1958): 1–3, King Papers, Boston University; From Wayne Morse to James A. Pike and Martin Luther King Jr. (12 November 1957), ACOA Collection, Amistad Center, Tulane University; and From George M. Houser to Mrs. Jo Ann List-

Israel (18 September 1957), ACOA Collection, Amistad Center, Tulane University.

52. Some important Americans refused to sign the *Declaration* or to publicly support it in other ways, believing perhaps that such support was not politically expedient, or that it would prove controversial. See From Margaret Chase Smith to Eleanor Roosevelt, James A. Pike, and Martin Luther King Jr. (23 August 1957), ACOA Collection, Amistad Center, Tulane University; and From Keith Spalding to Eleanor Roosevelt, James A. Pike, and Martin Luther King Jr. (21 August 1957), ACOA Collection, Amistad Center, Tulane University. Despite the failure of many public figures in America to support the *Declaration,* it is important to note that endorsements did come from four U.S. senators, sixteen members of the House of Representatives—Republican and Democrat, two university presidents, eight national religious leaders, and eleven authors and scholars.

53. *The A.C.O.A. Reports on the Declaration,* 1–3.

54. Scott, who had discussed South Africa at length with King in Ghana in 1957, suggested to the civil rights leader that steps be taken to exclude South Africa from the Olympic Games, to encourage representative bodies of the nursing profession worldwide to press the issue of the mistreatment of black and Colored members of their profession in South Africa, and to work through inter-university councils and other academic networks to change the apartheid government's policy of preventing universities in South Africa from accepting non-European students. Scott to King (23 January 1958).

55. *The A.C.O.A Reports on the Declaration,* 3; Hughes, "South Africa Retorts to Racial Critics," 16; and "Bias Appeal Scored by South Africans," 17.

56. From L. Marquard to the *Cape Times,* Cape Town, South Africa (23 November 1965); From N. M. Nel to Martin Luther King Jr. (17 March 1966), King Center Archives; and Baldwin, ed., *Toward the Beloved Community,* 90–92, 288–91, 306.

57. *The A.C.O.A. Reports on the Declaration,* 1–3.

58. From Oliver R. Tambo to Martin Luther King Jr. (18 November 1957), King Papers, Boston University.

59. *The A.C.O.A. Reports on the Declaration,* 3; and Baldwin ed., *Toward the Beloved Community,* 306–8.

60. Bryan to King (10 October 1959); and Bryan, "Statement on South Africa," 5–6.

61. King's earliest perspective on the situation confronting South African political prisoners most likely grew out of his reading of George M. Houser, *Report on South Africa's Treason Trials* (11 February 1958): 1–2, King Papers, Boston University; and "South Africa Frees 61 in Treason Case," *New York Times,* 18 December 1957, 15. One source reports that the ACOA, "with sponsorship of major church leaders including Dr. Martin Luther King, provided financial sup-

port for Mandela and others at the famous 'Treason Trials.'" See George W. Shepherd, "*Africa Today* in the Early Years: The Debate over Strategy for the Liberation of South Africa," *Africa Today* 41, no. 1 (first quarter 1994): 13.

62. Roosevelt, Pike, and King to Friends and Supporters of the ACOA (July 1957); From James A. Pike and Martin Luther King Jr. to the Honorable Paul H. Douglas (4 November 1957), ACOA Collection, Amistad Center, Tulane University; Pike and King to Friends and Supporters of the ACOA (25 February 1958); From J. B. Abrahamsen to Martin Luther King Jr. (2 March 1958), ACOA Collection, Amistad Center, Tulane University; and From James A. Pike to Martin Luther King Jr. (14 March 1958), ACOA Collection, Amistad Center, Tulane University.

63. Pike and King to Douglas (4 November 1957); and Martin Luther King Jr. et al., "A Letter to the Religious Press," unpublished document prepared under the auspices of the ACOA (5 March 1958): 1–2, ACOA Collection, Amistad Center, Tulane University.

64. From Martin Luther King Jr. to Friends and Supporters of the American Committee on Africa (12 November 1959), King Papers, Boston University.

65. Ibid.; Morrissett to King (10 December 1959); From Martin Luther King Jr. to Ann Morrissett (23 December 1959), ACOA Collection, Amistad Center, Tulane University; and Houser, *No One Can Stop the Rain,* 85, 127.

66. For examples, see From George M. Houser to Martin Luther King Jr. (9 November 1959), ACOA Collection, Amistad Center, Tulane University; and From Isidore W. Ruskin to Martin Luther King Jr. (30 November 1959), ACOA Collection, Amistad Center, Tulane University.

67. Smith to Roosevelt, Pike, and King (23 August 1957); and From Robert B. Meyner to Martin Luther King Jr. (6 December 1957), ACOA Collection, Amistad Center, Tulane University.

68. From Donald Harrington to George M. Houser (4 March 1958), ACOA Collection, Amistad Center, Tulane University; and "Africa and the United States," *Annual Report of the American Committee on Africa* (1 June 1959–31 May 1960): 2, King Papers, Boston University.

69. King, *Stride Toward Freedom,* 71–224; Martin Luther King Jr., "Statement Regarding the Little Rock Decision," Washington, D.C. (23 June 1958): 1, King Papers, Boston University; and Watley, *Roots of Resistance,* 101.

70. Luthuli, *Let My People Go,* 185–87.

71. Ibid, 135, 140, 185–87; and Pike and King to Douglass (4 November 1957).

72. Bryan to King (10 October 1959); and Bryan, "Statement on South Africa," 5–6. Bryan recently wrote: "When I encouraged him (Luthuli) to write a book clarifying his people's and his party's position in South Africa, he said, 'You know the greatest thrill of my life at the moment is reading Martin Luther King's

Stride Toward Freedom. I wish that I had a dozen copies to put in the hands of my party leaders.'" Bryan continued: "When he learned that I knew King personally, he pumped me with questions. I ended by telling him that I thought he was 'the King of South Africa.' Nothing could have pleased him more. I added that I thought he was up against more odds than King; he replied, 'May God grant me just half the courage and insight.'" Bryan later reported that Luthuli confided, "I want to be the King of South Africa." See G. McLeod Bryan, "Two Birmingham Letters," Thirtieth Anniversary, Winston-Salem, North Carolina (1993), 4.

73. King to Luthuli (8 December 1959).

74. Luthuli, *Let My People Go,* 152–55; and Baldwin, ed., *Toward the Beloved Community,* 322.

75. Luthuli, *Let My People Go,* 12, 37, 64, 87, 135; and Smith and Zepp, *Search for the Beloved Community,* 119–40. For a brief but interesting treatment of significant parallels in the philosophies of King, Luthuli, and Gandhi, see William R. Duggan, "Three Men of Peace," *The Crisis* 81, no. 10 (December 1974): 331–37.

76. Baldwin, ed., *Toward the Beloved Community,* 2–3.

77. Philip S. Foner, ed., *W. E. B. Du Bois Speaks: Speeches and Addresses, 1920–1963* (New York: Pathfinder Press, 1970): 125, 131–32, 203; Foner, ed., *Paul Robeson Speaks,* 288, 307–8; King to Dumas (11 January 1960); King, "Apartheid in South Africa," 2–3; and Stuckey, *Slave Culture,* 356. Robeson "was very well known to South African blacks" as early as the 1930s. He exchanged letters with ANC leaders in the 1950s. See Sterling Stuckey, *Going Through the Storm: The Influence of African American Art in History* (New York: Oxford University Press, 1994), 219; and Harvey, "Struggle Recalls King's," D-2.

78. Milfred C. Fierce, "Selected Black American Leaders and Organizations and South Africa, 1900–1977: Some Notes," *Journal of Black Studies* 17, no. 3 (March 1987): 315–16; Stuckey, *Slave Culture,* 356–57; Foner, ed., *Paul Robeson Speaks,* 10–11; and Albert and Hoffman, eds., *We Shall Overcome,* 175.

79. Fierce, "Selected Black American Leaders," 315–16; Foner, ed., *W. E. B. Du Bois Speaks,* 69, 125, 131–32, and *Paul Robeson Speaks,* 10, 288, 308. King's belief in an interracial coalition of blacks, Asians, and Coloreds to fight apartheid in South Africa was unmistakable in the 1950s and, if recent scholarship is accurate, his subscription to democratic socialism as an economic and political philosophy during the last three years of his life would have brought him closer ideologically to Robeson and Du Bois. See Smith, "The Radicalization of Martin Luther King Jr.," 270–88; and Fairclough, "Was Martin Luther King a Marxist?," 117–25. One source notes that "Booker T. Washington, W. E. B. Du Bois, and later Martin Luther King Jr. had their admirers in South Africa." See Peter Walshe, "The African National Congress: Part of the Solution in South Africa," *Christianity and Crisis* 47, no. 7 (4 May 1987): 164.

80. Foner, ed., *W. E. B. Du Bois Speaks,* 197, and *Paul Robeson Speaks,* 288; and King, "On South African Independence," 1–2.

81. Foner, ed., *Paul Robeson Speaks,* 169, 181–82, 277, 308, 319, 345, 350, 385.

82. Fierce, "Selected Black American Leaders," 314–15; and Martin B. Duberman, *Paul Robeson* (New York: Alfred A. Knopf, 1988), 206.

83. Quoted in Duberman, *Paul Robeson,* 333.

84. Ibid.

85. Roosevelt, Pike, and King to Friends and Supporters of the ACOA (July 1957); Pike and King to Friends and Supporters of the ACOA (25 February 1958); and Morrissett to King (10 December 1959).

86. From Joel R. Jacobson to Friends and Supporters of the ACOA (30 March 1959), ACOA Collection, Amistad Center, Tulane University. Boxes 14–17 in the ACOA Collection provide information on contributors to the Africa Defense and Aid Fund.

87. See partial list of signatories in *Declaration of Conscience,* 1–5.

88. For a brilliant discussion of Du Bois's "Talented Tenth" model, see Stuckey, *Slave Culture,* 266–69, 293–94.

89. Baldwin, *There Is a Balm in Gilead,* 15–336, and *To Make the Wounded Whole,* 7–313. The idea that the leader in the struggle should be an intellectual or "man of learning" stretches at least as far back as Henry H. Garnet in the 1840s, and it remains one of the main ingredients of black nationalist theory. However, black intellectuals, influenced by the white Western intellectual tradition, and determined to preserve what little they have achieved while avoiding economic and political reprisals, have tended not to devote themselves entirely to the struggle of their people. See Stuckey, *Slave Culture,* 187, 266–69, 293–94; and Gayraud S. Wilmore, *Black Religion and Black Radicalism: An Interpretation of the Religious History of Afro-American People* (Maryknoll, N.Y.: Orbis Books, 1983), 113.

2. A Common Destiny

1. Quoted in Colin Legum and Margaret Legum, *South Africa: Crisis for the West* (New York: Frederick A. Praeger, 1965), 178.

2. Albert J. Luthuli, *Let My People Go* (New York: McGraw-Hill, 1962), 83. One source claims that Luthuli "entitled his autobiography, *The Way to Freedom Is Via the Cross.*" This title does surface at points in *Let My People Go.* See Peter Walshe, "The African National Congress: Part of the Solution in South Africa," *Christianity and Crisis* 47, no. 7 (4 May 1987): 164.

3. Martin Luther King Jr., "Apartheid in South Africa," an unpublished speech (12 July 1963): 1–3, Archives of the Martin Luther King Jr. Center for Nonviolent Social Change, Inc., Atlanta, Georgia.

4. It could be argued that King's articulation and practical application of non-violent methods represented something new in America on three grounds. First,

nonviolence for King was very radical, confrontational, manipulative, coercive, and tied to social action and a broad sense of social responsibility, whereas nonviolence in America before him—as revealed in the lives of the Quakers in colonial America, the abolitionists and peace crusaders of the antebellum period, the pacifist progressives of the early twentieth century, and the conscientious objectors of World Wars I and II—tended to be individualistic and quietistic. Second, King was the first American to employ various forms of nonviolence consistently in addressing a range of problems that afflicted, and continue to afflict, the American society. Finally, King was the first American to consistently challenge the nations of the world to experiment with nonviolence in their relations with each other. These points are not emphasized in Staughton Lynd, ed., *Nonviolence in America: A Documentary History* (New York: Bobbs-Merrill, 1966): 3–530; and James H. Evans, "'Study War No More': Martin Luther King Jr. and Nonviolent Resistance," *A.M.E. Zion Quarterly Review* XCVIL, no. 4 (January 1988): 2–7. Eleanor Roosevelt, an ex-president's wife, once contended that King developed "a philosophy which is new to most of us in this country." Quoted in From Eleanor Roosevelt to a Mr. Canfield (15 August 1958), Martin Luther King Jr. Papers, Special Collections, Mugar Memorial Library, Boston University, Boston, Mass.

5. Martin Luther King Jr., *The Trumpet of Conscience* (New York: Harper and Row, 1967), xi–xii (foreword), 3–78; and *Where Do We Go from Here: Chaos or Community?* (Boston: Beacon Press, 1968): 167–91; Lewis V. Baldwin, *To Make the Wounded Whole: The Cultural Legacy of Martin Luther King Jr.* (Minneapolis: Fortress Press, 1992): 245–313.

6. Steve Harvey, "Struggle Recalls King's, but Strategies Differ," *Atlanta Journal and Constitution,* 17 June 1990, D-2; and Mark Sherman and Marcia Kunstel, "Activist Continues Push for Black South Africans' Political Freedom," *Atlanta Journal,* 27 June 1990, A-9.

7. George W. Shepherd, "Who Killed Martin Luther King's Dream?: An Afro-American Tragedy," *Africa Today* 15, no. 3 (April–May 1968): 2. The ties between the freedom struggles in the United States and South Africa evoked interest and concern from people around the world. The anti-apartheid activist Enuga S. Reddy has said that "I have been curious to learn what contact and interaction there had been between the two great nonviolent movements in South Africa and the United States." He continued: "To us in India, they were the greatest such movements after the struggles led by Gandhi in South Africa and India. There were parallels in methods also—e.g. bus boycott." From E. S. Reddy to Lewis V. Baldwin (14 September 1993).

8. Martin Luther King Jr., "An Address at the 47th Annual NAACP Convention," San Francisco, California (27 June 1956): 2–3, King Papers, Boston University; and Baldwin, *To Make the Wounded Whole,* 256–57.

9. From Martin Luther King Jr. to Enoch Dumas (11 January 1960), King Papers, Boston University.

10. "African Leader Visits Atlanta," *Atlanta Daily World,* 6 May 1960, 1.

11. King to Dumas (11 January 1960); Philip S. Foner, ed., *W. E. B. Du Bois Speaks: Speeches and Addresses, 1920–1963* (New York: Pathfinder Press, 1970): 131–32; Foner, ed., *Paul Robeson Speaks: Writings, Speeches, Interviews, 1918–1974* (Secaucus, N.J.: Citadel Press, 1978), 288; Paul Robeson, *Here I Stand* (Boston: Beacon Press, 1958), 64; and Martin Luther King Jr., "On South African Independence," a speech in London, England (7 December 1964): 1–2, King Center Archives.

12. From Harold Courlander to Martin Luther King Jr. (30 August 1961), King Papers, Boston University; and From Martin Luther King Jr. to Harold Courlander (30 October 1961), King Papers, Boston University.

13. King, *Where Do We Go from Here?,* 173.

14. Ibid.

15. "Doubts and Certainties Link: A Transcript of an Interview with Martin Luther King Jr.," London, England (winter 1968): 1, King Center Archives.

16. King, "On South African Independence," 1–2; "Apartheid in South Africa," 1–3; and "The Negro Looks at Africa," *New York Amsterdam News* (8 December 1962): 1 ff.

17. Martin Luther King Jr., "South Africa Benefit Speech," an unpublished speech, New York (10 December 1965): 1–5, King Center Archives. This speech also appears under the title "Call for an International Boycott on Apartheid South Africa," in *Four Decades of Concern: Martin Luther King Jr.* (Atlanta: Martin Luther King Jr. Center for Nonviolent Social Change, Inc., 1986), 19–22.

18. Walter E. Fluker, *They Looked for a City: A Comparative Analysis of the Ideal of Community in the Thought of Howard Thurman and Martin Luther King Jr.* (Lanham, Md.: University Press of America, 1989), 159–60.

19. Martin Luther King Jr., "A Knock at Midnight," sermon given at All-Saints Community Church, Los Angeles, California (25 June 1967): 1, King Center Archives.

20. Ibid.; and Fluker, *They Looked for a City,* 150–52.

21. King, "On South African Independence," 1–2, and "Apartheid in South Africa," 1–2.

22. King, "On South African Independence," 1–2.

23. King, "South Africa Benefit Speech," 1–5.

24. Martin Luther King Jr., "Speech at a Rally," unpublished document, Savannah, Ga. (1 January 1961): 6, King Papers, Boston University; "The Rising Tide," unpublished speech, National Urban League (6 September 1960): 1 ff., King Papers, Boston University; and "Transcript of a Radio Interview with Martin Luther King Jr. Regarding the Nobel Peace Prize," Oslo, Norway (9 December 1964): 1–4, King Center Archives. Interestingly enough, King's meeting with Adelaide Tambo and other ANC representatives at Africa Unity House in London was not widely covered by the press. It is possible that the reception

was not publicized, especially since, given the ANC's association with armed resistance, it could have perhaps embroiled King in controversy.

25. "Transcript of a Radio Interview with King," 1–4.

26. King, "On South African Independence," 1–2.

27. King, "The Negro Looks at Africa," 1 ff.

28. King, "Apartheid in South Africa," 1–3.

29. Ibid.; and King, "On South African Independence," 1–2.

30. King, "South Africa Benefit Speech," 1–5.

31. King, "Apartheid in South Africa," 1; King, "On South African Independence," 1–2; and Lewis V. Baldwin, ed., *Toward the Beloved Community: Martin Luther King Jr. and South African Apartheid,* unpublished manuscript (1994), 13, King Center Archives.

32. King, "South Africa Benefit Speech," 1–5; and King to Dumas (11 January 1960).

33. King, "South Africa Benefit Speech," 1–5.

34. George M. Houser, *No One Can Stop the Rain: Glimpses of Africa's Liberation Struggle* (New York: The Pilgrim Press, 1989), 108, 120, 124, 265–66, 349; and Interview with George M. Houser (26 May 1993).

35. Martin Luther King Jr., "Why We Must Go to Washington II," unpublished manuscript (15 January 1968): 15, King Center Archives; From Hope R. Stevens to Friends and Supporters of Africa Freedom Day of the ACOA (April 1960), The ACOA Collection, Amistad Center, Tulane University, New Orleans, La.; and "Americans Protest South African Massacre," *Atlanta Daily World,* 24 March 24 1960, 1 ff. King was also undoubtedly upset with the South African government's violent put-down of the Pan-Africanist Congress's Positive Action Campaign, a nonviolent movement that occurred shortly after the Sharpeville massacre in 1960. However, no mention of this campaign is made in King's most important papers on South Africa.

36. "Liberals Urge Ambassador to South Africa Be Recalled for Consultation—Suspension of Gold Purchases," *Press Release* of Americans for Democratic Action, Washington, D.C. (17 April 1960): 1–3, King Center Archives; Paul W. Ward, "Liberals Bid U.S. Censure South Africa: A.D.A. Petition Urges Envoy's Recall, Halt in Gold-Buying," *Baltimore Sun,* 17 April 1960, 1; and "A.D.A. Asks U.S. Protest on African Apartheid," *Sunday Star,* 17 April 1960, 1 ff.

37. "South Africa Emergency Committee Formed by Key Organization Leaders," *Press Release,* American Committee on Africa (23 April 1960): 1, ACOA Collection, Amistad Center, Tulane University.

38. King, "Apartheid in South Africa," 1–3; "On South African Independence," 1–2; and "South Africa Benefit Speech," 1–5.

39. Roger Omond, *The Apartheid Handbook: A Guide to South Africa's Every-*

day Racial Policies (New York: Viking Penguin, 1985): 19; and James Leatt et al., eds., *Contending Ideologies in South Africa* (Grand Rapids, Mich.: William B. Eerdmans, 1986), 99–100. Interestingly enough, the black nationalist Malcolm X had a more favorable view than King of the ANC's shift to armed struggle. In December 1964, Malcolm characterized Nelson Mandela as "a man who advocated nonviolence in South Africa, until he saw that it wasn't getting anywhere, and then Mandela stepped up and had to resort to tactical violence." For Malcolm, this "showed that Mandela was for the freedom of his people." "He was more interested in the end than he was the means," continued Malcolm, "whereas many of the Negro leaders" in the United States "are more strait-jacketed by the means rather than the end." Quoted in David Gallen, *A Malcolm X Reader* (New York: Carroll and Graf Publishers, Inc., 1994), 203.

40. Luthuli must have had King, among others, in mind when he accepted the Nobel Peace Prize. He said: "In this acknowledgment, I include also many South Africans and friends abroad who have sympathized with the liberation struggle and in their own way have labored for the realization of cordial relations in our land, especially between black and white." See "Hammarskjöld, Zulu Chief Given Nobel Peace Prize: '61 Award Made Posthumously to U.N. Secretary— Albert Luthuli, a Foe of Apartheid, Gets Delayed '60 Honor," *New York Times,* 24 October 1961, 1, 22; "Foe of Apartheid: Albert John Luthuli," *New York Times,* 24 October 1961, 1, 22; Liane Rozzell, "A Gesture of Honor," *Sojourners* (December 1984): 4; and *The Road to Oslo . . . and Beyond,* pamphlet (1962), 1–21, King Center Archives. In a letter to friends and supporters of the ACOA, Luthuli, after receiving the Nobel Prize, noted that "our methods" are "patterned on Gandhi's." Although Luthuli was influenced by both Gandhi and King, it is more correct to say that he inherited a nonviolent tradition from the historical beginnings of the African National Congress in 1912. From Albert J. Luthuli to Friends of the American Committee on Africa (10 December 1961): King Papers, Boston University.

41. King, "On South African Independence," 1; and Interview with Houser (26 May 1993).

42. From James W. King to Martin Luther King Jr. (25 March 1964), King Center Archives.

43. From Martin Luther King Jr. to James W. King (6 April 1964), King Center Archives.

44. Luthuli, *Let My People Go,* 101, 153, 160, 183, 185–88, 211, 221–23. Colin Morris, *Unyoung, Uncolored, Unpoor* (Nashville and New York: Abingdon Press, 1969), 63, 90–91; and William L. Van Deburg, *New Day in Babylon: The Black Power Movement and American Culture, 1965–1975* (Chicago: University of Chicago Press, 1992), 45. Nelson Mandela, one of those young radical voices in the ANC under Luthuli's leadership, was convinced after 1960 that King's meth-

ods in the United States were not applicable to South Africa. When two Americans attempted to show that Mandela "was not a Christian" by "asserting that the Reverend Martin Luther King never resorted to violence," the brilliant South African activist promptly lectured them. "I told them that the conditions in which Martin Luther King struggled were totally different from my own." Pointing out the differences, Mandela declared: "The United States was a democracy with constitutional guarantees of equal rights that protected nonviolent protest (though there was still prejudice against blacks); South Africa was a police state with a constitution that enshrined inequality and an army that responded to nonviolence with force." Mandela continued: "I told them that I was a Christian and had always been a Christian. Even Christ, I said, when he was left with no alternative, used force to the expel the moneylenders from the temple. He was not a man of violence, but had no choice but to use force against evil. I do not think I persuaded them." See Nelson Mandela, *Long Walk to Freedom: The Autobiography of Nelson Mandela* (Boston: Little, Brown, 1994), 453–54.

45. King to King (25 March 1964); and quoted in Winnie Mandela, *Part of My Soul Went with Him*, ed. Anne Benjamin (New York: W. W. Norton and Company, 1984), 125. Luthuli was more of a "pragmatic pacifist" than a "thoroughgoing pacifist." Here he was consistent with the tradition of the ANC. King called himself "a realistic pacifist." King wrote: "I am no doctrinaire pacifist. I have tried to embrace a realistic pacifism. Moreover, I see the pacifist position not as sinless but as the lesser evil in the circumstances. Therefore, I do not claim to be free from the moral dilemmas that the Christian nonpacifist confronts." The label of "realistic pacifist" may be applied to Luthuli as well. However, King was more thoroughgoing in his pacifism than Luthuli, especially since King accepted nonviolence as a personal ethic or as a way of life. See James M. Washington, ed., *A Testament of Hope: The Essential Writings and Speeches of Martin Luther King Jr.* (San Francisco: HarperCollins, 1968), 39.

46. "Chief Albert John Mvumbi Lituli Isitwalandwe, 1898–1967," *Sechaba: Official Organ of the African National Congress of South Africa,* supplement to I, no. 8 (1967): 1–8. Young militants such as Nelson Mandela and Oliver Tambo became disillusioned with the lack of militancy on the part of the ANC under Luthuli's leadership. They founded the ANC Youth League, and "Within five years of infighting and maneuvering, the young rebels succeeded in purging the older, more conservative ANC leadership and taking over the organization." "We are going to keep to nonviolence, but we give you permission to go and start the organization to embark on armed actions," said Luthuli to Mandela and other organizers of the Youth League in 1960. Luthuli also told Mandela: "You will report to us from time to time on the progress you're making, with the understanding that the organization as such is not going to be involved." See Hans J. Massaquoi, "From Prisoner to President: Twenty-Seven Year Ordeal Behind Bars Prepared

Freedom Fighter for the Tough Job that Lies Ahead," *Ebony* XLIX, no. 10 (August 1994): 41; and Paul Gray, "Nelson Mandela and F. W. de Klerk," *Time,* 3 January 1994, 55.

47. Luthuli, *Let My People Go,* 92, 138, 140, 153–55, 170, 230; Martin Luther King Jr., "A Response to J. Edgar Hoover's Charge that Communists Have Infiltrated the Civil Rights Movement," unpublished statement (23 April 1964): 1–3, King Center Archives; King, "A Statement in Response to *The Atlanta Constitution*'s Article Alleging Communist Ties," unpublished document (25 July 1963): 1–2, King Center Archives; and "A Transcript of the Martin Luther King Jr. Interview on 'Face the Nation,'" broadcast on CBS Television (10 May 1964): 18–20, King Center Archives.

48. Luthuli to Friends of the ACOA (10 December 1961); and From Albert J. Luthuli to Friends of the American Committee on Africa (6 August 1962), ACOA Collection, Amistad Center, Tulane University.

49. From Donald Harrington to Martin Luther King Jr. (16 February 1960), King Papers, Boston University; From Maude L. W. Ballou to Donald Harrington (24 February 1960), ACOA Collection, Amistad Center, Tulane University; From George M. Houser to Martin Luther King Jr. (31 March 1960), King Papers, Boston University; Stevens to Friends and Supporters of the ACOA (April 1960); From Martin Luther King Jr. to the American Committee on Africa (24 July 1961), ACOA Collection, Amistad Center, Tulane University; From George M. Houser to Martin Luther King Jr. (12 December 1961), ACOA Collection, Amistad Center, Tulane University; Statement of Consent from Martin Luther King Jr. to the American Committee on Africa (20 December 1961), ACOA Collection, Amistad Center, Tulane University; From Martin Luther King Jr. to George Houser (21 December 1961), King Papers, Boston University; and From Dora McDonald to George M. Houser (8 February 1962), King Papers, Boston University. During the 1960s, King served as a sponsor of the ACOA's Africa Defense and Aid Fund along with many of his friends, mentors, and former professors, among whom were Mordecai Johnson, Benjamin Mays, Howard Thurman, Adam C. Powell Jr., Reinhold Niebuhr, Walter Muelder, Sandy Ray, and Charles Diggs. See From Alan Paton to Friends and Supporters of the Africa Defense and Aid Fund of the ACOA (May 1960), ACOA Collection, Amistad Center, Tulane University.

50. From George M. Houser to Martin Luther King Jr. (6 February 1962), ACOA Collection, Amistad Center, Tulane University.

51. Ibid.; and From Eleanor Roosevelt to George M. Houser (19 July 1962), ACOA Collection, Amistad Center, Tulane University.

52. Luthuli to Friends of the ACOA (6 August 1962). Hundreds of letters were sent to world leaders and supporters by George Houser, Martin Luther King Jr., Albert J. Luthuli, and others, soliciting support for the *Appeal for Action*

Against Apartheid. See From George M. Houser to Maida Springer (26 July 1962), ACOA Collection, Amistad Center, Tulane University; and From Donald S. Harrington to Friends of the ACOA (26 November 1962), King Papers, Boston University. African American civil rights activists who received letters included Charles C. Diggs Jr., Jackie Robinson, Whitney Young, Wyatt T. Walker, Dorothy Height, and Rosa L. Gragg, National President of the National Association of Colored Women.

53. See *Appeal for Action Against Apartheid,* an ACOA Campaign (1962), 1–4, King Center Archives.

54. Ibid.; From David Reisman to George Houser (27 August 1962), ACOA Collection, Amistad Center, Tulane University; From Deborah Kallen to Martin Luther King Jr. (30 August 1962), ACOA Collection, Amistad Center, Tulane University; From George M. Houser to Lillian Smith (27 September 1962), ACOA Collection, Amistad Center, Tulane University; From Clifford Case to George M. Houser (4 October 1962), ACOA Collection, Amistad Center, Tulane University; and From Adam C. Powell Jr. to George M. Houser (9 October 1962), ACOA Collection, Amistad Center, Tulane University. Some public officials in the United Stats refused to sign the appeal for reasons that are unclear. See from Margaret C. Fowler to George M. Houser (27 August 1962), ACOA Collection, Amistad Center, Tulane University; and From the American Committee on Africa to John F. Kennedy (7 December 1962), The King Center Archives.

55. *Appeal for Action Against Apartheid,* 1–4; and Houser, *No One Can Stop the Rain,* 266.

56. Houser, *No One Can Stop the Rain,* 266.

57. Ibid.; and Milfred C. Fierce, "Selected Black American Leaders and Organizations and South Africa, 1900–1977: Some Notes," *Journal of Black Studies* 17, no. 3 (March 1987): 317–18. The idea for this organization actually grew out of a "small meeting" which included George M. Houser, John Morsell of the NAACP, John Davis of the American Society of African Culture, attorney Hope R. Stevens, James Farmer of the Congress of Racial Equality, and Frank Montero, an ACOA board member and activist in the National Urban League. In a letter to King, Houser explained: "We felt the idea of holding a conference of perhaps 100 to 200 Negro leaders across the country to give consideration to some of the pressing problems, particularly in southern Africa, could be very important and needed further exploration." Houser noted further, "The role of the American Committee on Africa is simply to get the ball rolling." From George M. Houser to Martin Luther King Jr. (5 June 1962), ACOA Collection, Amistad Center, Tulane University.

58. Houser, *No One Can Stop the Rain,* 266. Sponsoring organizations included The African-American Institute, the ACOA, Alpha Kappa Alpha Sorority,

Inc., Alpha Phi Alpha Fraternity, Inc., The American Society of African Culture, the Brotherhood of Sleeping Car Porters, AFL-CIO, Congress of Racial Equality, Delta Sigma Theta Sorority, Inc., Gandhi Society for Human Rights, the NAACP, the National Council of Negro Women, the National Urban League, Operation Crossroads Africa, Phelps-Stokes Fund, the SCLC, and several others.

59. Houser, *No One Can Stop the Rain,* 266; and Fierce, "Selected Black American Leaders," 317–18. A call meeting of the ANLCA took place in New York in the summer of 1962, and Martin Luther King Jr., Whitney Young, Hobson Reynolds, C. B. Powell, Dorothy Height, Jeanne Noble, Maida Springer, James H. Robinson, and Thomas Kilgore were among those invited. King did not attend, but told Houser to "feel free to use my name on the letter calling for the American Negro Leadership Conference on Africa." From Houser to King (5 June 1962); From Dora McDonald to George Houser (18 June 1962), King Papers, Boston University; From George M. Houser to Clarence Jones (26 June 1962), ACOA Collection, Amistad Center, Tulane University; From Martin Luther King Jr. to George M. Houser (2 July 1962), King Papers, Boston University; and "Call to the American Negro Leadership Conference on Africa," unpublished document (June 1962), 1, King Center Archives.

60. "Call to the ANLCA," 1.

61. *The American Negro Leadership Conference on Africa: Resolutions,* presented at Arden House, Columbia University, Harriman, New York (23–25 November 1962): 1–6, King Center Archives.

62. Martin Luther King Jr., "Statement on Africa," presented at the ANLCA Meeting, Arden House Campus, Columbia University, Harriman, New York (24 November 1962): 1–2, King Center Archives; and King, "The Negro Looks at Africa," 1 ff.

63. King, "Statement on Africa," 1–2; M. S. Handler, "U.S. Negroes Link Aid to Sub-Sahara African Nations with Rights Struggle," *New York Times,* 25 November 1962, 64; Handler, "Leading Negroes Agree on Goals: Arden House Session Asks South Africa Sanctions," *New York Times,* 26 November 1962, 17; and From George M. Houser to Martin Luther King Jr. (26 November 1962), King Papers, Boston University.

64. Handler, "U.S. Negroes Link Aid to Sub-Sahara African Nations," 64; Handler, "Leading Negroes Agree on Goals," 17; ACOA to Kennedy (7 December 1962); Memorandum form George M. Houser to the American Negro Leadership Conference on Africa (14 December 1962), King Papers, Boston University; From the American Negro Leadership Conference to John F. Kennedy (17 December 1962), King Center Archives; and "Africa 'Marshall Plan' Asked by Negro Leaders," *Washington Post,* 18 December 1962, 1 ff.

65. ANLCA to Kennedy (17 December 1962); ACOA to Kennedy (7 December 1962); and Interview with Houser (26 May 1993).

66. King, "The Negro Looks at Africa," 1 ff.

67. This story involving Beyers Naudé's "radical turn-about" is told in G. McLeod Bryan, "Two Birmingham Letters," Thirtieth Anniversary, Winston-Salem, N.C. (1993), 3; and Bryan, *Naudé: Prophet to South Africa* (1978).

68. Baldwin, *To Make the Wounded Whole*, 163–44.

69. From Theodore E. Brown to Martin Luther King Jr. (27 February 1963), King Papers, Boston University; From Martin Luther King Jr. to George M. Houser (21 March 1963), King Center Archives; From George M. Houser to Martin Luther King Jr. (8 March 1963), ACOA Collection, Amistad Center, Tulane University; From Martin Luther King Jr. to Theodore E. Brown (1 April 1963), King Papers, Boston University; M. S. Handler, "U.S. Negroes Plan Active Link with Peoples of African Nations," *New York Times*, 4 April 1963, 20; From George M. Houser to Martin Luther King Jr. (5 November 1963), ACOA Collection, Amistad Center, Tulane University; From Dora McDonald to George M. Houser (14 November 1963), King Papers, Boston University; and "Minutes of the Call Committee of the ANLCA," unpublished (16 December 1963): 1–3, King Papers, Boston University.

70. King to Brown (1 April 1963).

71. According to E. S. Reddy, "The U.N. Special Committee Against Apartheid (it had a long title at that time) was established in 1963 and had its first meeting on 2 April 1963. It was the first U.N. Committee boycotted by the Western Powers, and there was a feeling that it would be a flop. I was appointed its Principal Secretary." Reddy to Baldwin (14 September 1993). Also see From George M. Houser to Martin Luther King Jr. (9 April 1963), ACOA Collection, Amistad Center, Tulane University. Building on his comments, Houser told King that "there was never a time more than the present when solidarity between African nationalist leaders and American civil rights leaders was more needed than at the present time." From George M. Houser to Martin Luther King Jr. (6 September 1963), ACOA Collection, Amistad Center, Tulane University.

72. E. S. Reddy reports that "I met George Houser, whom I had known, and we discussed ways to obtain to the Committee and the issue of apartheid. As a result of this, the Chairman of the Special Committee, the late Diallo Telli of Guinea, received the letter (requesting a hearing) of 10 June 1963, from Dr. King—on the stationery of the American Committee on Africa." The letter from Dr. King stated, "As one of the two co-sponsors, with Chief Lutuli, of the Appeal for Action Against Apartheid last December, I would appreciate an opportunity to appear before your Committee, at its convenience, to testify on the policies of apartheid of the Government of the Republic of South Africa." Reddy added: "After the request was considered by the Committee, I sent the reply of 28 June. We did not hear from Dr. King." Reddy to Baldwin (14 September 1993); From E. S. Reddy to Martin Luther King Jr. (28 June 1963), King Center Archives;

From Martin Luther King Jr. to the Sub-Committee of the Special Committee on the Policies of Apartheid of the Government of the Republic of South Africa (10 June 1963), The Personal Papers of E. S. Reddy, New York, N.Y.; and From E. S. Reddy to Lewis V. Baldwin (15 May 1994).

73. See King, "Apartheid in South Africa," 1–6; and From George M. Houser to Wyatt T. Walker (11 July 1963), ACOA Collection, Amistad Center, Tulane University.

74. From Wyatt T. Walker to George M. Houser (10 July 1963), ACOA Collection, Amistad Center, Tulane University; and Interview with Houser (26 May 1993). Concerning efforts to get King before the U.N. Committee on Apartheid, E. S. Reddy recalls: "I called his representative in New York—I believe Rev. Wyatt Walker—twice to remind him, but there was no response. We felt that perhaps Dr. King was prevailed upon by the State Department not to speak before the U.N. Committee. But I believe we were wrong." Reddy to Baldwin (14 September 1993); and From George M. Houser to Lewis V. Baldwin (9 October 1987).

75. Ibid.; and From George M. Houser to Martin Luther King Jr. (4 September 1963), ACOA Collection, Amistad Center, Tulane University.

76. From Theodore E. Brown to Members of the Call Committee of the ANLCA (25 January 1964), King Papers, Boston University; From George M. Houser to Martin Luther King Jr. (22 June 1964), The King Center Archives; From Dora McDonald to George M. Houser (1 July 1964), ACOA Collection, Amistad Center, Tulane University; M. S. Handler, "Negroes Ask Role in Foreign Policy: Leaders to Meet in Capital—White House Interested," *New York Times,* 9 July 1964, 15; From Dora McDonald to Theodore E. Brown (30 July 1964), King Papers, Boston University; From Dorothy Gaines to Theodore E. Brown (31 July 1964), ACOA Collection, Amistad Center, Tulane University; and From Theodore E. Brown to Martin Luther King Jr. (21 July 1964), King Center Archives.

77. Brown to Members of the Call Committee of the ANLCA (25 January 1964); Handler, "Negroes Ask Role in Foreign Policy," 15; and Interview with Houser (26 May 1993).

78. Handler, "Negroes Ask Role in Foreign Policy," 15; Interview with Houser (26 May 1993); and *The American Negro Leadership Conference on Africa: Resolutions,* presented at Shoreham Hotel, Washington, D.C. (24–27 September 1964): 1–9.

79. *The A.N.L.C.A.: Resolutions* (1964), 4.

80. Ibid., 9; and Fierce, "Selected Black American Leaders," 318.

81. Baldwin, ed., *Toward the Beloved Community,* 335–424.

82. King, "On South African Independence," 1–2; and "King Accuses U.S.A. and Britain of Bolstering Racial Segregation in South Africa," *Relay News in English,* London, England (8 December 1964): 1–2.

83. King, "On South African Independence," 1–2. On this occasion, King also cautioned against a "growing color or race problem in England" caused by "the large numbers of persons that migrated here from various points of the British Commonwealth." See "Transcript of a Radio Interview with Martin Luther King Jr. Regarding the Nobel Peace Prize," Oslo, Norway (9 December 1964): 1–2, King Center Archives.

84. King, "On South African Independence," 1–2; and "King Accuses U.S.A. and Britain of Bolstering Racial Segregation," 1–2.

85. King, "On South African Independence," 1–2.

86. Quoted in Washington, ed. *A Testament of Hope,* 225. In a radio interview on 9 December 1964, the day before the awarding of the Nobel Prize, King, with the American South and South Africa very much in view, observed that "racial injustice is a constant threat to the peace and to the harmony of the world." He further noted that racism "is just as great a threat to the human race as the atomic bomb." See "Transcript of Radio Interview with Martin Luther King Jr.," 4.

87. From George M. Houser to Martin Luther King Jr. (5 January 1965), King Center Archives; From Martin Luther King Jr. to George M. Houser (19 January 1965), King Center Archives; From Roy Wilkins to Martin Luther King Jr. (7 July 1965), King Center Archives; From Martin Luther King Jr. to Roy Wilkins (20 July 1965), King Center Archives; and From Theodore E. Brown to Martin Luther King Jr. (9 August 1965), King Center Archives.

88. "U.S. Negroes' Goal: To Set Africa Policy," *U.S. News and World Report* LVIII, no. 2 (11 July 1965): 60–61.

89. From George M. Houser to Martin Luther King Jr. (14 July 1965), ACOA Collection, Amistad Center, Tulane University.

90. Ibid.

91. From Dora McDonald to George M. Houser (10 September 1965), King Center Archives; From George M. Houser to Martin Luther King Jr. (17 September 1965), King Center Archives; From Mary Louise Hooper to Charlton Heston (5 October 1965), ACOA Collection, Amistad Center, Tulane University; from Mary Louise Hooper to Martin Luther King Jr. (12 October 1965), King Center Archives; From George M. Houser to Martin Luther King Jr. (22 October 1965), King Center Archives; From George M. Houser to Martin Luther King Jr. (10 November 1965), King Center Archives; From Dora McDonald to George M. Houser (15 November 1965), ACOA Collection, Amistad Center, Tulane University; From George M. Houser to Martin Luther King Jr. (23 November 1965), King Center Archives; and From Mary Louise Hooper to Dora McDonald (29 November 1964), King Center Archives. Mary Louise Hooper said in one letter to King: "In my mind I have for years somehow associated you with my dear friend Chief Luthuli, with whom I worked, as I told you, for two years in South Africa. You are two men cut out of very much the same cloth, if I may say so." See

From Mary Louise Hooper to Martin Luther King Jr. (17 December 1965), King Center Archives.

92. King, "South Africa Benefit Speech," 1. The U.N. Centre Against Apartheid, at the request of the Special Committee, published King's speech and an appeal as a pamphlet. Reddy to Baldwin (14 September 1993). One source reports that King "entitled his address, 'Let My People Go,' in honour of Chief Albert Luthuli—President-General of the A.N.C." See *South Africa Freedom News,* issued by the African National Congress (South Africa), Dar Es Salaam (14 June 1966): 1–2.

93. Ibid., 3. James H. Cone has speculated on the possibility that there might have been a "relationship between King's perspective on Africa and his need for the support of the Federal Government in the civil rights movement." There is no strong evidence to substantiate this view, especially for the period 1965 to 1968, when King made it clear, by his positions on Vietnam and capitalism, that he attached very little significance to what the federal government thought about him. See From James H. Cone to Lewis V. Baldwin (18 February 1987).

94. King, "South Africa Benefit Speech," 4–5; and Herb Goldstein, "King Urges Boycott of Africa Racists," *New York Post,* 12 December 1965, 1 ff.

95. King, "South Africa Benefit Speech," 5–6. For brief assessments of the impact of King's presence and speech on the success of the ACOA's Human Rights Day activities in December 1965, see From George M. Houser to Martin Luther King Jr. (13 December 1965), King Center Archives; and Hooper to King (17 December 1965).

96. From George M. Houser to Martin Luther King Jr. (6 January 1966), King Center Archives; Interview with Houser (26 May 1993); George M. Houser, "Memorandum to Concerned Individuals and Organizations Regarding Hearings on Apartheid in the Sub-Committee on Africa of the House of Representatives Foreign Affairs Committee," unpublished document (5 January 1966), King Center Archives; From Dora McDonald to George M. Houser (14 January 1966), ACOA Collection, Amistad Center, Tulane University; From George M. Houser to Martin Luther King Jr. (2 February 1966), King Center Archives; and From George M. Houser to Martin Luther King Jr. (5 April 1966), King Center Archives.

97. Baldwin, *To Make the Wounded Whole,* 283–84.

98. Ibid., 276–78, 283–84. The harassment and isolation of King in this period happened as he was becoming more radical. Kenneth L. Smith persuasively argues that this "radicalization" process occurred on two levels. First, King broadened his vision "of the kind of society required to eliminate racism and achieve justice for everyone" (democratic socialism). Second, he broadened "his view of the tactics necessary to actualize such a society" (mass civil disobedience). I submit that King was also radicalized at a third level. More specifically, he broadened

his conception of how the African American struggle related to the struggles of oppressed peoples in other parts of the world. See Kenneth L. Smith, "The Radicalization of Martin Luther King Jr.: The Last Three Years," *Journal of Ecumenical Studies* 26, no. 2 (spring 1989): 270–87.

99. King treated all of these disturbing developments in his very last book. See King, *Where Do We Go from Here?*, 1–101.

100. "Same Dreary Old Distortions: Dr. Luther King Is No Communist," *Cape Times* (15 November 1965): 1 ff.; "No Reply to Luther King Invitation," *Cape Times,* 23 November 1965, 1 ff.; "Dr. Luther King in Bad Company," *Cape Times,* 22 November 1965, 1 ff.; and "Dr. Luther King Cause of U.S. Violence," *Cape Times,* 25 November 1965, 1 ff. Copies of these accounts exist in the King Center Archives.

101. "The Racial Scene," *Christian Century* LXXXIII, no. 30 (20 July 1966): 930.

102. A common view among scholars is that by the end of 1966, King's optimism regarding the possibility of the realization of the "American Dream" for all citizens in this country "had been shattered." Although King's optimism was severely challenged, it is excessive to claim that it was completely shattered. Up to the time of his death in 1968, King believed deeply that his people would ultimately reach the Promised Land. See Adam Fairclough, "Was Martin Luther King a Marxist?," *History Workshop,* vol. 15 (spring 1983): 120; and James H. Cone, *Martin and Malcolm and America: A Dream or a Nightmare* (Maryknoll, N.Y.: Orbis Books, 1991): 213–43.

103. Baldwin, *To Make the Wounded Whole,* 245–313; and King, *Where Do We Go from Here?*, 167–191.

104. King, *Where Do We Go from Here?*, 173; and Martin Luther King Jr., "On the World Taking a Stand on Rhodesia," transcript of an Interview, Paris, France (25 October 1965): 1, King Center Archives.

105. From T. Wendell Foster to Martin Luther King Jr. (10 April 1967), King Center Archives; and From Jackie Robinson to Martin Luther King Jr. (10 April 1967), King Center Archives.

106. From Dennis Brutus to Martin Luther King Jr. (20 October 1967), King Center Archives; and From Dennis Brutus to Lewis V. Baldwin (6 October 1987).

107. Brutus to Baldwin (6 October 1987); and Baldwin, ed., *Toward the Beloved Community,* 330.

108. Houser, *No One Can Stop the Rain,* 260; and Interview with Houser (26 May 1993).

109. Luthuli, *Let My People Go,* 37, 87, 135, 185, 236; King, "South Africa Benefit Speech," 5–6; "On South African Independence," 1–2; and *Where Do We Go from Here?*, 167–91; and Lewis V. Baldwin, *There Is a Balm in Gilead: The*

Cultural Roots of Martin Luther King Jr. (Minneapolis: Fortress Press, 1991), 63–90.

110. Luthuli, *Let My People Go,* 42, 47, 80, 82–83, 131–32; Houser, *No One Can Stop the Rain,* 52; King to King (25 March 1964); King, "A Knock at Midnight," 6–7, and "South Africa Benefit Speech," 5–6.

111. Fierce, "Selected Black American Leaders," 318.

112. Houser, *No One Can Stop the Rain,* 266, and "Freedom's Struggle Crosses Oceans and Mountains: Martin Luther King Jr. and the Liberation Struggles in Africa and America," in Peter J. Albert and Ronald Hoffman, eds., *We Shall Overcome: Martin Luther King Jr., and the Black Freedom Struggle* (New York: Pantheon Books, 1990), 186–87; Telephone Interview with George M. Houser (23 July 1987); and Interview with Houser (26 May 1993).

113. King, *Where Do We Go from Here?,* 57. For important reflections on where Robeson and Malcolm stood on this matter, see Sterling Stuckey, *Slave Culture: Nationalist Theory and the Foundations of Black America* (New York: Oxford University Press, 1987), 341; Stuckey, *Going Through the Storm: The Influence of African-American Art in History* (New York: Oxford University Press, 1994), 217–18, 223; and George Breitman, ed., *Malcolm X Speaks: Selected Speeches and Statements* (New York: Pathfinder, 1989), 36, 53, 72–77. King's view of the leadership role African Americans could possibly play in the worldwide struggle reflected his tendency toward *Pan-Negroism,* a concern that still awaits adequate treatment in the scholarship on King. See John H. Bracey Jr. et al., eds., *Black Nationalism in America* (New York: Bobbs-Merrill, 1970), xxix (introduction).

114. Baldwin, ed., *Toward the Beloved Community,* 320; Shepherd, "Who Killed Martin Luther King's Dream?," 2; and quoted in Washington, ed., *A Testament of Hope,* 23–30.

115. Fierce, "Selected Black American Leaders," 318–19; From James H. Robinson to Martin Luther King Jr. (22 June 1965), King Center Archives; From Sylvester A. Okereke to Martin Luther King Jr. (27 July 1965), King Center Archives; From Sylvester Okereke to Martin Luther King Jr. (10 June 1965), King Center Archives; From Martin Luther King Jr. to Sylvester A. Okereke (6 August 1965), King Center Archives; and From the PASOA to Martin Luther King Jr. (10 July 1967), King Center Archives.

116. "Doubts and Certainties Link," 1–9.

117. King, "South Africa Benefit Speech," 1–6; King, "On South African Independence," 1–2; quoted in Washington, ed., *A Testament of Hope,* 50; and King, "Why We Must Go to Washington," 14–15. King continued to believe that nonviolence was the only hope for South Africa. He felt that nonviolence as employed by an "international coalition of socially aware forces, operating outside governmental frameworks," remained the best approach to that country's "en-

trenched problems." See King, *The Trumpet of Conscience*, 63.

118. "Doubts and Certainties Link," 1–2.

119. Ibid.; Baldwin, *There Is a Balm in Gilead*, 50; and Fairclough, "Was Martin Luther King a Marxist?," 120.

120. King, "A Knock at Midnight," 6–7; and *Where Do We Go from Here?*, 167–68.

121. King, *Where Do We Go from Here?*, 167–68.

122. From Raymond Hoffenberg to Martin Luther King Jr. (8 April 1965), King Center Archives. In this letter, Hoffenberg referred to Davie as "Principal of the University until his death about ten years ago. He was a fearless and forceful critic of apartheid and a defender of the principles of academic freedom." Though living in South Africa at this time, Hoffenberg listed his address as Flat One, 25 Avenue Road, London, N.W. 8., England. In a recent letter to this author, he explained: "The address in London was temporary. I did this to avoid the scrutiny of the South African Security Police who would most certainly have opened and stopped any letter addressed to Dr. King." From Raymond Hoffenberg to Lewis V. Baldwin (13 July 1993).

123. Ibid.; From Martin Luther King Jr. to Raymond Hoffenberg (11 June 1965), King Center Archives; and From Raymond Hoffenberg to Martin Luther King Jr. (8 April 1965), King Center Archives.

124. From C. W. de Kiewiet to Martin Luther King Jr. (13 July 1965), The King Center Archives; From Dora McDonald to C. W. de Kiewiet (5 August 1965), King Center Archives; From Monica Wilson to Martin Luther King Jr. (12 November 1965), King Center Archives; and From Monica Wilson to Martin Luther King Jr. (18 February 1966), King Center Archives.

125. C. W. de Kiewiet told King that this invitation from SVLTF "is a more emphatic note of protest by the student body against apartheid, but also represents a tribute to the great transformation in our American life with which you are identified." de Kiewiet to King (13 July 1965); From Dora McDonald to Monica Wilson (3 December 1965), King Center Archives; From Dora McDonald to H. Baum (28 February 1966), King Center Archives; From M. Battsek to Dora McDonald (4 March 1966), King Center Archives; From Monica Wilson to Martin Luther King Jr. (11 March 1966), King Center Archives; and From King to Hoffenberg (11 June 1965).

126. From Peter Mansfield to Martin Luther King Jr. (26 October 1965), King Center Archives. The NUSAS was founded in 1924 to represent students studying in South Africa, to advance their common interests, and to cater to their multitude of needs. In 1965, the organization was called "the largest, and one of the few remaining, non-racial organizations in the country." Aside from Cape Town, branches of the NUSAS existed at the University of the Witwatersrand in Johannesburg and at other institutions.

127. From Martin E. West to Martin Luther King Jr. (2 April 1965), King Center Archives; From Martin Luther King Jr. to Martin West (24 May 1965), King Center Archives; From Claudie Erleigh to Martin Luther King Jr. (5 October 1966), King Center Archives; and From Martin Luther King Jr. to Claudie Erleigh (28 October 1966), King Center Archives.

128. Mansfield to King (26 October 1965).

129. From Martin Luther King Jr. to Peter Mansfield (3 November 1965), King Center Archives; and Mansfield to King (26 October 1965).

130. Mansfield to King (26 October 1965). Mansfield sent King a copy of Laurence Gandar's speech, titled "Old Myths and New Realities," delivered at the Annual Congress of the NUSAS in 1965. The speech launched a withering assault on South African apartheid. Also see *Martin Luther King Jr.: A Pamphlet* (Cape Town: NUSAS, 1965): 1–35, King Center Archives.

131. Mansfield to King (26 October 1965).

132. See Hoffenberg to King (8 April 1965); King to Hoffenberg (11 June 1965); Hoffenberg to Baldwin (13 July 1993); Wilson to King (28 February 1966); McDonald to Baum (28 February 1966); Battsek to McDonald (4 March 1966); Wilson to McDonald (11 March 1966); Mansfield to King (26 October 1965); From H. Baum to Martin Luther King Jr. (1 November 1965), King Center Archives; From Dora McDonald to H. Baum (18 November 1965), King Center Archives; From Peter Mansfield to Martin Luther King Jr. (18 November 1965), King Center Archives; and From Ian Robertson to Martin Luther King Jr. (26 January 1966), King Center Archives.

133. Mansfield to King (26 October 1965).

134. "Same Dreary Old Distortions," 1 ff.; and "No Reply to Luther King Invitation," 1 ff.

135. "DRC Pastor Replies: King 'Dark Brother' of 'Cape Times,'" *Cape Times,* 15 November 1965, 1 ff.; and "Dr. Luther King in Bad Company," 1 ff.

136. "Dr. Luther King Cause of U.S. Violence," 1 ff. Numerous statements of this kind were sent to King by the NUSAS president Peter Mansfield. Mansfield also sent King letters written to *Cape Times* in defense of him. See "Same Dreary Old Distortions," 1 ff.; "Challenge on Luther King," *Cape Times,* 18 November 1965, 1 ff.; "Be Reasonable," *Cape Times,* 18 November 1965, 1 ff.; "No Light Thrown on Dr. Luther King," *Cape Times,* 19 November 1965, 1 ff.; and "Another Saying," *Cape Times,* 19 November 1965, 1 ff. Mansfield also invited King to reply to the accusations against him, but King, as was so often the case with his critics in America, refused. See From Peter Mansfield to Martin Luther King Jr. (25 November 1965), King Center Archives.

137. From Ian Robertson to Lewis V. Baldwin (6 July 1993).

138. Mansfield to King (18 November 1965). Ian Robertson sent King a letter with almost the identical statement. See Robertson to King (26 January 1966).

Robertson reports, "We never found out if Dr. King received it or prepared a taped message." Robertson to Baldwin (6 July 1993).

139. From Stephen Hayes to Martin Luther King Jr. (17 August 1965), King Center Archives.

140. Ibid.

141. From Martin Luther King Jr. to South African Embassy (9 February 1966), King Center Archives.

142. From N. M. Nel to Martin Luther King Jr. (17 March 1966), King Center Archives. For other sources that refer to King's unsuccessful application for a South African visa, see From N. M. Nel to Martin Luther King Jr. (11 February 1966), King Center Archives; *News Release,* The Student Nonviolent Coordinating Committee, Atlanta, Ga. (24 March 1966): 1, King Center Archives; "The Racial Scene," 930; and Omond, *The Apartheid Handbook,* 209.

143. "'I Knew I Must Record It for the World,'" *Life* 64, no. 16 (19 April 1968): 1 ff.

144. Shepherd, "Who Killed Martin Luther King's Dream?," 2.

145. "Roundup: Foreign Tributes to Dr. King," *Christian Century* LXXXV, no. 19 (8 May 1968): 629–30; and quoted in Shirley DuBoulay, *Tutu: Voice of the Voiceless* (Grand Rapids, Mich.: William B. Eerdmans, 1988), 126; and John W. de Gruchy, *The Church Struggle in South Africa* (Grand Rapids, Mich.: William B. Eerdmans, 1986), 118.

146. "Roundup: Foreign Tributes to Dr. King," 630.

147. Press statement issued by the delegates at the Annual General Conference of the International Defence and Aid Fund, London, England (19–21 April 1968): 1, ACOA Collection, Amistad Center, Tulane University.

148. These developments were clearly reflected in the circles of liberation theology. For example, see Baldwin, *To Make the Wounded Whole,* 59–244; and Jim Galloway, "King's Passive Philosophy Faces Hard Sell in Africa," *St. Paul Pioneer Press Dispatch* (18 January 1987): 8A.

149. Morris, *Unyoung, Uncolored, Unpoor,* 9–157.

3. On Different Terms

1. Quoted in Mokgethi Motlhabi, *Challenge to Apartheid: Toward a Moral National Resistance* (Grand Rapids, Mich.: William B. Eerdmans, 1988), 37.

2. Allan A. Boesak, *Farewell to Innocence: A Socio-Ethical Study on Black Theology and Black Power* (Maryknoll, N.Y.: Orbis Books, 1977), 66.

3. Quoted in John W. de Gruchy, *The Church Struggle in South Africa* (Grand Rapids, Mich.: William B. Eerdmans, 1986), 233.

4. Jim Galloway, "King's Passive Philosophy Faces Hard Sell in Africa," *St. Paul Pioneer Press Dispatch,* 18 January 1987, 8A; and James Leatt et al., eds., *Contending Ideologies in South Africa* (Grand Rapids, Mich.: William B. Eerdmans, 1986), 99–104.

5. *International Tribute to Martin Luther King Jr.: A Booklet* (New York: United Nations Special Committee Against Apartheid, 1979), 27. This booklet consists of speeches given by world leaders at the King Center in Atlanta, Georgia, on 16 January 1979. Also see Lewis V. Baldwin, ed., *Toward the Beloved Community: Martin Luther King Jr. and South African Apartheid,* unpublished manuscript (1994), 341–48, King Center Archives.

6. George M. Houser, *No One Can Stop the Rain: Glimpses of Africa's Liberation Struggle* (New York: The Pilgrim Press, 1989), 266; Houser, "Freedom's Struggle Crosses Oceans and Mountains: Martin Luther King Jr. and the Liberation Struggles in Africa and America," in Peter J. Albert and Ronald Hoffman, ed., *We Shall Overcome: Martin Luther King Jr. and the Black Freedom Struggle* (New York: Pantheon Books, 1990), 187; and Milfred C. Fierce, "Selected Black American Leaders and Organizations and South Africa, 1900–1977: Some Notes," *Journal of Black Studies* 17, no. 3 (March 1987): 318.

7. Galloway, "King's Passive Philosophy Faces Hard Sell," 8A; and Baldwin, ed., *Toward the Beloved Community,* 333.

8. Leatt et al., eds., *Contending Ideologies in South Africa,* 102–3; Motlhabi, *Challenge to Apartheid,* 143–56; Galloway, "King's Passive Philosophy Faces Hard Sell," 8A; and Baldwin, ed., *Toward the Beloved Community,* 333.

9. Galloway, "King's Passive Philosophy Faces Hard Sell," 8A.

10. Ibid.; and Leatt et al., eds., *Contending Ideologies in South Africa,* 83–107.

11. Baldwin, ed., *Toward the Beloved Community,* 333–34; and Galloway, "King's Passive Philosophy Faces Hard Sell," 8A.

12. Leatt et al., eds., *Contending Ideologies in South Africa,* 107–19; and Motlhabi, *Challenge to Apartheid,* 27, 33, 67–68.

13. Donald Woods, *Biko* (New York: Vintage Books, 1978), 45–46.

14. Ibid.; Leatt et al., eds., *Contending Ideologies in South Africa,* 107; Motlhabi, *Challenge to Apartheid,* 27; and Roger Omond, *The Apartheid Handbook: A Guide to South Africa's Everyday Racial Policies* (New York: Penguin Books, 1986), 20.

15. Woods, *Biko,* 46.

16. Ibid.

17. Motlhabi, *Challenge to Apartheid,* 27–28.

18. Baldwin, ed., *Toward the Beloved Community,* 335. James H. Cone makes the same point regarding King and black power advocates in America. See James H. Cone, *Black Theology and Black Power* (New York: Seabury Press, 1969), 109. It is not excessive to speculate that Biko was influenced by the whole history of the black struggle in America, a point seemingly borne out by his acceptance of the slave spirituals as music reflective of the African heritage and struggle. See Aelred Stubbs, ed., *Steve Biko—I Write What I Like: A Selection of His Writings Edited with a Personal Memoir and a New Preface* (San Francisco: Harper and Row, 1978), 42–43.

19. Galloway, "King's Passive Philosophy Faces Hard Sell," 8A; and Leatt et al., eds., *Contending Ideologies in South Africa*, 105. Despite his differences with King on nonviolence, Biko preferred peaceful means over armed struggle in the South African freedom movement. He was as adamant as King in arguing that the effectiveness of nonviolent protest inside South Africa depended on the extent of the pressure imposed by the outside world. See Woods, *Biko*, 206, 216, 226, 236; and Stubbs, ed., *Steve Biko—I Write What I Like*, 143.

20. Baldwin, ed., *Toward the Beloved Community*, 335; and Cone, *Black Theology and Black Power*, 109.

21. Leatt et al., eds., *Contending Ideologies in South Africa*, 105–6.

22. Stubbs, ed., *Steve Biko—I Write What I Like*, 139, 147.

23. Ibid., 20–21, 121; Steve Biko, "Black Consciousness and the Quest for a True Humanity," in Basil Moore, ed., *The Challenge of Black Theology in South Africa* (Atlanta: John Knox Press, 1974), 40; Paul R. Garber, "Black Theology: The Latter Day Legacy of Martin Luther King Jr.," *The Journal of the Interdenominational Theological Center* 2, no. 2 (spring 1975): 100–113; and Garber, "King Was a Black Theologian," *Journal of Religious Thought* 31, no. 2 (fall/winter 1974–75): 16–32.

24. Stubbs, ed., *Steve Biko—I Write What I Like*, 146–47.

25. While black Americans had to deal with divisions in their own ranks at the points of ideology and methods, they did not have the deeply rooted traditions of tribalism that were typical of black South Africans, traditions that were reinforced to some extent by the existence and politics of the bantustans, or homelands. See ibid.

26. Leatt et al., eds., *Contending Ideologies in South Africa*, 59.

27. *New York Amsterdam News*, 2 January 1971, 1 ff.

28. Motlhabi, *Challenge to Apartheid*, 27–28, 33, 82.

29. Stubbs, ed., *Steve Biko—I Write What I Like*, 146–47; and Richard J. Neuhaus, *Dispensations: The Future of South Africa As South Africans See It* (Grand Rapids, Mich.: William B. Eerdmans, 1986), 237.

30. Woods, *Biko*, 9; Motlhabi, *Challenge to Apartheid*, 82–83; and Baldwin, ed., *Toward the Beloved Community*, 336.

31. Motlhabi, *Challenge to Apartheid*, 82–93; Leatt et al., eds., *Contending Ideologies in South Africa*, 107, 114–15; and Martin Luther King Jr., *Where Do We Go from Here: Chaos or Community?*, (Boston: Beacon Press, 1967), 173.

32. Galloway, "King's Passive Philosophy Faces Hard Sell," 8A.

33. Ibid.; and Gayraud S. Wilmore, "Steve Biko, Martyr," *Christianity and Crisis* 37, no. 16 (17 October 1977): 239–240.

34. Even James H. Cone failed to mention King in the brief article he contributed to this volume. See Moore, ed., *The Challenge of Black Theology in South Africa*, 49–51, 59, 63.

35. See "'Black Power': A Statement by the National Committee of Negro Churchmen," in Gayraud S. Wilmore and James H. Cone, ed., *Black Theology: A Documentary History, 1966–1979* (Maryknoll, N.Y.: Orbis Books, 1977), 23–30. This first significant statement on contemporary black theology in the United States was signed by many of the best-known black clergymen in America. King did not sign it.

36. Wilmore, "Steve Biko, Martyr," 239–40; and Baldwin, ed., *Toward the Beloved Community,* 337.

37. Wilmore, "Steve Biko, Martyr," 239–40.

38. Ibid., 240; and Stubbs, ed., *Steve Biko—I Write What I Like,* 213. Though it is important to point out that Biko, on fundamental grounds, preferred a nonviolent struggle in South Africa, arguing, in words quite similar to King's, that "violence brings too many residues of hate into the reconstruction period. If at all possible, we want the revolution to be peaceful and reconciliatory." Quoted in Leatt et al., eds., *Contending Ideologies in South Africa,* 112.

39. Baldwin, ed., *Toward the Beloved Community,* 388; and "James Cone Interview: Liberation, Black Theology, and the Church," *Radix* 14, no. 2 (September/October 1982): 9–11.

40. Tutu treats black theology in both contexts as emerging out of the black Christian experience, a context from which he was not likely to exclude King. See Desmond Tutu, "Black Theology/African Theology: Soul Mates or Antagonists?," *Journal of Religious Thought* XXXII, no. 2 (fall/winter 1975): 25–33; and Allan Boesak, *Coming in Out of the Wilderness: A Comparative Interpretation of the Ethics of Martin Luther King Jr. and Malcolm X* (Kampen, Holland: J. H. Kok, 1976), 1–48.

41. Desmond Tutu, "The South African Struggle," speech delivered at the Partners in Ecumenism Conference of the National Council of Churches, Washington, D.C. (26 September 1984): 1; and Boesak, *Farewell to Innocence,* 15.

42. Naomi Tutu, Comp., *The Words of Desmond Tutu* (New York: Newmarket Press, 1989), 101; Desmond Tutu, *Crying in the Wilderness: The Struggle for Justice in South Africa,* ed. John Webster (Grand Rapids, Mich.: William B. Eerdmans, 1982), 113; and Tutu, "The Struggle in South Africa," 1.

43. Tutu, comp., *The Words of Desmond Tutu,* 26–91.

44. Desmond M. Tutu, *Hope and Suffering: Sermons and Speeches,* ed. John Webster (Grand Rapids, Mich.: William B. Eerdmans, 1983), 69.

45. Ibid.; Tutu, *Crying in the Wilderness,* 113; and Tutu, comp., *The Words of Desmond Tutu,* 33, 38–39, 72–73, 83–91.

46. Tutu, comp., *The Words of Desmond Tutu,* 29, 32, 41.

47. De Gruchy, *The Church Struggle in South Africa,* 232–33.

48. Ibid.

49. See Boesak, "Coming in Out of the Wilderness," 1–48.

50. Ibid., 1–5; Galloway, "King's Passive Philosophy Faces Hard Sell," 8A; and Leatt et al., eds., *Contending Ideologies in South Africa,* 105.

51. Boesak, *Farewell to Innocence,* 6, 55, 74, 145–46; Tutu, "The Struggle in South Africa," 1; and Tutu, *Hope and Suffering,* 48–56.

52. Boesak, *Farewell to Innocence,* 15.

53. Ibid., 53, 58–62, 65, 137, 149.

54. Ibid., 39–40, 63–64, 69.

55. Ibid., 56–71.

56. Ibid., 58–71.

57. Ibid., 66–67.

58. Ibid., 39.

59. Ibid., 7.

60. Peter J. Paris, "Reflections on Recent South African Theological Writings," *Princeton Seminary Bulletin* 9, no. 1 (New Series, 1988), 45.

61. Baldwin, ed., *Toward the Beloved Community,* 341. See Dennis Brutus, *Stubborn Hope: New Poems and Selections from China Poems and Strains* (Washington, D.C.: Three Continents Press, 1978), 1–97; and Peter Abrahams, *Tell Freedom: Memories of Africa* (New York: Collier Books, 1970), 1–304.

62. Joseph Beam, "The Elder of the Village: An Interview with Bayard Rustin," *B/Out* (1987): 17; Baldwin, ed., *Toward the Beloved Community,* 342; and Baldwin, *To Make the Wounded Whole: The Cultural Legacy of Martin Luther King Jr.* (Minneapolis: Fortress Press, 1992), 230.

63. "SCLC V.P. Demands U.N. Peace Force in South Africa," *Jet* (16 September 1976): 18; and Baldwin, ed., *Toward the Beloved Community,* 343.

64. "SCLC V.P. Demands U.N. Peace Force in South Africa," 18.

65. Houser, *No One Can Stop the Rain,* 357.

66. Ibid., 266; Houser, "Freedom's Struggle Crosses Oceans and Mountains," 186–87; and Telephone Interview with George M. Houser (23 July 1987).

67. Fierce, "Selected Black American Leaders," 321; "Diggs Renews Drive Against South Africa," *Jet,* 21 March 1974, 14; and "Representative Diggs Halted in South Africa Airport," *Jet,* 20 February 1975, 12.

68. Fierce, "Selected Black American Leaders," 321; and "Representative Diggs Halted in South Africa Airport," 12.

69. Ranganath Murthy, "Good Intentions Aren't Enough: A Critique of the Sullivan Principles," unpublished paper (24 April 1986), 1–6; and Baldwin, ed., *Toward the Beloved Community,* 341–342.

70. Fierce, "Selected Black American Leaders," 318, 322.

71. Ibid., 322–23.

72. Quoted in *Four Decades of Concern: Martin Luther King Jr.* (Atlanta: King Center for Nonviolent Social Change, Inc., 1986), 27–28.

73. Ibid.

74. "A.M.E. Bishops' Council to Seek Kissinger Meeting," *Jet*, 25 September 1975, 31.

75. "Black Churches Tell Banks to Halt South African Loans," *Jet*, 30 March 1978, 31.

76. See Gayraud S. Wilmore, *Black Religion and Black Radicalism: An Interpretation of the Religious History of Afro-American People* (Maryknoll, N.Y.: Orbis Books, 1983), 99–134.

77. "We All Need a New Heart: Rev. Graham to South Africa," *Jet*, 5 April 1973, 13.

78. "South Africa Segregation Doomed, Graham Says," *Atlanta Constitution*, 30 March 1960, 3.

79. See Edward Lee Moore, "Billy Graham and Martin Luther King Jr.: An Inquiry Into White and Black Revivalistic Traditions," Ph.D. dissertation, Vanderbilt University, Nashville, Tenn., April 1979, 454, 457.

80. Ibid.

81. For examples, see John Pullock, *Billy Graham: The Authorized Biography* (New York: McGraw-Hill, 1966), 97–99, 214, 221–25; and Richard Quebedeaux, *The Young Evangelicals: The Story of the Emergence of a New Generation of Evangelicals* (New York: Harper and Row, 1974), 82–86. This tendency to ignore the impact that King had on the developing moderation of Graham and other white preachers toward race is suggestive of the depth of racism in the American society, and particularly in scholarly circles.

82. George W. Shepherd Jr., "Does the Carter Administration Have a Strategy for Southern Africa?," *Christian Century* XCIV, no. 28 (14 September 1977): 784. Also see "President Clinton, Former President Carter Tell: 'What Dr. Martin Luther King Means to Me,'" *Jet*, 17 January 1994, 4–6.

83. Shepherd, "Does the Carter Administration Have a Strategy?," 782–86.

84. Ibid., 785.

85. From Enuga S. Reddy to Lewis Baldwin (15 May 1994); and *International Tribute to Martin Luther King Jr.,* 63. Reddy is currently writing *Gandhi and America,* a book that will discuss Gandhi's contacts with African Americans. This book should afford information and insights not available in Sudarshan Kapur, *Raising Up a Prophet: The African-American Encounter with Gandhi* (Boston: Beacon Press, 1992).

86. Reddy to Baldwin (15 May 1994).

87. *International Tribute to Martin Luther King Jr.,* 1–65.

88. Quoted in ibid., 1–2.

89. Quoted in ibid., 3.

90. Quoted in ibid., 37–38.

91. Miss Challenor read the message sent by Amadou Mahtar M'bow, director-general of UNESCO. See ibid., 43–44.

92. Quoted in ibid., 4–5.

93. Quoted in ibid., 10, 12.

94. Quoted in ibid., 13.

95. Quoted in ibid., 13–14.

96. Quoted in ibid., 26.

97. Quoted in ibid., 32–33.

98. Ibid., 36.

99. Quoted in ibid., 40–42.

100. Quoted in ibid., 59.

101. Quoted in ibid., 47. Collins's name had long been associated with King through the American Committee on Africa. See From George M. Houser to Martin Luther King Jr. (1 February 1968), The ACOA Collection, Amistad Research Center, Tulane University, New Orleans, La.; and *Press Statement* issued by the Delegates of the Annual General Conference of the International Defence and Aid Fund, London, England (19–21 April 1968): 1, ACOA Collection, Amistad Center, Tulane University.

102. Quoted in *International Tribute to Martin Luther King Jr.,* 46.

103. Quoted in ibid., 29–31.

104. Jaipal read from the message sent by Morarji Desai, the Prime Minister of India. Quoted in ibid., 19.

105. Siddiqui shared this message from the Government of Pakistan. Quoted in ibid., 25–26.

106. Osman related this message from H. E. Gaafar Mohamed Nimeiri, president of the Democratic Republic of the Sudan, and, at that time, chairman of the Organization of African Unity (OAU). Quoted in ibid., 22.

107. Quoted in ibid., 27.

108. Quoted in ibid., 53.

109. Quoted in ibid., 48–51.

110. Quoted in ibid., 52.

111. Ibid.

112. Bomani carried this message from H. E. Mwalimu Julius Nyerere, president of the Republic of Tanzania. Quoted in ibid., 24.

113. Hussen's statement came from H. E. Mohamed Siad Barre, President of the Somali Democratic Republic. Quoted in ibid., 21.

114. Quoted in ibid., 15–17.

4. A Question of Options

1. Winnie Mandela, *Part of My Soul Went with Him,* ed. Anne Benjamin (New York: W. W. Norton, 1984), 125–26.

2. "A South African Fights from Exile," *New York Times,* 6 December 1985, A35.

3. "South Africa Discussed This Week," *Vanderbilt Register,* Vanderbilt University (Nashville, Tenn.), 24 January 1986, 1.

4. Jim Galloway, "King's Passive Philosophy Faces Hard Sell in Africa," *St. Paul Pioneer Press Dispatch,* 18 January 1987, 8A; Beyers Naudé, "Where Is South Africa Going?," *Africa Report* (May–June 1985): 4–9; Mark A. Uhlig, ed., *Apartheid in Crisis* (New York: Vintage Books, 1986), 1–12; and Charles Villa-Vicencio, ed., *Theology and Violence: The South African Debate* (Grand Rapids, Mich.: William B. Eerdmans, 1987), 1–308.

5. Uhlig, ed., *Apartheid in Crisis,* 15; and Villa-Vicencio, ed., *Theology and Violence,* 71–78.

6. Carole Collins, "Chronology of South Africa: A History of Black Struggle," *National Catholic Reporter* (22 March 1985): 16.

7. Naudé, "Where Is South Africa Going?," 4.

8. Collins, "Chronology of South Africa," 16; and Uhlig, ed., *Apartheid in Crisis,* 7.

9. Collins, "Chronology of South Africa," 16.

10. Ibid.

11. Jim Wallis and Joyce Hollyday, eds., *Crucible of Fire: The Church Confronts Apartheid* (Maryknoll, N.Y.: Orbis Books, 1989), 21–39, 92–101; and Frank Chikane, *No Life of My Own: An Autobiography* (Maryknoll, N.Y.: Orbis Books, 1988), 69–70.

12. Galloway, "King's Passive Philosophy Faces Hard Sell," 8A; and Lewis V. Baldwin, ed., *Toward the Beloved Community: Martin Luther King Jr. and South African Apartheid;* unpublished manuscript (1994), 348, Archives of the Martin Luther King Jr. Center for Nonviolent Social Change, Inc., Atlanta, Georgia.

13. Richard J. Neuhaus, *Dispensations: The Future of South Africa As South Africans See It* (Grand Rapids, Mich.: William B. Eerdmans, 1986), 214.

14. Galloway, "King's Passive Philosophy Faces Hard Sell," 8A; and Quoted in Wallis and Hollyday eds., *Crucible of Fire,* 99. One biblical scholar in America was told in the mid-eighties that "the two dirtiest words in black South Africa today are 'nonviolence' and 'reconciliation.'" See Walter Wink, *Violence and Nonviolence in South Africa: Jesus' Third Way* (Philadelphia: New Society Publishers, 1987), 7.

15. Quoted in Uhlig, ed., *Apartheid in Crisis,* 135–36.

16. This can be seen in the series of articles by white and black South Africans in Villa-Vicencio, ed., *Theology and Violence,* 1–308. Also see sources like Wink, *Violence and Nonviolence in South Africa,* 2–107; and Charles Villa-Vicencio, *Civil Disobedience and Beyond: Law, Resistance, and Religion in South Africa* (Grand Rapids, Mich.: William B. Eerdmans, 1990), 1–144.

17. "South Africa Discussed This Week," 1.

18. Galloway, "King's Passive Philosophy Faces Hard Sell," 8A.

19. Ibid.

20. Ibid.

21. Ibid.

22. Ibid.

23. Uhlig, ed., *Apartheid in Crisis,* 135.

24. James Leatt et al., eds., *Contending Ideologies in South Africa* (Grand Rapids, Mich.: William B. Eerdmans, 1986), 102–4; and Collins, "Chronology of South Africa," 16.

25. Leatt et al., eds., *Contending Ideologies in South Africa,* 102.

26. Uhlig, ed., *Apartheid in Crisis,* 134–35.

27. Ibid.; and "A South African Fights from Exile," A35. King held the view of war as a possible "negative good" before the Montgomery bus boycott in 1955–56. Given his own intellectual journey on the whole question of war, he would have been at least open to hear and understand the ANC's position in the 1980s. See Martin Luther King Jr., "Interview on World Peace," *Red Book,* November 1964, 3–7.

28. Uhlig, ed., *Apartheid in Crisis,* 135.

29. "A South African Fights from Exile," A35.

30. ANC leaders would not have interpreted classical Just War theory in the same ways as most South African whites. Some of the most interesting debates on nonresistance versus the Just War theory are carried in *Christianity Today* XXIV, no. 19 (7 November 1980): 14–25.

31. Uhlig, ed., *Apartheid in Crisis,* 135; Leatt et al., eds., *Contending Ideologies in South Africa,* 103–4, 118; Interview with Keith Appolis (26 February 1990); Mokgethi Motlhabi, *Challenge to Apartheid: Toward a Moral National Resistance* (Grand Rapids, Mich.: William B. Eerdmans, 1988), 79–117.

32. Uhlig, ed., *Apartheid in Crisis,* 39.

33. Leatt et al., eds., *Contending Ideologies in South Africa,* 102–3; and Motlhabi, *Challenge to Apartheid,* 89, 100.

34. Uhlig, ed., *Apartheid in Crisis,* 141–42.

35. Leatt et al., eds., *Contending Ideologies in South Africa,* 104, 115, 149.

36. Uhlig, ed., *Apartheid in Crisis,* 129–30; "May Day in South Africa: 15 Million Black Workers Strike," *Workers' Vanguard,* no. 403 (9 May 1986): 1, 3–4; and "South Africa's Top Black Labor Leader Calls on Workers to 'Seize Power,'" *Los Angeles Times,* 16 July 1987, Part I, 8.

37. "South Africa's Top Black Labor Leader Calls on Workers," 8.

38. Motlhabi's argument is strikingly similar to the one put forth consistently by Malcolm X in the United States in the 1960s. Both questioned the moral capacity of white racists to respond to nonviolence, an issue not typically raised by King and Gandhi. Motlhabi, *Challenge to Apartheid,* 151.

39. In supporting the violence of the government, while denouncing the self-defense or counterviolence of the oppressed, the white churches in South Africa were essentially no different from the white churches African Americans encountered in the United States in the 1950s and 1960s. Indeed, the critique set forth

in *The Kairos Document* recalls Malcolm X's complaints regarding the responses of white American churches to riots in the ghettoes. See *The Kairos Document—Challenge to the Church: A Theological Comment on the Political Crisis in South Africa*, rev. 2d ed. (Grand Rapids, Mich.: William B. Eerdmans, 1986), 13–15; Willis H. Logan, ed., *The Kairos Covenant: Standing with South African Christians* (New York: Meyer Stone Books and Friendship Press, 1988), 2–178; and "South African Theologians: Taking a Stand," *Christianity and Crisis* (11 November 1985): 435–37.

40. See Villa-Vicencio, ed., *Theology and Violence*, 1–309. Some twenty-five churchmen and theologians, white and black, contributed to this volume, thus providing a vivid indication of the level of attention devoted to issues of violence and nonviolence in the 1980s in South Africa.

41. See the essays by de Gruchy, Villa-Vicencio, and other whites in Villa-Vicencio, ed., *Theology and Violence*. Also see "South Africa Discussed This Week," 1; Wallis and Hollyday, eds., *Crucible of Fire*, 1–163; Uhlig, ed., *Apartheid in Crisis*, 5–332; Charles Villa-Vicencio and John W. de Gruchy, eds., *Resistance and Hope: South African Essays in Honour of Beyers Naudé* (Grand Rapids, Mich.: William B. Eerdmans, 1986), 3–198; Wink, *Violence and Nonviolence in South Africa*, 2–86; C. F. Beyers Naudé and Dorothee Sölle, *Hope for Faith: A Conversation* (Grand Rapids, Mich.: William B. Eerdmans, 1986), 2–38; Villa-Vicencio, *Civil Disobedience and Beyond*, 1–144; Chikane, *No Life of My Own*, 1–132; Neuhaus, *dispensations*, 1–310; Itumeleng J. Mosala and Buti Tlhagale, eds., *The Unquestionable Right to Be Free: Black Theology from South Africa* (Maryknoll, N.Y.: Orbis Books, 1986), 1–197; J. A. Loubser, *The Apartheid Bible: A Critical Review of Radical Theology in South Africa* (Cape Town, South Africa: Maskew Miller Longman, 1987), 135–43; and *Evangelical Witness in South Africa: A Critique of Evangelical Theology and Practice by South African Evangelicals* (Grand Rapids, Mich.: William B. Eerdmans, 1986), 7–48.

42. Villa-Vicencio, ed., *Theology and Violence*, 246–50; and "South Africa Discussed This Week," 1.

43. Much of what Villa-Vicencio says here calls to mind points made by Colin Morris almost a decade earlier. See Villa-Vicencio, ed., *Theology and Violence*, 246; and Colin Morris, *Unyoung, Uncolored, Unpoor* (Nashville and New York: Abingdon Press, 1969), 63, 90–91, and 94–95.

44. Mosala and Tlhagale, eds., *The Unquestionable Right to Be Free*, 135, 139. The attention given to King by black South African Theologians in discussions of violence and nonviolence in the 1980s was the primary inspiration for my series of essays on King and South Africa. See Lewis V. Baldwin, "Martin Luther King, Jr.'s 'Beloved Community' Ideal and the Apartheid System in South Africa," *Western Journal of Black Studies* 10, no. 4 (winter 1986): 211–22; "The Deferred Dream of Martin Luther King Jr.: The United States and South Africa," Part I,

National Baptist Union-Review 91, no. 9 (August 1987): 4, 6; "The Deferred Dream of Martin Luther King Jr.: The United States and South Africa," Part II, *National Baptist Union-Review* 91, no. 12 (October 1987): 6–7; "Toward the Dawn of Freedom: Martin Luther King Jr.'s Vision of an Independent Africa," *African Commentary* II, issue 3 (March 1990): 6–8; and "The Vision of Martin Luther King Jr. and the Apartheid System in South Africa," *Journal of Religious Studies* 16, nos. 1 and 2 (winter 1991): 22–45.

45. Cornel West implies that King and Boesak cannot be separated on the issue of nonviolence. Quoted in Logan, ed., *The Kairos Covenant,* 121. Some attention to how the nonviolent tradition in South Africa influenced Boesak, over and apart from King's influence on him, would have shown that the two men are not "pragmatic" or "realistic" pacifists in the same sense. The different contexts in which they operated must be seriously considered.

46. Interestingly enough, Boesak treats King's and Luthuli's "theology of refusal" in the same vein as that of Denmark Vesey, Frederick Douglass, W. E. B. Du Bois, Nehemiah Tile, and Mangana Mokone. See Allan Boesak, *Black and Reformed: Apartheid, Liberation and the Calvinist Tradition,* ed. Leonard Sweetman (Maryknoll, N.Y.: Orbis Books, 1984), 26, 48–49.

47. Boesak held that given the hypocrisy of white Christians on the question of nonviolence, "the question of 'just revolution,' raised by the French Huguenots many years ago (it was not thought up by black revolutionaries), must be faced." Ibid., 44, 49. King often assumed in the 1960s that with the proper international pressure from the outside, the nonviolent means he employed in America could work inside South Africa. At other times, he seemed to really understand that the South African situation was a unique one requiring methods beyond anything that he, as an American, was prepared to suggest or offer.

48. Villa-Vicencio, ed., *Theology and Violence,* 71–78.

49. Quoted in Logan, ed., *The Kairos Covenant,* 91.

50. Quoted in Villa-Vicencio, ed., *Theology and Violence,* 74; and Uhlig, ed., *Apartheid in Crisis,* 25.

51. Quoted in Villa-Vicencio, ed., *Theology and Violence,* 73.

52. Ibid., 72-73 and 76.

53. Ibid., 77; "'We Will Be Free' Says Bishop Tutu; Seeks International Community Aid," *Up-Date on the Black Church* (summer 1981): 1; Meg Voorhes, "Black South African Views on Divestment," *South Africa Review Service* (Washington D.C.: Investor Responsibility Research Center, 1986), 13; and Desmond Tutu, *Crying in the Wilderness: The Struggle for Justice in South Africa,* ed. John Webster (Grand Rapids, Mich.: William B. Eerdmans, 1982), 53. Tutu said frequently in the 1980s that the South African situation could possibly trigger a global confrontation, a view quite similar to the one King had in the 1960s. See Desmond Tutu, *Hope and Suffering: Sermons and Speeches,* ed. John Webster

(Grand Rapids, Mich.: William B. Eerdmans, 1984), 130; and Villa-Vicencio, ed., *Theology and Violence,* 77.

54. Quoted in Tutu, *Hope and Suffering,* 22.

55. Quoted in Villa-Vicencio, ed., *Theology and Violence,* 77. Like Tutu, Arun Gandhi, the grandson of Mohandas K. Gandhi, believed that apartheid would have been eliminated years ago had the world community, and especially the South African government, understood nonviolence and the true benefits that reconciliation and interracial community bring. An Interview with Arun Gandhi (3 April 1990).

56. Mandela, *Part of My Soul Went with Him,* 125–28.

57. Quoted in Wallis and Hollyday, eds., *Crucible of Fire,* 95, 98–99.

58. Boesak, *Black and Reformed,* 48.

59. Ibid., 30–31, 48–49.

60. *The Kairos Document* dealt in some measure with how the church should respond to the issue of violence in South Africa. The challenge put before the church about the violence of apartheid calls to mind King's challenge to white churches concerning the violence of segregation in his "Letter from the Birmingham City Jail" (1963). See Villa-Vicencio, ed., *Theology and Violence,* 305–6; Logan, ed., *The Kairos Covenant,* 7–160; *The Kairos Document,* 5–31; "South African Theologians: Taking a Stand," 435–37; and Martin Luther King Jr., *Why We Can't Wait* (New York: New American Library, 1964), 89–93.

61. Chikane, *No Life of My Own,* 55–56.

62. Quoted in Wallis and Hollyday, eds., *Crucible of Fire,* 66.

63. "South Africa Discussed This Week," 1.

64. Humphrey Tyler, "S. African Churches Vow to Undo Apartheid: One Urges Breaking Law," *Christian Science Monitor,* 27 October 1981, 11.

65. *Evangelical Witness in South Africa,* 7–45.

66. Ibid.

67. Voorhes, "Black South African Views on Divestment," 13.

68. King, *Why We Can't Wait,* 90.

69. Villa-Vicencio, *Civil Disobedience and Beyond,* 60–61; "Apartheid Victims Will Suffer White Christmas," *National Catholic Reporter* (19 December 1986): 3; and Wallis and Hollyday, eds., *Crucible of Fire,* xvi (introduction).

70. Wallis and Hollyday, eds., *Crucible of Fire,* xvi (introduction).

71. Ibid., 19.

72. Tutu, *Hope and Suffering,* 69, and *Crying in the Wilderness,* 113.

73. For Tutu, as for King, the traditional concept of "the Kingdom of God" is synonymous with the "beloved community" ideal. See "An Interview with Bishop Desmond Tutu: 1984 Nobel Peace Prize Winner," conducted by Delbert W. Baker, *Message,* 52, no. 1 (January–February 1986): 11.

74. Ibid.; Naomi Tutu, Comp., *The Words of Desmond Tutu* (New York:

Newmarket Press, 1989), 71-79; Tutu, *Crying in the Wilderness,* 113, and *Hope and Suffering,* 69.

75. Boesak, *Black and Reformed,* 30, 67.

76. Chikane, *No Life of My Own,* 42–43, 46, 56.

77. Tyler, "S. African Churches Vow to Undo Apartheid," 11.

78. Voorhes, "Black South African Views on Divestment," 13–14; *The Kairos Document,* 7–31; Naudé and Sölle, *Hope for Faith,* 2–38; and Roxanne Jordaan, "Religion: An Opium of the Masses or a Catalyst for Social Change?," unpublished paper, Vanderbilt University, Nashville, Tenn. (fall 1991): 10.

79. Uhlig, ed., *Apartheid in Crisis,* 136.

80. The UDF's *Declaration* in 1983 affirmed Boesak's vision of a "single nonracial, unfragmented South Africa . . . free of Bantustans and Group Areas." See Motlhabi, *Challenge to Apartheid,* 89–90; and Chikane, *No Life of My Own,* 56.

81. Uhlig, ed., *Apartheid in Crisis,* 136.

82. Roger Omond, *The Apartheid Handbook: A Guide to South Africa's Everyday Racial Policies* (New York: Penguin Books, 1985), 20; and Leatt et al., eds., *Contending Ideologies in South Africa,* 35.

83. Mandela, *Part of My Soul Went with Him,* 123.

84. "A South African Fights from Exile," A35.

85. Leatt, et al., eds., *Contending Ideologies in South Africa,* 59, 107–8, 114–16.

86. Ibid. Mokgethi Motlhabi reports that "The BCM rejected integration, especially if this was understood to mean assimilation of black people into an already existing white society with preestablished values and norms." See Motlhabi, *Challenge to Apartheid,* 49; and Leatt et al., eds., *Contending Ideologies in South Africa,* 108.

87. Uhlig, ed., *Apartheid in Crisis,* 136.

88. Leatt et al., eds., *Contending Ideologies in South Africa,* 114.

89. Ibid., 115.

90. Ibid., 105–19; and Uhlig, ed., *Apartheid in Crisis,* 136–137.

91. Uhlig, ed., *Apartheid in Crisis,* 136; Leatt et al., eds., *Contending Ideologies in South Africa,* 105, 114–19; and Motlhabi, *Challenge to Apartheid,* 50, 55.

92. Leatt et al., eds., *Contending Ideologies in South Africa,* 129–33.

93. Uhlig, ed., *Apartheid in Crisis,* 39, 127, 135–38, 140–48; Leatt et al., eds., *Contending Ideologies in South Africa,* 129–33; and Collins, "Chronology of South Africa," 16.

94. A solid work on King by a black South African scholar, taking into account the civil rights leader's impact on blacks in South Africa, has yet to be written. Such a study would be a valuable contribution to our understanding of King's significance for liberation movements beyond the United States over time. Moreover, such a study would have to draw on oral sources and the scattered writ-

ings and speeches of black South African clergymen, educators, and activists since the time of Albert Luthuli. Unfortunately, the closest source we have so far to such a study is Allan Boesak, *Coming In Out of the Wilderness: A Comparative Interpretation of the Ethics of Martin Luther King Jr. and Malcolm X* (Kampen, Holland: J. H. Kok, 1976).

95. Desmond Tutu, "The South African Struggle," speech delivered at the Partners in Ecumenism Conference of the National Council of Churches, Washington, D.C. (26 September 1984): 1 ff.

96. Tutu, *Hope and Suffering*, 22, 69, and *Crying in the Wilderness*, 113; Tutu, Comp., *The Words of Desmond Tutu*, 43, 72–73; Villa-Vicencio, *Civil Disobedience and Beyond*, 71; and Interview with Appolis (26 February 1990).

97. Shirley Du Boulay, *Tutu: Voice of the Voiceless* (Grand Rapids, Mich.: William B. Eerdmans, 1988), 198.

98. Ibid., 225; and *Four Decades of Concern: Martin Luther King, Jr.* (Atlanta: Martin Luther King Jr. Center for Nonviolent Social Change, 1986), 34. After Tutu received the Nobel Peace Prize, his picture appeared on the cover of a number of American publications with King's. See, for example, *Message*, 52, no. 1 (January–February, 1986).

99. Preston N. Williams, "A Review of Allan Boesak's *Black and Reformed: Apartheid, Liberation and the Calvinist Tradition* (1984)," in *The Princeton Seminary Bulletin* VI, no. 3 (New Series, 1985): 239.

100. Paul R. Spickard, "A Review of Allan Boesak's *Black and Reformed: Apartheid, Liberation, and the Calvinist Tradition* (1984)," in *Christian Scholars Review* 15, no. 1 (1985): 56.

101. Quoted in Wallis and Hollyday, eds., *Crucible of Fire*, 53. King consistently made this comment in the 1960s. See Coretta Scott King, *My Life with Martin Luther King Jr.* (New York: Avon Books, 1969), 327.

102. Wallis and Hollyday, eds., *Crucible of Fire*, 15–16.

103. Ibid., 8.

104. Ibid.

105. Boesak, *Black and Reformed*, 121.

106. Louise Kretzschmar, *The Voice of Black Theology in South Africa* (Johannesburg, South Africa: Ravan Press, 1986), 17 and 59.

107. Only fleeting references are made to King in Mosala and Tlhagale, eds., *The Unquestionable Right to Be Free*, 139. For a perfect example of the failure of scholars to sufficiently link King to black theology in South Africa in the 1980s, see Dwight N. Hopkins, *Black Theology USA and South Africa: Politics, Culture, and Liberation* (Maryknoll, N.Y.: Orbis Books, 1989), 8, 35, 42.

108. Mark Mathabane, *Kaffir Boy: The True Story of a Black Youth's Coming of Age in Apartheid South Africa* (New York: New American Library, 1986), 157. A sense of King's impact on black South Africans also comes through Mathabane,

Kaffir Boy in America: An Encounter with Apartheid (New York: Scribner's, 1989), 9, 32, 48, 81, 120; and Mark and Gail Mathabane, *Love in Black and White: The Triumph of Love over Prejudice and Taboo* (New York: HarperCollins, 1992), 53, 260.

109. Neuhaus, *Dispensations,* 34–35.

110. Ibid., 237–57. Many black South Africans, particularly strong anti-apartheid activists, would have insisted that any comparison between the Buthelezi of the 1980s and King was so insulting as to border on blasphemy. During the eighties, Buthelezi was commonly seen as a collaborator with the South African government, an image quite at odds with King's reputation as one who consistently challenged evil governments. Interview with Appolis (26 February 1990).

111. One source contends that King became "the black messiah, the singular and exclusive pattern not only for blacks in America to imitate but also for other liberation movements throughout the world," a point that lends some support to my conclusion. See William R. Jones, "Martin Luther King Jr.: Black Messiah or White Guardian?," unpublished paper presented before the First Unitarian Society of Minneapolis, Minn. (6 April 1986): 1.

112. Quoted in *Jet,* 14 October 1985, 40; and in Alex Ayres, ed., *The Wisdom of Martin Luther King Jr.: An A-to-Z Guide to the Ideas and Ideals of the Great Civil Rights Leader* (New York: Penguin Books USA, Inc., 1993), xi.

113. *Annual Report of the U.N. Special Committee Against Apartheid,* unpublished document (1982), 39, The Personal Collection of E. S. Reddy, New York, N.Y.; and From E. S. Reddy to Lewis V. Baldwin (10 April 1994).

114. Reddy to Baldwin (10 April 1994); From E. S. Reddy to Lewis V. Baldwin (17 August 1994); and *Annual Report of the U.N. Special Committee Against Apartheid,* 39.

115. *Annual Report of the U.N. Special Committee Against Apartheid,* 39.

116. From Coretta Scott King to E. S. Reddy (4 February 1982), personal collection of E. S. Reddy.

117. Ibid.

118. Reddy to Baldwin (10 April 1994); and *Official Records of the United Nations General Assembly,* Thirty-Seventh Session, 56th Plenary Meeting, New York, New York (5 November 1982): 963–76, personal collection of E. S. Reddy.

119. Reddy to Baldwin (10 April 1994); and *Official Records of the United Nations,* 964–76.

120. *Official Records of the United Nations,* 970.

121. Ibid., 971–72.

122. Baldwin, "Martin Luther King Jr.'s 'Beloved Community' Ideal and the Apartheid System in South Africa," 215–16, and *To Make the Wounded Whole: The Cultural Legacy of Martin Luther King Jr.* (Minneapolis: Fortress Press, 1992), 233–44.

123. Baldwin, *To Make the Wounded Whole*, 234.

124. Ibid., 233–44; and Joseph E. Lowery, "An Appeal to Eliminate Apartheid on Human Rights Day," a speech (10 December 1983): 1–3.

125. Lowery, "An Appeal to Eliminate Apartheid," 1–3.

126. "Lowery Suggests Reagan Show Concern for S. Africa," *Jet*, 27 June 1988, 38.

127. Lowery, "An Appeal to Eliminate Apartheid," 1–3.

128. Roger D. Hatch and Frank E. Watkins, eds., *Reverend Jesse L. Jackson: Straight from the Heart* (Philadelphia: Fortress Press, 1987), 232.

129. Ibid., 232–45.

130. D. Michael Cheers, "Jackson Tours Europe and Joins Marches Against South Africa," *Jet*, 3 June 1985, 30–33; and Naudé and Sölle, *Hope for Faith*, 27–28.

131. Cheers, "Jackson Tours Europe and Joins Marches," 30–33.

132. Michael Lerner, "A Dialogue with Jesse Jackson," *Tikkun* 2, no. 5 (November/December 1987): 40.

133. D. Michael Cheers, "Jesse Jackson: Rebuilding Bridges to Africa—P.U.S.H. Founder Renews Spiritual Bond between U.S. Blacks and Africans," *Ebony* 42, no. 2 (December 1986): 132–33, 136, 138; and Cheers, "After Visit to African Nations, Jesse Jackson Urges Joint Partnership," *Jet*, 30 January 1989, 12–16.

134. Cheers, "Jesse Jackson: Rebuilding Bridges," 136, 138; and "What Black Americans and Africans Can Do for Each Other," *Ebony* 41, no. 6 (April 1986): 156.

135. "U.S. Negroes' Goal: To Set Africa Policy," *U.S. News and World Report* LVIII, no. 2 (11 July 1965): 60–61.

136. Quoted in *Four Decades of Concern*, 28.

137. Ibid., 27–36 and 43–56; and Tutu, Comp., *The Words of Desmond Tutu*, 103.

138. Quoted in *Four Decades of Concern*, 31; "What Black Americans and Africans Can Do," 155; and "King Family Arrested and Jailed for Embassy Protest," *Jet*, 15 July 1985, 5.

139. "Coretta King Urges World Peace on King's Birthday," *Jet* (7 October 1985): 4; and "Heirs of Nobel Peace Prize Winners," *Jet* (2 December 1985): 44.

140. "Transcript of a Television Interview with Coretta Scott King," aired on ABC's *Good Morning America*, 18 September 1986, 1; and Villa-Vicencio, ed., *Theology and Violence*, 303.

141. Quoted in *Four Decades of Concern*, 31.

142. Ibid., 32.

143. Ibid., 33–35.

144. Ibid., 33.

145. Ibid., 35.

146. Ibid., 30–31.

147. King, *My Life with Martin Luther King Jr.*, 73, 83.

148. Quoted in *Four Decades of Concern*, 29.

149. Ibid., 31.

150. Ibid., 32.

151. Ibid., 30.

152. Ibid., 32-33.

153. Ibid.; and "Transcript of a Television Interview with Coretta Scott King," 1.

154. Quoted in *Four Decades of Concern*, 27–35.

155. Ibid., 31.

156. Ibid., 30.

157. Ranganath Murthy, "Good Intentions Aren't Enough: A Critique of the Sullivan Principles," unpublished paper (24 April 1986): 1–6.

158. Michele N. K. Collison, "Colleges See Pressure on South African Investments Following Sullivan's Call for U.S. Withdrawal," *Chronicle of Higher Education* 33, no. 39 (10 June 1987): 2.

159. Christopher A. Coons, *The Response of Colleges and Universities to Calls for Divestment* (Washington, D.C.: Investor Responsibility Research Center, 1986), 1 ff.; and From David Riesman to Lewis V. Baldwin (28 June 1993). Having witnessed the same situation in my work as adviser of Vanderbilt University Students Against Apartheid (VAA), I find Riesman's comments very much on the mark.

160. "Congressmen Blast Reagan Executive Order Applying Sanctions to South Africa," *Jet*, 23 September 1985, 5; and Baldwin, *To Make the Wounded Whole*, 234.

161. A Letter from William H. Gray III to Friends of the Free South Africa Movement (April 1988).

162. D. Michael Cheers, "TransAfrica: The Black World's Voice on Capitol Hill," *Ebony* 42, no. 9 (July 1987): 108, 110; and "What Black Americans and Africans Can Do," 155.

163. Cheers, "TransAfrica: The Black World's Voice," 108, 110, 112, 114; *Four Decades of Concern*, 33, 35; "What Black Americans and Africans Can Do," 155–56; and Martin Luther King Jr., "On South African Independence," a speech in London, England (7 December 1964), 18. For interesting reflections on TransAfrica's role in the black South African struggle, see "Randall Robinson's TransAfrica Dedicates New Building," *Jet*, 7 June 1993, 34–36, 38.

164. Quoted in Gray to Friends of the Free South Africa Movement (April 1988).

165. Ibid.

166. "National Baptist Confab Raps South African Racism: Gears for Economic Growth," *Jet,* 30 September 1985, 24–25; and *National Baptist Union-Review* 89, no. 20 (October 1985): 2.

167. "Final Statement of Black Church Summit on Southern Africa," *A.M.E. Church Review,* 104, no. 333 (January/March 1989): 53–54.

168. The extent to which black churches and their leadership have addressed black South African concerns since the King years has not been seriously treated even by scholars whose approaches are Afrocentric. Such a study would have to begin with King and his influence upon the attitudes of black churchpersons toward South Africa in particular and Africa in general. See Baldwin, *To Make the Wounded Whole,* 163–244.

169. "A Resolution of the National Council of Churches of Christ in the U.S.A.: Current Developments in Southern Africa," Chicago, Ill. (5–7 November 1986): 1–2.

170. Denise Johnson Stovall, "Methodist Leaders Rejoice at Mandela Release," *United Methodist Reporter of the Tennessee Conference* 136, no. 39 (23 February 1990): 3; John A. Lovelace, "World Methodist Group to Meet de Klerk," *United Methodist Reporter of the Tennesse Conference* 137, no. 11 (10 August 1990): 4; and "Religious Leaders Call for New South Africa Policy," *Report to Presbyterians from Washington* 6, no. 6 (March/April 1985): 1–4.

171. One of the most enlightening and thought-provoking discussions of Reagan's "Constructive Engagement" policy is afforded in Robert Fatton, "The Reagan Foreign Policy Toward South Africa: The Ideology of the New Cold War," *African Studies Review* 27, no. 1 (March 1984): 57–82.

172. "Falwell Raises a Stir by Opposing Sanctions Against South Africa," *Christianity Today* 29, no. 14 (4 October 1985): 52–54. Most white American churches either supported Falwell's views or engaged in a conspiracy of silence and nonaction with respect to the question of sanctions against South Africa.

173. "Falwell Raises a Stir by Opposing Sanctions Against South Africa," 52–54. At least 90 percent of South Africa's blacks favored sanctions against their country in 1985–86, a statistic which challenged Falwell's claims. See "Improving Life's Quality Is Dream," *Vanderbilt Register,* 24 January 1986, 3. Falwell's position was essentially no different from that of the American evangelical leader Jimmy Swaggart, "who actually sided with the South African government against the interest of suffering blacks in the name of the gospel." See *Evangelical Witness in South Africa,* 11.

174. D. Michael Cheers, "Rev. Jesse Jackson Travels to Lynchburg to Take Issue with Rev. Jerry Falwell," *Jet,* 23 September 1985, 6–9.

175. Ibid.; and "Falwell Lambasted for His Remarks about Tutu," *Jet,* 9 September 1985, 16.

176. Cheers, "Rev. Jesse Jackson Travels to Lynchburg," 6–9; and Flo Conway

and Jim Siegelman, *Holy Terror: The Fundamentalist War on America's Freedoms in Religion, Politics and Our Private Lives* (New York: Dell Publishing Company, 1984): 85–86.

177. "Lowery Chides Robertson on South Africa Comments and on Killing Libya's Gadhafi," *Jet,* 29 February 1988, 54.

178. Ibid.

179. Lowery, "An Appeal to Eliminate Apartheid," 1 ff.; and Cheers, "Jackson Tours Europe and Joins Marches," 30–33.

180. "Sullivan Critiques Churches' Inactivity in South Africa," *National Catholic Reporter* (19 December 1986): 4.

181. "Conversation in Ghana," *Christian Century* LXXIV, no. 15 (10 April 1957): 447.

182. William K. Quick, "Resolution of the World Methodist Conference on South Africa," *A.M.E. Zion Quarterly Review* XCVIII, no. 3 (October 1986): 16–17.

183. "Pope Blasts U.S. Racism; Urges Church to Continue Fight for Black Equality," *Jet,* 28 September 1987, 4. Although Pope John Paul II was not speaking directly about South African apartheid, his comments certainly had implications for the struggle against that system.

184. Martin Luther King Jr., *Where Do We Go from Here?: Chaos or Community* (Boston: Beacon Press, 1968), 167; and Baldwin, *To Make the Wounded Whole,* 247–86.

185. Du Boulay, *Tutu,* 192, 232; and Roger D. Hatch, *Beyond Opportunity: Jesse Jackson's Vision for America* (Philadelphia: Fortress Press, 1988), 121.

186. Andrew Meldrum, "The Bush Agenda in Southern Africa," *Africa Report* 34, no. 1 (January/February, 1989): 16–17.

187. King, "Call for an International Boycott on Apartheid," 21–22.

188. "70,000 Greet Released Leaders in South Africa," *Tennessean,* 30 October 1989, 1, 2A; Charles Villa-Vicencio, "South Africa: Options for the Future," *Africa Report* 35, no. 2 (May–June 1990): 29; and Sebastian Mallaby, *After Apartheid: The Future of South Africa* (New York: Time Books, 1992), 1–36.

5. Envisioning a New Order

1. Quoted in *New York Times,* 30 January 1991, 2A.

2. Quoted in *Time,* 3 January 1994, 54.

3. Quoted in *New York Times,* 10 May 1994, 1.

4. Martin Luther King Jr., "A Proposed Statement to the South," presented at the Southern Negro Leadership Conference on Transportation and Nonviolent Integration, Atlanta, Ga. (10 January 1957): 1, Martin Luther King Jr. Papers, Special Collections, Mugar Memorial Library, Boston University, Boston, Mass.

5. "70,000 Greet Released Leaders in South Africa," *Tennessean,* 30 October

1989, 1 and 2A; Charles Villa-Vicencio, "South Africa: Options for the Future," *Africa Report* 35, no 2 (May/June 1990): 29; and Sebastian Mallaby, *After Apartheid: The Future of South Africa* (New York: Times Books, 1992), 3, 6, 11, 15–16, 27, 100–1, 103, 252.

6. "In Mandela's Garden: An Interview," *Africa Report* 35, no. 2 (May/June, 1990): 34; Leonard Madu, "South Africa: New Realities," *Nashville Pride,* 25 October 1991, 2A; "South African Clash Kills Two Right-Wingers," *Nashville Banner,* 10 August 1991, 1, A2; Christopher S. Wren, "Two Black Factions in South Africa Will End Rivalry: Breakthrough Accord," *New York Times,* 30 January 1991, 1; and "Church Leaders Hasten South African Summit," *United Methodist Reporter of the Tennessee Conference* 140, no. 7 (9 July 1993): 3.

7. "Churches Seen Continuing as Reconcilers," *United Methodist Reporter of the Tennessee Conference* 140, no. 3 (11 June 1993): 3; and Cynthia B. Astle and Denise J. Stovall, "Methodist Pastor Quietly Trains South African Peace Workers," in ibid.

8. Such writers have shown a stunning lack of knowledge concerning the depth of racism in South African society. See Ray S. Anderson, "Toward a Post-Apartheid Theology," *The Reformed Journal* 38, issue 5 (May 1988): 23–26; James M. Wall, "South African Changes: Hope for a Region as Well as a Nation," *Christian Century* III, no. 16 (11 May 1994): 483; "A New South Africa: Editorial Comment II," *The Month: A Review of Christian Thought and World Affairs* CCLV, no. 1517 (May 1994): 171–72; and "Sullivan Urges Business Commitment to South Africa," *Jet,* 8 November 1993, 4. Writing in 1992, one scholar clearly exaggerated when he compared changes in South Africa at that point to the collapse of communism in Eastern Europe. His assertion that "apartheid has been defeated" was, and still is, absurd, and it feeds into the kind of misguided or erroneous assumptions that still pervade much of the global community. See Mallaby, *After Apartheid,* 3–9; and Paul Ruffins, "A Review of Sebastian Mallaby's *After Apartheid,*" *Washington Post Book World,* 14 June 1992, 4.

9. Lewis V. Baldwin, *To Make the Wounded Whole: The Cultural Legacy of Martin Luther King Jr.* (Minneapolis: Fortress Press, 1992), 302–7; Jewelle T. Gibbs, "British Black and Blue: Discrimination against Black British Youth in Education, Employment, and the Administration of Justice Impedes Their Upward Mobility," *Focus* 21, no. 14 (April 1993): 3–5; Harry Stein, "Fashioning a Human Face for Today's Young Fascists," *TV Guide,* 8–14 May 1993, 48; "New Report Reveals Young Whites Are More Biased Against Blacks Than Older Whites Are," *Jet,* 5 July 1993, 26–29; and Michael E. Cottman, "Racism in Japan: Negative Images of Blacks Fuel Friction and Misunderstanding," *Emerge* 4, issue 9 (July–August 1993): 24–25.

10. Mallaby, *After Apartheid,* 6, 15–16; "What Next Mandela?," *New African,*

no. 270 (March 1990): 9; and Ruffins, "A Review of Sebastian Mallaby's *After Apartheid*," 4.

11. "70,000 Greet Released Leaders," 1, 2A; and Villa-Vicencio, "South Africa: Options for the Future," 29.

12. Mallaby, *After Apartheid*, 11–12.

13. Lewis V. Baldwin, ed., *Toward the Beloved Community: Martin Luther King Jr. and South African Apartheid*, unpublished manuscript (1994), 393; and Interview with Keith Appolis (26 February 1990).

14. Mallaby, *After Apartheid*, 101, 252; and Interview with Appolis (26 February 1990).

15. See Martin Luther King Jr., *Stride Toward Freedom: The Montgomery Story* (New York: Harper and Row, 1958), 219–20; and Lewis V. Baldwin, *There Is a Balm in Gilead: The Cultural Roots of Martin Luther King Jr.* (Minneapolis: Fortress Press, 1991), 66.

16. "What Next Mandela?," 9; and Mallaby, *After Apartheid*, 15–16.

17. Sebastian Mallaby reported in 1992 that the sanctions caused South Africa's gross domestic product to decline from 20 percent to 35 "percent lower than would otherwise have been the case." See Mallaby, *After Apartheid*, 44–46, 48, 196–98; and George M. Fredrickson, "No Going Back for Either Side: A Review of Sebastian Mallaby's *After Apartheid*," *New York Times Book Review*, 5 April 1992, 3.

18. Mallaby, *After Apartheid*, 15, and From George M. Houser to Lewis V. Baldwin (9 October 1987).

19. Interview with Appolis (26 February 1990); Houser to Baldwin (9 October 1987); Fredrickson, "No Going Back for Either Side," 3; Steve Harvey, "Struggle Recalls King's, but Strategies Differ," *Atlanta Journal and Constitution*, 17 June 1990, D-2; and Peter Walshe, "The African National Congress: Part of the Solution in South Africa," *Christianity and Crisis* 47, no. 7 (4 May 1987): 166.

20. Mallaby, *After Apartheid*, 100–3; and "South African Clash Kills Two Right-Wingers," 1, A2.

21. Mallaby, *After Apartheid*, 100–103.

22. Ibid., 32; and Paul Gray, "Nelson Mandela and F. W. de Klerk," *Time* 143, no. 1 (3 January 1994): 57.

23. "What Next Mandela?," 9. One source notes: "Mandela had always been willing to talk; violence was his recourse when the other side would not listen." See Gray, "Nelson Mandela and F. W. de Klerk," 55; and Nelson Mandela, *Intensify the Struggle to Abolish Apartheid: Speeches, 1990*, ed. Greg McCartan (New York: Pathfinder Press, 1990), 11, 13, 21.

24. Martin Luther King Jr. considered *negotiation* one of the four basic steps in any truly nonviolent direct action campaign. The other three involve a collection

of facts to determine if injustice exists, self-purification, and direct action, steps that correspond with Mohandas K. Gandhi's forms of direct satyagraha action. See John J. Ansbro, *Martin Luther King Jr.: The Making of a Mind* (Maryknoll, N.Y.: Orbis Books, 1982), 132; and Martin Luther King Jr., *Why We Can't Wait* (New York: The New American Library, 1963), 78. In 1990, Oliver Tambo "was glad to renounce guerrilla tactics when the de Klerk government lifted its ban and asked for open negotiations." See "A Great Tree Falls in Africa: Oliver Tambo Dies at 75," *The Crisis* 100, issue 4 (April/May 1993): 28.

25. Christopher S. Wren, "Zulu Ex-Aide Tells of Arms Training: New Testimony of Help by Pretoria for the ANC's Foe, Inkatha," *New York Times,* 1 March 1992, 3; Mallaby, *After Apartheid,* 31–32, 100; "In Mandela's Garden," 34; and Madu, "South Africa: New Realities," 2A.

26. "In Mandela's Garden," 34; "What Next Mandela?," 10; and D. Michael Cheers, "Nelson Mandela Reveals Private Side of His Life as a Prisoner for 27 Years," *Jet,* 12 March 1990, 12–17.

27. "What Next Mandela?," 10.

28. "De Klerk's Mandate Frees South Africa for a New Day," *New York Times,* 22 March 1992, 2; Fredrickson, "No Going Back for Either Side," 3. One source seems to give more credit to the South African government than to black political pressure for such reforms, a conclusion not supported by the evidence. See Mallaby, *After Apartheid,* 16–154.

29. Patrick Laurence, "The Year of Negotiations," *Africa Report* 37, no. 1 (January/February, 1992): 50; Bill Keller, "South African Massacre: Fingers Point at the Police," *New York Times,* 20 June 1992, 1, 3; and "Massacre Leaves Talks 'in Tatters': ANC Breaks Off with de Klerk," *Tennessean,* 22 June 1992, 1. Nelson Mandela and Desmond Tutu urged the International Olympic Committee to ban South Africa from competition in Barcelona because of the apartheid government's involvement in the Boipatong massacre. See *Jet,* 13 July 1992, 48.

30. "Interviews with Nelson Mandela and F. W. de Klerk," *Time,* 3 January 1994, 53–57; and "Black South Africans Protest to Commemorate 1976 Soweto Uprising," *Jet,* 6 July 1992, 5.

31. King, *Why We Can't Wait,* 78.

32. Gray, "Nelson Mandela and F. W. de Klerk," 54–57.

33. Mallaby, *After Apartheid,* 32.

34. Gray, "Nelson Mandela and F. W. de Klerk," 54.

35. "Mandela Makes Plea for U.S. to End Sanctions Against South Africa," *Jet,* 18 October 1993, 56; "Johannesburg, South Africa," *Emerge* 5, no. 4 (December 1993–January 1994): 60; and "Mandela: We Stand Here Not as Guests, but as Comrades in Arms," *The Crisis* 100, issue 6 (August/September 1993): 31.

36. Gray, "Nelson Mandela and F. W. de Klerk," 57.

37. "Mandela, De Klerk Accept Nobel Peace Prize While Toni Morrison Picks

Up Top Honor for Literature," *Jet,* 27 December 1993–3 January 1994, 6; and "Winnie Mandela Calls Joint Nobel Peace Prize 'Insult,'" *Jet,* 15 November 1993, 17.

38. Gray, "Nelson Mandela and F. W. de Klerk," 52, 57.

39. Martin Luther King Jr., *Where Do We Go from Here: Chaos or Community?* (Boston: Beacon Press, 1967), 173, 186; D. Michael Cheers, "Nelson Mandela: A Special Message to Black Americans," *Ebony* XLV, no. 7 (May 1990): 180–82; and Gray, "Nelson Mandela and F. W. de Klerk," 52–53.

40. Mallaby, *After Apartheid,* 100–103; and Christopher S. Wren, "Fewer Options for South Africa's Rightists," *New York Times,* 1 March 1992, 5. Throughout 1993, the idea of a separate homeland was heavily supported by many South African whites, and Nelson Mandela and others in the ANC agreed to compromise with them, but only "within the framework of a unitary South Africa ruled by a black majority." See Deborah Scroggins, "Mandela Hints at Compromise with Whites Seeking Homeland," *Atlanta Constitution,* 12 July 1993, A1; and Scroggins, "Whites Demanding Homeland in South Africa: Mandela Offers Talks with Separatists," *Atlanta Journal,* 12 July 1993, A1, C1–C3. According to one account, conservative whites saw Mandela "as a man who will expel whites, nationalize businesses and cause South Africa to be as economically hopeless as Tanzania or Zambia." "It could be," the account continued in 1990, that Mandela "would like to establish a hardline Marxist-Leninist State. But it is equally likely that a Mandela-led South Africa would resemble Jomo Kenyatta's Kenya, and become a somewhat capitalist, somewhat multiracial, somewhat democratic nation." See Martin M. Wooster, "South Africa is Not the U.S. and A.N.C. Leader Is Not King," *Atlanta Journal and Constitution,* 17 June 1990, D-10.

41. Mallaby, *After Apartheid,* 100–103, 216, 231; "Violence Erupts in South Africa after Slaying of Leader," *Jet,* 26 April 1993, 10; "Massacre Leaves Talks 'in Tatters,'" 1; "Mob chases de Klerk Away: Police Kill Three in Crowd," *Tennessean,* 21 June 1992, 1, 2A; "ANC Statement: The Death of Chris Hani," unpublished document issued by the ANC (10 April 1993): 1; and Jim Cason, "Push for Speedier South African Transition Follows Hani's Death," *Africa News* 38, no. 6 (April 26–May 8, 1993): 5.

42. Mallaby, *After Apartheid,* 225–31, 235–36, 239–40; Keller, "South African Massacre," 1, 3; and Christopher S. Wren, "Judge Convicts Winnie Mandela of Accessory in Assault on Youths," *New York Times,* 14 May 1991, 1, A7.

43. Gray, "Nelson Mandela and F. W. de Klerk," 55.

44. Baldwin, ed., *Toward the Beloved Community,* 396–97, 399–400. De Klerk said in 1990, "The United States Constitution would be the model for the protection of minority rights under black majority rule in South Africa," *Atlanta Daily World,* 24 June 1990, 1.

45. Roger Omond, *The Apartheid Handbook: A Guide to South Africa's Everyday Racial Policies* (New York: Penguin Books, 1985), 20; James Leatt et al., eds., *Contending Ideologies in South Africa* (Grand Rapids, Mich.: William B. Eerdmans, 1986), 35; Mallaby, *After Apartheid,* 55–58, 156; *The African National Congress Constitution,* adopted at ANC National Conference (June 1991), 1–18; and David Garrow, "About People: Mandela, for All Seasons," *Newsday,* 5 March 1990, 38, 40.

46. "In Mandela's Garden," 34. King's belief in the capacity of the masses, at least on a theoretical level, explains why he rejected W. E. B. Du Bois's "Talented Tenth" idea, a position with which Mandela would have fully agreed in 1990. The Talented Tenth concept, which holds that the best 10 percent of the race should guide the masses, contradicts those African-based communal values that apparently influenced Mandela and King in ways perhaps unconscious to both. For a brilliant discussion that is useful for placing both men in that tradition, see Sterling Stuckey, *Slave Culture: Nationalist Theory and the Foundations of Black America* (New York: Oxford University Press, 1987), 268–270, 293–294. Also see King, *Why We Can't Wait,* 33.

47. "In Mandela's Garden," 34.

48. King, *Why We Can't Wait,* 77. King's conviction concerning the interrelationship and interdependence of humans was generally accepted by all sectors of black South African society, particularly as a matter of principle, in the early 1990s.

49. Leatt et al., eds., *Contending Ideologies in South Africa,* 114–15; King, *Where Do We Go from Here?,* 173; and Mallaby, *After Apartheid,* 55–58.

50. Leatt et al., eds., *Contending Ideologies in South Africa,* 43, 114–15.

51. See Martin Luther King Jr., "Address to a Meeting of Operation Breadbasket," Chicago Theological Seminary, Chicago, Ill. (25 March 1967): 3, Archives of the Martin Luther King Jr. Center for Nonviolent Social Change, Inc., Atlanta; *The Chicago Plan of SCLC* (7 January 1966): 3, King Center Archives; *The African Fund News,* no. 1, issue 1 (spring 1992): 3; Mallaby, *After Apartheid,* 55–58; and Leatt et al., eds., *Contending Ideologies in South Africa,* 43, 114–15.

52. "In Mandela's Garden," 34; Mallaby, *After Apartheid,* 55–59, 140, 146–47, 149–50, 153–56, 158; and Kenneth L. Smith, "Equality and Justice: A Dream or Vision of Reality," *Report from the Capital,* Washington, D.C., vol. 39, no. 1 (January 1984): 5.

53. "In Mandela's Garden," 34.

54. Ibid.; Wooster, "South Africa Is Not the U.S. and A.N.C. Leader Is Not King," D-10; Kenneth L. Smith, "The Radicalization of Martin Luther King Jr.: The Last Three Years," *Journal of Ecumenical Studies* 26, no. 2 (spring 1989): 278; Leatt et al., eds., *Contending Ideologies in South Africa,* 35, 107, 115; Mandela,

Intensify the Struggle, 27; and Villa-Vincencio, "South Africa: Options for the Future," 27–30. According to a 1991 report, Buthelezi advocated a market economy and was very much opposed to the ANC's call for nationalization measures. See *New York Times,* 30 January 1991, 1, A2.

55. Leatt et al., eds., *Contending Ideologies in South Africa,* 115.

56. Mandela, *Intensify the Struggle,* 27.

57. Leatt et al., eds., *Contending Ideologies in South Africa,* 107, 114–15; Mandela, *Intensify the Struggle,* 27–28; Smith "The Radicalization of Martin Luther King Jr.," 278; "In Mandela's Garden," 34; and Villa-Vincencio, "South Africa: Options for the Future," 30.

58. Baldwin, ed., *Toward the Beloved Community,* 406; and *The Africa Fund News,* no. 1, issue 1 (spring 1992): 3.

59. Baldwin, *There Is a Balm in Gilead,* 62–63, 74, 206; and idem, ed., *Toward the Beloved Community,* 406.

60. "In Mandela's Garden," 34; Baldwin, ed., *Toward the Beloved Community,* 407; and Mandela, *Intensify the Struggle,* 13.

61. Interview with Appolis (26 February 1990). One American newspaper declared in bold terms: "Make way for the New ANC. Mr. Mandela's revolution has gone high-tech and high-cost." The newspaper described Mandela's 1993 trip to Atlanta as "a high society affair," and noted that the ANC had "made the transition from freedom fighters to fundraisers just fine." See John Blake, "New ANC in Evidence As Funds Pour In," *Atlanta Journal,* 12 July 1993, C1.

62. "Street Crime: Africa Style," from comments made by Nelson Mandela on the CBS News program *60 Minutes* (3 April 1994); and Quoted in Ansbro, *Martin Luther King Jr.,* 232.

63. Nelson Mandela attributed some of this criminal violence to youths who had been encouraged by the ANC to start self-defense units to protect ANC leaders. Some in these units turned into gangs. See "Street Crime: Africa Style"; Mark A. Uhlig, ed., *Apartheid in Crisis: Perspectives on the Coming Battle for South Africa* (New York: Vintage Books, 1986), 25; Mandela, *Intensify the Struggle,* 11, 13, 45–46; and Charles Villa-Vicencio, ed., *Theology and Violence: The South African Debate* (Grand Rapids, Mich.: William B. Eerdmans, 1987), 71–78.

64. "Street Crime: Africa Style"; and Villa-Vicencio, ed., *Theology and Violence,* 71–78.

65. Much of this violence had its roots in tribal loyalties. Buthelezi and the Zulus in Inkatha did not like the possibility of being ruled by a Xhosa member like Mandela. See Wren, "Two Black Factions in South Africa Will End Rivalry," 1; Keller, "South African Massacre," 1, 3; Wren, "Zulu Ex-Aide Tells of Arms Training," 3; James T. Campbell, "Inkatha and 'Tribal Violence' in South Africa," *Program of African Studies: News and Events* 1, no. 2 (fall/winter, 1990): 4; Christopher S. Wren, "Factional Strife in Township Near Johannesburg Kills

Ten," *New York Times,* 10 March 1991, 4; "ANC Concern About Continuing Revelations Regarding Covert Activities," media release of the African National Congress's Department of Information and Publicity, Johannesburg, South Africa (27 November 1992): 1–2; *ANC Negotiations Bulletin,* no. 18 (26 November 1992), 1–2; and "Violence and Political Action in South Africa: Five Comrades Speak," *Passages: A Chronicle of the Humanities,* issue 4 (1992): 1–3.

66. Wren, "Two Black Factions in South Africa Will End Rivalry," 1; "Church Leaders Hasten South African Summit," 3; and "Mandela and Buthelezi Reach an Accord," *Jet,* 21 March 1994, 23. Aside from the fact of Mandela's membership in the Xhosa tribe and Buthelezi's in the Zulu tribe, other issues of a political and economic nature separated the two men. Buthelezi criticized the ANC's reliance on economic sanctions, its armed struggle against apartheid, its support for nationalization policies, its call for the election of a constituent assembly to draft a new nonracial constitution, and its insistence on an interim government to oversee South Africa's transition to majority rule. See *New York Times,* 30 January 1991, 1, A2. Many whites supported Buthelezi's drive for a separate state because this would have justified their desire to secede and set up all-white areas. Such whites saw that democracy would threaten their very existence, especially given the scarcity of their numbers in comparison to blacks. Zulu leaders insisted that they would oppose the April 1994 elections "unless they receive guarantees that their Kwa-Zulu homeland will be preserved." See Scroggins, "Mandela Hints at Compromise with Whites," A1; and *The Africa Fund News,* no. 1, issue 1 (spring 1992): 1.

67. Interview with Appolis (26 February 1990); Wren, "Two Black Factions in South Will End Rivalry," 1 and A2; "Sunrise and Sunset: Negotiations in the New Phase," *Mayibuye* 3, no. 10 (November 1992): 8–9; "P.A.C. Betrayed Us, Says A.Z.A.P.O.," *Work in Progress,* no. 79 (December 1991): 20; King, *Where Do We Go from Here?,* 123–25; and Baldwin, *There is a Balm in Gilead,* 46–59.

68. Quoted in Harvey, "Struggle Recalls King's," D-2. John W. de Gruchy reported in 1992 that "With the unbanning of liberation movements, it is now acceptable by most that the use of violence to transform South African society is no longer morally or practically justifiable." See John W. de Gruchy, "Christian Witness in South Africa in a Time of Transition," *Union Seminary Quarterly Review* 46, nos. 1–4 (1992): 285.

69. Interview with Appolis (26 February 1990); and Mandela, *Intensify the Struggle,* 11–13, 46.

70. "Interviews with Mandela and de Klerk," 54.

71. Mandela, *Intensify the Struggle,* 11–13; "In Mandela's Garden," 34; Malcolm X, *By Any Means Necessary: Speeches, Interviews, and a Letter by Malcolm X,* ed. George Breitman (New York: Pathfinder Press, 1970), 41–43; and Interview with Appolis (26 February 1990).

72. Garrow, "About People: Mandela, for All Seasons," 40; and Interview with Appolis (26 February 1990). For a very recent and strikingly interesting work that treats Nelson Mandela and Martin Luther King Jr. as "moral exemplars of the African and African American ethic respectively," see Peter J. Paris, *The Spirituality of African Peoples: The Search for a Common Moral Discourse* (Minneapolis: Fortress Press, 1995), 132–55.

73. Garrow, "About People: Mandela, for All Seasons," 38.

74. Ibid., 40; Interview with Appolis (26 February 1990); and Harvey, "Struggle Recalls King's," D-2. Responding to the view that "Nelson Mandela is the South African equivalent of Martin Luther King Jr.," one source contends: "Comparisons between Mr. Mandela and Dr. King are misleading. Prior to 1964, Mr. Mandela was best known as the lawyer who defended other ANC leaders. If comparisons to Americans must be made, Mr. Mandela is the South African equivalent of Thurgood Marshall not Dr. King." See Wooster, "South Africa Is Not the U.S. and A.N.C. Leader Is Not King," D-10. Mandela himself refused to draw parallels between himself and black American leaders. In a 1990 interview, he said that "I can't say I was influenced by any particular international leader. But I certainly have heard of, and admire greatly, these men (W. E. B. Du Bois, Marcus Garvey, and Paul Robeson). Also, Dr. Martin Luther King Jr., Malcolm X, and Booker T. Washington were [African Americans] that I admire because of their work done in the interest of freedom. They are our heroes, too." See "Interview with Nelson Mandela," *Ebony* XLV, no. 7 (May 1990): 180.

75. This perception grew out of the understanding that as long as blacks and whites were unequal in terms of their access to the material and nonmaterial goods of the society, such questions would always be settled on terms dictated by white oppressors. Interview with Appolis (26 February 1990).

76. Villa-Vicencio, ed., *Theology and Violence,* 1–10; and Baldwin, ed., *Toward the Beloved Community,* 415.

77. "Nelson Mandela's ANC Group Rejects Proposed Amnesty," *Jet,* 7 September 1992, 13. My treatment of this issue benefited enormously from extensive conversation with Danny and Roxanne Jordaan, black South Africans who have remained very much in touch with their people's struggle. This amnesty question was seriously addressed in the early 1990s by the SACC. See "Implementation Committee on Emergency Summit on Violence Meets," press release from the South African Council of Churches, Johannesburg, South Africa (7 May 1992): 1–3.

78. Winnie Mandela, "Comments on Black Americans and Apartheid," Morehouse College, Atlanta (27 June 1990); my reflections on this subject were influenced by my Interview with Appolis (26 February 1990).

79. Mandela, "Comments on Black Americans and Apartheid"; and Baldwin, *There Is a Balm in Gilead,* 268–70.

80. Of course, this was not so true of many white churches and their leaders. For a highly informed discussion of the full range of responses to apartheid by white South African churches, see Martin Prozesky, ed., *Christianity Amidst Apartheid: Selected Perspectives on the Church in South Africa* (New York: St. Martin's Press, 1990), 1–244. In their leadership roles, black South African Christians reaffirmed the critical statements on apartheid found earlier in essays by Paul R. Spickard and Nyameko Pityana, and they also added proof to Desmond Tutu's view that the struggle against apartheid "is a profoundly spiritual and theological matter." See Paul R. Spickard, "A Review of Allan Boesak's *Black and Reformed*," *Christian Scholars Review* 15, no. 1 (1985): 55; Nyameko Pityana, "Theological Perspective from Apartheid South Africa," *Third World Book Review* 1, nos. 4 and 5 (1985): 65; and John W. de Gruchy, *Bonhoeffer and South Africa* (Grand Rapids, Mich.: William B. Eerdmans, 1984), 124.

81. "Implementation Committee on Emergency Summit on Violence Meets," 1–3.

82. Ibid.

83. "Church Leaders Hasten South African Summit," 3.

84. Astle and Stoval, "Methodist Pastor Quietly Trains South African Peace Workers," 3.

85. "Churches Seen Continuing as Reconcilers," 3.

86. A brief conversation with Bernard Lafayette (7 May 1993). Church leaders' roles as agents of peace and reconciliation in South Africa provided insights into how religious leaders might address the continuing problem of American racism. See "World Church Leaders Will Probe U.S. Racism," *Jet*, 8 June 1992, 17.

87. Derek Ingram, "Conflict Over Sanctions," *New African*, no. 270 (March 1990): 12; and "South Africa," *Africa Report* 37, no. 3 (May–June, 1992): 12.

88. Dennis Brutus, "Thoughts on the Shaping of Post-Apartheid South Africa," reprinted from *Journal of Law and Religion* 5, no. 2 (1987): 524; and Margaret C. Lee, *SADCC: The Political Economy of Development in Southern Africa* (Nashville: Winston-Derek Publishers, 1989), 1–279.

89. Sanford J. Ungar, "America's Welcome is Steeped in Irony," *Atlanta Journal and Constitution*, 17 June 1990, D-4; Andrew J. Glass, "Visit Can Help Restore Black Pride in U.S.," *Atlanta Journal and Constitution*, 17 June 1990, D-10; and Mark Sherman, "The Mandela Crusade: Bound for America," in *Atlanta Journal and Constitution*, 17 June 1990, D-1, D-2.

90. "Interview with Nelson Mandela," 180.

91. Ibid., 180, 182.

92. Nelson Mandela, "Address to the Congress of the United States: From a Contemporary Perspective," *AME Church Review* CVI, no. 339 (July–September 1990): 28–29; and Nelson Mandela, *Long Walk to Freedom: The Autobiography of Nelson Mandela* (Boston: Little, Brown, 1994), 508.

93. Two newspaper writers reported that "Mr. Mandela's visit" to Atlanta "is designed to link the South African nationalist to the memory of Dr. King and the civil rights movement." See Mark Sherman and Marcia Kunstel, "Activist Continues Push for Black South Africans' Political Freedom," *Atlanta Journal and Constitution,* 27 June 1990, A-1, A-9; and "Welcome, Nelson Mandela!: 'Great Honor' to Visit King's Hometown," *Atlanta Journal and Constitution,* 27 June 1990, A-1.

94. Harvey, "Struggle Recalls King's," D-2; Glass, "Visit Can Help Restore Black Pride," D-10; and Sherman, "The Mandela Crusade," D-1.

95. Nelson Mandela, "An Address to African-Americans," Morehouse College, Atlanta (27 June 1990); and Sherman and Kunstel, "Activist Continues Push for Black South Africans' Political Freedom," A-9.

96. Quoted in *Nelson Mandela U.S. Freedom Tour—Academic Convocation: Commemorative Booklet,* issued at the Martin Luther King Jr. International Chapel, Atlanta University Center, Atlanta, Ga. (27 June 1990): 15.

97. Ibid., 61.

98. Ibid., 59.

99. Ibid., 62.

100. Ibid., 149.

101. Ibid., 39.

102. *The Africa Fund News,* no. 1, issue 1 (spring 1992): 1–2; and Baldwin, ed., *Toward the Beloved Community,* 423–24.

103. "Mandela: We Stand Here Not as Guests," 29.

104. Ibid.

105. Ibid., 28–31; and "Excerpts from Some of Dr. Hooks' Speeches," *The Crisis* 83, no. 1 (January 1993): 102.

106. "Mandela Solicits Aid of Civil Rights Groups: Hopes A.N.C., N.A.A.C.P. Will Unite in Future," *Tennessean,* 11 July 1993, 18A. "Mandela: We Stand Here Not as Guests," 28–29, 31; and "Sullivan Urges Business Commitment to South Africa," *Jet,* 8 November 1993, 4.

107. "Sec. Brown's Trip Opens Trade with South Africa," *Jet,* 20 December 1993, 28–29.

108. "Blacks Have Chance to Invest in South Africa," *Jet,* 7 February 1994, 28; "Veteran Diplomat Horace Dawson Heads Effort to Train South Africa's New Foreign Service Corps," *Jet,* 14 February 1994, 46–47; and "Glover Returns from Aiding South Africa Election," *Jet,* 21 February 1994, 47.

109. "Rep. Lewis Tours South Africa, Compares Moments to U.S. Civil Rights Movement," *Jet,* 25 April 1994, 6, 8.

110. "South African in U.S. Detects Many Parallels," *Jet,* 7 September 1992, 12–13.

111. "Mandela: We Stand Here Not as Guests," 29, 31.

112. "Sec. Brown's Trip Opens Trade with South Africa," 29.

113. "South Africa: Sharing Power," *Africa Confidential* 35, no. 10 (20 May 1994): 1; and "South Africans Hail President Mandela: First Black Leader Pledges Racial Unity," *New York Times,* 11 May 1994, A1, A4.

114. See *New York Times,* 10 May 1994, 1.

115. Anthony Egan, "The Making of a President, 1994: Nelson Mandela," *The Month: A Review of Christian Thought and World Affairs* CCLV, no. 1517 (May 1994): 173; and "Nelson Mandela and South Africa Celebrate Freedom at Last," *Jet,* 23 May 1994, 12.

116. Bill Keller, "Mandela Is Named President, Closing the Era of Apartheid," *New York Times,* 10 May 1994, 1; and Francis X. Clines, "Apartheid's Outcasts Have Come to the Fore," in *New York Times,* 10 May 1994, A6.

117. Clines, "Apartheid's Outcasts Have Come to the Fore," A6; "South Africans Hail President Mandela," A1 and A4; and Francis X. Clines, "Dance for Joy!: Come Dance a Toyi-Toyi," *New York Times,* 11 May 1994, A1, A4.

118. Clines, "Apartheid's Outcasts Have Come to the Fore," A6, and "Dance for Joy!" A1, A4.

119. "Nelson Mandela and South Africa Celebrate," 6.

120. James M. Wall, "South African Changes: Hope for a Region as Well as a Nation," *Christian Century* III, no. 16 (11 May 1994): 483.

121. "South Africa: The End of the Beginning," *Africa Confidential* 35, no. 1 (January 7, 1994): 3–5; Patrick Laurence, "After Victory, What?," *Africa Report* 39, no. 1 (January–February, 1994): 62–64; "South Africa: The Generals Are Nervous," *Africa Confidential* 35. no. 4 (18 February 1994): 3–4; Patrick Laurence, "South Africa: The 11th Hour," *Africa Report* 39, no. 2 (March–April, 1994): 36–39; and "South Africa: Waiting for Kwa Zulu," *Africa Confidential* 35, no. 6 (18 March 1994): 1–2. Drawing on the thought of Heraclitus and Hegel, King wrote and spoke a lot about the dialectic that is always at work in social movements. See Ansbro, *Martin Luther King Jr.,* 119–28.

122. Laurence, "South Africa: The 11th Hour," 36–39; "South Africa: Waiting for Kwa Zulu," 1–2; and Laurence, "South Africa: Acceding to the Inevitable," *Africa Report* 39, no. 3 (May–June 1994): 67–70.

123. "South Africa: All Right for the Right," *Africa Confidential* 35, no. 7 (1 April 1994): 1–2; "South Africa: Sharing Power," 2–3; and Laurence, "South Africa: Acceding to the Inevitable," 69.

124. Laurence, "South Africa: Acceding to the Inevitable," 68–70; and Steven A. Holmes, "South African Commission to Investigate Past Political Violence," *New York Times,* 8 June 1994, A5.

125. Laurence, "South Africa: The 11th Hour," 37; and Ansbro, *Martin Luther King Jr.,* 119–20.

126. Jim Cason, "South African Electioneering Gains Momentum: Campaign

for First Democratic Election Gears Up As Negotiations on Procedures Continue," *Africa News* 38, no. 5 (5–18 April 1993): 1.

127. Conversation with Lafayette (7 May 1993); and Tsitsi Wakhisi, "African-American Settlers Flock to South Africa," *The Crisis* 101, no. 5 (July 1994): 18, 38, 40, 47.

128. "Nelson Mandela and South Africa Celebrate," 6–7; and Keller, "Mandela Is Named President," A1, A6. Referring to the occasion of his victory speech, Mandela said: "Mrs. Coretta Scott King, the wife of the great freedom fighter Martin Luther King Jr., was on the podium that night, and I looked over to her as I made reference to her husband's immortal words: . . . 'Free at Last! Free at Last!'" See Mandela, *Long Walk to Freedom,* 539–40.

129. Quoted on the local CBS News, Nashville, Tenn., 27 April 1994.

130. "South Africans Hail President Mandela," A4; and Lerone Bennett Jr., "Vice President Gore Leads Delegation of Blacks to Mandela's Inaugural Events," *Jet,* 30 May 1994, 14. For a listing of the African Americans who attended Mandela's inauguration, see "Nelson Mandela and South Africa Celebrate," 54–56.

131. "South Africa: The Mandate for Mandela," *Africa Confidential* 35, no. 9 (6 May 1994): 1–2.

132. A listing of those included in the Government of National Unity can be found in "South Africa: Sharing Power," 1–4. Also see Bill Keller, "Mandela Completes Cabinet, Giving Buthelezi Post," *New York Times,* 12 May 1994, A4.

133. "South Africa: Sharing Power," 1–2.

134. Keller, "Mandela Completes Cabinet," A4.

135. Bill Keller, "Mandela Tells His Nation of the Hard Work to Come," *New York Times,* 25 May 1994, A6.

136. Wakhisi, "African-American Settlers Flock to South Africa," 17–18, 38, 40, 47; and "Nelson Mandela Leads South Africa to Free Elections," *Jet,* 16 May 1994, 13. For references to "an interesting African and African American bonding ceremony" that occurred in Johannesburg in early 1994, see Bennett, "Vice President Gore Leads Delegation of Blacks," 10.

6. King and the Future of South Africa

1. Quoted in Charles F. Whitaker, "The Cultural Explosion: Freedom Cry of South African Artists and Writers Deepens the Music and Art of the World," *Ebony* XLIX, no. 10 (August 1994): 110.

2. Lynn Norment, "The Women of South Africa," *Ebony* XLIX, no. 10 (August 1994): 101.

3. Donna Bryson, "S. Africans Await Wonders 'Guaranteed' by Freedom," *Tennessean,* 16 April 1995, 7A.

4. Alton B. Pollard, III, "No Easy Walk to Freedom: A Review of Steve Clark,

ed., *Nelson Mandela Speaks: Forging a Democratic, Nonracial South Africa* (1993)," in *Africa Today* 41, no. 1 (first quarter 1994): 80; and Martin Luther King Jr., "To Chart Our Course for the Future," an address delivered at an SCLC retreat, Frogmore, South Carolina (29–31 May 1967), 4–5.

5. "The Pulse of the ANC: The Apparent Policy Consensus in Mandela's Party Could Crack As Pressure to Deliver Grows," *Africa Confidential* 36, no. 2 (20 January 1995): 3–4; "Economic with the Truth: The Row over Indemnities Is Just the Start of Growing Disenchantment with Coalition Politics," *Africa Confidential* 36, no. 3 (3 February 1995): 4–6; "Buthelezi Bounces Back: Shoring Up Its Support in KwaZulu/Natal Means Inkatha Is Set to Challenge the ANC Again," *Africa Confidential* 36, no. 5 (3 March 1995): 1–4; Richard J. Payne, "African-Americans and U.S. Policy Toward Post-Apartheid South Africa," *Africa Today* 41, no. 3 (third quarter 1994): 65–69; "Mandela Warns Against Anarchy," *Tennessean*, 18 February 1995, 6A; Paul Taylor, "Mandela Fires Estranged Wife: Outspoken Government Critic, Accused of Graft, Dropped from Cabinet," *Washington Post*, 28 March 1995, A10; and Bill Keller, "Nelson Mandela Moves to Expel Winnie Mandela from Cabinet," *New York Times*, 28 March 1995, A1, A5.

6. James Ainsworth, "Smile, the Beloved Country: Your Time Has Come," *Africa Today* 41, no. 1 (first quarter 1994); 66; and Donald Will, "South African History at Its Best: A Review of Leonard Thompson's *A History of South Africa* (1992)," in *Africa Today* 41, no. 1 (first quarter 1994): 76.

7. Nelson Mandela, *Long Walk to Freedom: The Autobiography of Nelson Mandela* (Boston: Little, Brown, 1994), 544.

8. "South Africans Hail President Mandela: First Black Leader Pledges Racial Unity," *New York Times*, 11 May 1994, A1, A4.

9. Muriel L. Whetstone, "Mandela in America: Blacks and Whites Give South African Hero a Royal Welcome," *Ebony* XLIX, no. 10 (August 1994): 47–48; and Ainsworth, "Smile, the Beloved Country," 66.

10. "President Mandela Leads Team of Racial and Ethnic Diversity," *Ebony* XLIX, no. 10 (August 1994), 86, 88, 90; and "South Africans Hail President Mandela," A1, A4.

11. "Economic with the Truth," 4–6; Taylor, "Mandela Fires Estranged Wife," A10; Keller, "Nelson Mandela Moves to Expel Winnie Mandela," A1, A5; Bill Keller, "Is Winnie Mandela South Africa's Future?," *Tennessean*, 2 April 1995, 1D; and "The Pulse of the ANC," 3–4.

12. "The Pulse of the ANC," 3–4; and Jendayi Frazer, "Interview with M. C. Ramaphosa, Secretary General of the African National Congress (ANC)," in *Africa Today* 41, no. 1 (first quarter 1994), 9.

13. Frazer, "Interview with M. C. Ramaphosa," 9.

14. Linda E. Thomas, "African Indigenous Churches as a Source of Socio-

Political Transformation in South Africa," *Africa Today* 41, no. 1 (first quarter 1994), 39; and "Economic with the Truth," 4–5.

15. Frank James, "The Black Middle Class: Small Group Has Same Lifestyles—and Same Problems—As U.S. Counterpart," *Ebony* XLIX, no. 10 (August 1994): 92–94, 96; and Interview with Keith Appolis (27 April 1995).

16. Taylor, "Mandela Fires Estranged Wife," A10; Keller, "Is Winnie Mandela South Africa's Future?," D1; and Keller, "Nelson Mandela Moves to Expel Winnie Mandela," A1, A5.

17. Payne, "African-Americans and U.S. Policy," 68; and Alton B. Pollard, III, "'The Dawn of Freedom': A South African Diary," *Africa Today* 41, no. 1 (first quarter 1994), 59.

18. William D. Watley, *Roots of Resistance: The Nonviolent Ethic of Martin Luther King, Jr.* (Valley Forge, Pa.: Judson Press, 1985), 89.

19. Norment, "The Women of South Africa," 98–101, 134; and Interview with Appolis (27 April 1995).

20. "South Africans Hail President Mandela," A1, A4; Norment, "The Women of South Africa," 98; Quoted in *Ebony* XLIX, no. 10 (August 1994): 85; and "Mandela Honored by UNICEF," *Tennessean* (2 April 1995), 4A.

21. Whitaker, "The Cultural Explosion," 110–11.

22. Ibid., 110–12, 114.

23. Ibid.; and Lerone Bennett Jr., "Fifteen Days That Shook the World," *Ebony* XLIX, no. 10 (August 1994), 74, 76.

24. Lewis V. Baldwin, *To Make the Wounded Whole: The Cultural Legacy of Martin Luther King Jr.* (Minneapolis: Fortress Press, 1992), 200–218.

25. Colleen Lowe Morna, "Joe Slovo, 1926–1995, Principled Pragmatist," *Africa Report* 40, no. 2 (March–April 1995): 44–45.

26. Taylor, "Mandela Fires Estranged Wife," A10; and Keller, "Nelson Mandela Moves to Expel Winnie Mandela," A1, A5.

27. "Buthelezi Bounces Back," 1–4.

28. Martin Luther King Jr., *Where Do We Go from Here?: Chaos or Community* (Boston: Beacon Press, 1967), 179.

29. "Mandela Warns Against Anarchy," 6A.

30. Ibid.

31. Norment, "The Women of South Africa," 98.

32. Laura B. Randolph, "Sisters in the Struggle," *Ebony* XLIX, no. 10 (August 1994), 18.

33. Ibid.; and Norment, "The Women of South Africa," 98.

34. Norment, "The Women of South Africa," 98–99.

35. Randolph, "Sisters in the Struggle," 18.

36. Ibid.

37. Ibid.

38. Ibid.

39. Quoted in ibid.

40. Ibid. For Interesting Treatments of gender issues in South Africa, see John Sharp, "A World Upside Down: Households and Differentiation in a South African Bantustan in the 1980s," *African Studies* 53, no. 1 (1994): 71–88; and Leslie Bank, "Angry Men and Working Women: Gender, Violence, and Economic Change in Qwaqwa in the 1980s," *African Studies* 53, no. 1 (1994): 89–90.

41. Keller, "Mandela Is Named President," A1, A6.

42. Quoted in Norment, "The Women of South Africa," 100–101.

43. Ibid.; and Taylor, "Mandela Fires Estranged Wife," A10.

44. Keller, "Is Winnie Mandela South Africa's Future?," 3D.

45. Taylor, "Mandela Fires Estranged Wife," A10; and Keller, "Nelson Mandela Moves to Expel Winnie Mandela," A1, A5.

46. Norment, "The Women of South Africa," 98–101, 134.

47. Jim Wallis and Joyce Hollyday, eds., *Crucible of Fire: The Church Confronts Apartheid* (Maryknoll, N.Y.: Orbis Books, 1989), 95.

48. Bennett, "Fifteen Days That Shook the World," 70, 72, 74, 76.

49. See Katie G. Cannon, *Black Womanist Ethics* (Atlanta: Scholars Press, 1988), 160–74; Patricia Hill Collins, *Black Feminist Thought: Knowledge, Consciousness, and the Politics of Empowerment* (New York: Routledge, Chapman, and Hall, 1991), 197; and Baldwin, *To Make the Wounded Whole,* 156–59.

50. Jacquelyn Grant, "The Sin of Servanthood and the Deliverance of Discipleship," in Emilie M. Townes, ed., *A Troubling in My Soul: Womanist Perspectives on Evil and Suffering* (Maryknoll, N.Y.: Orbis Books, 1993), 213–14; and Delores S. Williams, *Sisters in the Wilderness: The Challenge of Womanist God-Talk* (Maryknoll, N.Y.: Orbis Books, 1993), 200.

51. Kelly Brown Douglas, *The Black Christ* (Maryknoll, N.Y.): Orbis Books, 1994), 3, 36–45, 48–52, 71–73, 88, 107.

52. Cheryl Townsend Gilkes, "We Have a Beautiful Mother: Womanist Musings on the Afrocentric Idea," in Cheryl J. Sanders, ed., *Living in the Intersection: Womanism and Afrocentrism in Theology* (Minneapolis: Fortress Press, 1995), 37. For significant references to the relationship of King to black womanism by African American male scholars, see Baldwin, *To Make the Wounded Whole,* 55, 156–59; and Noel Leo Erskine, *King Among the Theologians* (Cleveland: The Pilgrim Press, 1994), 164, 167, 169.

53. Baldwin, *To Make the Wounded Whole,* 203–4.

54. Taylor, "Mandela Fires Estranged Wife," A10. Mandela's recent efforts to begin divorce proceedings against his estranged wife have rekindled discussions concerning his attitude toward women. See "South African President Nelson Mandela Filing for Divorce," *Jet,* 4 September 1995, 4.

55. Pollard, "No Easy Walk to Freedom," 79. Perhaps the best evidence of the course Mandela will take was offered in his response to South Africa's first Women's Day, a new national holiday recently celebrated with a march to the presidential offices in Pretoria. The four thousand participants were commemorating the massive 1956 march by twenty thousand women in protest against the laws of South Africa's white minority government, an event that evoked no major responses from Martin Luther King Jr. and black male leaders in the anti-apartheid struggle inside South Africa. Recognizing the celebration, Mandela declared: "The constitution-writing process is well underway. As a tribute to the legions of women who navigated the path of fighting for justice before us, we ought to imprint in the supreme law of the land firm principles upholding the rights of women." See "South Africa Celebrates First Women's Day," *Jet*, 28 August 1995, 22.

56. Kenneth L. Smith, "The Radicalization of Martin Luther King Jr.: The Last Three Years," *Journal of Ecumenical Studies* 26, no. 2 (spring 1989): 278.

57. Anthony Egan, "The Making of a President, 1994: Nelson Mandela," *The Month: A Review of Christian Thought and World Affairs* CCLV, no. 1517 (May 1994): 176.

58. Martin Luther King Jr., *Strength to Love* (Philadelphia: Fortress Press, 1981), 98–99.

59. "South Africa: Sharing Power," *Africa Confidential* 35, no. 10 (20 May 1994): 1.

60. Ibid., 1–4; and "President Mandela Takes Office and Tells Plans for Future," *Jet*, 30 May 1994, 54.

61. "South Africa: Sharing Power," 2–3.

62. King, *Where Do We Go from Here?*, 124–25.

63. "Mandela's Address Promises Justice, Peace and Work for Country," *Jet*, 30 May 1994, 53. Nothing is more illustrative of Mandela's determination to promote racial reconciliation than his recent visit with 94-year-old Betsie Verwoerd, the widow of Hendrik Verwoerd, who "built apartheid and sent Mandela to prison for life in 1964 as punishment for fighting white rule." This gesture on Mandela's part fits into the best of that spirit of forgiveness and reconciliation for which Gandhi, Luthuli, and King were so well known. See "Mandela Visits Widow of Apartheid Architect Who Sent Him to Jail for Life," *Jet*, 4 September 1995, 40.

64. Bill Keller, "South Africa Faces the Hard Part: Integration (and Taxes) Locally," *New York Times*, 9 July 1994, 1.

65. Egan, "The Making of a President, 1994," 176; Patrick Laurence, "South Africa: The 11th Hour," *Africa Report* 39, no. 2 (March–April 1994): 38; and "South Africa: Acceding to the Inevitable," *Africa Report* 39, no. 3 (May–June 1994): 69.

66. Allistar Sparks, "Loyalty of Mixed-Race South Africans Up for Grabs," *Africa News* 38, nos. 2 and 3 (8–21 March 1993) 3.

67. The best and most extensive treatment of King's theory of human dignity is Garth Baker-Fletcher, *Somebodyness: Martin Luther King Jr., and the Theory of Dignity* (Minneapolis: Fortress Press, 1993), 1–193.

68. Fredrickson senses that the need to address party loyalties will remain even more important in the rural areas of South Africa. See George M. Fredrickson, "No Going Back for Either Side: A Review of Sebastian Mallaby's *After Apartheid*," *New York Times Book Review*, 5 April 1992, 3.

69. King, *Strength to Love*, 99; and Baldwin, *To Make the Wounded Whole*, 252–53.

70. King, *Where Do We Go from Here?*, 181; and Martin Luther King Jr., *The Trumpet of Conscience* (San Francisco: Harper and Row, 1968), 68–70. Mandela has consistently included in his vision of a new South Africa the building of what he terms a "nonsexism." See "Mandela's Address Promises Justice, Peace, and Work," 53.

71. "Nelson Mandela Leads South Africa to Free Elections," *Jet*, 16 May 1994, 10, 12–13.

72. Ibid.; and Sylvester Holmes, "Open for Business: Black South Africa's Next Important Quest Is for Economic Opportunity and Stability," *Emerge* 5, no. 10 (July–August 1994): 47.

73. Holmes, "Open for Business," 47.

74. "Nelson Mandela Leads South Africa to Free Elections," 12; and Holmes, "Open for Business," 46–47.

75. Holmes, "Open for Business," 46; Bill Keller, "Mandela Tells His Nation of the Hard Work to Come," *New York Times*, 25 May 1994, A6; and Fredrickson, "No Going Back for Either Side," 3.

76. "Nelson Mandela and South Africa Celebrate Freedom at Last," *Jet*, 23 May 1994, 11; and Keller, "South Africa Faces the Hard Part," 1–2.

77. Keller, "Mandela Tells His Nation of the Hard Work," A6.

78. Ibid.; and Holmes, "Open for Business," 47.

79. Egan, "The Making of a President, 1994," 176.

80. Holmes, "Open for Business," 46.

81. Ibid., 46–47.

82. Quoted in Holmes, "Open for Business," 46–47.

83. Vice President Gore's interest in a "Marshall Plan" for Africa squares with an issue raised by King in the 1960s, thus highlighting once again the timelessness of certain of King's concerns with respect to South Africa in particular and Africa in general. See Lerone Bennett Jr., "Vice President Gore Visits African Countries, Hears Call for Marshall Plan for Africa," *Jet*, 6 June 1994, 6–8; "Nelson Mandela Leads South Africa to Free Elections," 13; and Payne, "African-Americans and U.S. Policy Toward Post-Apartheid South Africa," 71.

84. These comments were made during a "Global Forum with President Clinton" on the CNN television network, 8 May 1994. For a discussion of how

Clinton's goals for South Africa compare with the ANC's Reconstruction and Development Programme, see Payne, "African-Americans and U.S. Policy Toward Post-Apartheid South Africa," 71.

85. African Americans are already developing business ventures in South Africa, involvements that may become more important and far-reaching than what they have experienced with other African countries. See, for an example, "New Business Venture," *Jet,* 13 June 1994, 26; and Tsitsi Wakhisi, "African-American Settlers Flock to South Africa," *The Crisis* 101, no. 5 (July 1994): 17–18, 38, 40, 47.

86. John W. De Gruchy, "Christian Witness in South Africa in a Time of Transition," *Union Seminary Quarterly Review* 46, nos. 1–4 (1992): 283–84.

87. Walter E. Fluker, *They Looked for a City: A Comparative Analysis of the Ideal of Community in the Thought of Howard Thurman and Martin Luther King Jr.* (Lanham, Md.: University Press of America, 1989), 48–64, 129–170; James M. Washington, ed., *A Testament of Hope: The Essential Writings of Martin Luther King Jr.* (San Francisco: Harper and Row, 1986), 107, 142; and Thomas, "African Indigenous Churches as a Source of Socio-Political Transformation in South Africa," 39–56.

88. For a keen sense of how King related education to human freedom and community, see Martin Luther King Jr., "Field of Education a Battleground," a speech delivered before the United Federation of Teachers, New York City, New York (15 July 1965): 1, King Center Archives; and "Revolution in the Classroom," an address presented before the Georgia Teachers and Education Association, Atlanta (31 April 1967): 2–8, King Center Archives.

89. "Nelson Mandela Talks About Discipline, Education on Anniversary of Soweto Student Uprising," *Jet,* 4 July 1994, 14.

90. "Apartheid's Collapse Finds Black Children Going Back to School," *Tennessean,* 16 June 1994, A7.

91. Ibid.

92. The ANC's current views on education were set forth with considerable clarity in the early 1990s. See "Discussion Paper for the ANC on Education Policy," unpublished document (4 September 1991): 1–32; and *Die Suid-Afrikaan: Politiek se Manne van Aksie,* no. 39 (June–July 1992): 27. For an interesting study of how education should be used to bring much-needed change and stability in the southern Africa context, instead of sustaining the old colonial paradigm, see Dickson A. Mungazi, *The Struggle for Social Change in Southern Africa: Visions of Liberty* (New York: Taylor and Frances, 1989). The Mungazi study is still most relevant for South Africa in its period of transition.

93. King, "Field of Education a Battleground," 1–4; "An Address at Syracuse University," Syracuse, New York (15 July 1965), 1, King Center Archives; "Revolution in the Classroom," 1–8; *Strength to Love,* 147; and Lewis V. Baldwin, ed.,

Toward the Beloved Community: Martin Luther King Jr. and South African Apartheid, unpublished manuscript (1994), 419, King Center Archives.

94. King, *The Trumpet of Conscience,* 70.

95. "Discussion Paper for the ANC on Education Policy," 21; and King, *Where Do We Go from Here?,* 122–23.

96. Amy Waldman, "Apartheid Reminders Quickly Fade," *New York Times,* 15 June 1994, A7.

97. "Witchcraft, Tribal Justice Alive in New South Africa," *Tennessean,* 19 June 1994, 9A.

98. A few "historians and survivors," according to one account, have already "assigned themselves to preserve the remnants of apartheid in a country focused single-mindedly on paving over its past to build the future." See Waldman, "Apartheid Reminders Quickly Fade," A7.

99. King, *Where Do We Go from Here?,* 122–23; and Lewis V. Baldwin, *There Is a Balm in Gilead: The Cultural Roots of Martin Luther King Jr.* (Minneapolis: Fortress Press, 1991), 44–50, 57–58, 60–61, 230–72, 301–2.

100. "Witchcraft, Tribal Justice Alive in New South Africa," 9A.

101. Martin Luther King Jr., *Stride Toward Freedom: The Montgomery Story* (New York: Harper and Row, 1958), 33–34; and Washington, ed., *A Testament of Hope,* 107, 142.

102. Gray, "Nelson Mandela and F. W. de Klerk," 57.

103. Tom Cohen, "ANC, Inkatha Backers Resume Fighting in Troubled Township," *Birmingham News,* 3 July 1994, 27A.

104. "South Africa: A Nuclear Nightmare," *Africa Confidential* 35, no. 3 (4 February 1994): 1–3; and "South Africa: Nuclear Reactions," *Africa Confidential* 35, no. 5 (4 March 1994): 1–2.

105. Harry Smith's Interview with Allan Boesak on the CBS News "This Morning" (29 April 1994).

106. Tim Smith, "Attacks on Black Unity," *Maryknoll* 85, no. 8 (August 1991): 18. Smith quotes Martin Luther King Jr. at the end of this article.

107. Steven A. Holmes, "South African Commission to Investigate Past Political Violence," *New York Times,* 8 June 1994, A5.

108. James M. Wall, "South African Changes: Hope for a Region as Well as a Nation," *Christian Century* 3, no. 16 (11 May 1994): 484; Colleen L. Morna, "South Africa: Reforming the Police," *Africa Report* 40, no. 1 (January–February 1995): 32–35; and Patrick Laurence, "South Africa: Unmasking the Third Force," *Africa Report* 40, no. 2 (March–April 1995): 41–49.

109. Nelson Mandela, "An Address to African-Americans," Morehouse College, Atlanta (27 June 1990).

INDEX